Born of the Spirit

John Sungchul Hong

Emeth Press
www.emethpress.com

Born of the Spirit

Copyright © 2013 John Sungchul Hong
Printed in the United States of America on acid-free paper

All rights reserved. No part of this book may be reproduced, or stored in a retrieval system or transmitted in any form or by any means, electronic, mechanical, photocopying, recording, scanning or otherwise, except as permitted by the 1976 United States Copyright Act, or with the prior written permission of Emeth Press. Requests for permission should be addressed to: Emeth Press, P. O. Box 23961, Lexington, KY 40523-3961.   http://www.emethpress.com.

Library of Congress Cataloging-in-Publication Data

Hong, Sung Chul.
  Born of the spirit / John Sungchul Hong.
    p. cm.
  ISBN 978-1-60947-051-7 (alk. paper)
  1. Bible. N.T. John III, 1-16--Meditations. I. Title.
  BS2615.54.H66 2013
  227'.9606--dc23
                                  2012048865

Contents

Foreword / v

Introduction / vii

1. There Was a Man / 1
2. A Man of the Pharisees / 9
3. A Member of the Jewish Ruling Council / 17
4. Knowing / 23
5. A Teacher from God / 29
6. The Miraculous Signs / 37
7. The Miraculous Signs (2) / 45
8. The Miraculous Signs (3) / 53
9. Born – Again / 59
10. The Background of Born – Again / 67
11. The Kingdom of God / 77
12. Nicodemus' Second Question / 83
13. Nicodemus' Second Question (2) / 89
14. The Secret of New Birth / 95
15. The Secret of New Birth (2) / 101
16. The Secret of New Birth (3) / 107

17. The Secret of New Birth (4) / 115
18. The Kingdom of God (2) / 123
19. The Necessity of New Birth / 131
20. Flesh and Spirit / 137
21. Flesh and Spirit (2) / 143
22. Man Born of the Spirit / 149
23. Man Born of the Spirit (2) / 157
24. Man Born of the Spirit (3) / 165
25. Man Born of the Spirit (4) / 173
26. Man Born of the Spirit (5) / 179
27. Man Born of the Spirit (6) / 187
28. The One Who Came from Heaven / 193
29. The One Who Has Gone into Heaven / 201
30. The One Who Is Lifted Up / 207
31. The One Who Is Lifted Up (2) / 213
32. The One Who Is Lifted Up (3) / 221
33. The One Who Is Lifted Up (4) / 227
34. God's Love / 235
35. God's Love (2) / 243
36. God's Love (3) / 249
37. God's Love (4) / 257
38. God's Love (5) / 265
39. God's Love (6) / 271
40. God's Love (7) / 277

Foreword

Decades ago, while studying geography in college, I read a small, early twentieth-century, historically-influential book in which the writer introduced his "heartland" theory. As I recall, he was developing a theory of world influence. Specifically, he said that whoever controls Europe influences the world; whoever controls Germany influences Europe; and whoever controls the "heartland" section of Germany influences Germany and, therefore, Europe and the wider world. He acknowledged that the world is much more than Germany, and is vast and differentiated but, for several reasons, Germany's "heartland" has a very disproportionate influence worldwide.

Our professor had us read the book because Hitler's *Third Reich* based its world strategy upon the theory. I have never forgotten the most important lessons: that theories matter, and Big Ideas have far-reaching consequences—for good or ill. I later learned Kurt Lewin's maxim: "There is nothing more practical than a good theory."

My friend and colleague, Dr. John Hong, has developed an idea analogous to the German heartland theory. The Gospel of John is not, of course, the whole of Scripture; but understanding the Fourth Gospel helps us understand much of the Bible, and much of Christianity's message. Furthermore, the third chapter of John's gospel is not the whole of John, but it is the hinge of his gospel; if you do not understand John 3, you do not understand John. Understanding John 3 is arguably the most important single key to understanding what Christianity has to offer to the peoples of the earth; and it is arguably the most important single biblical chapter for communicating the Gospel to most people. John 3 is Christianity's literary "heartland;" if we get that right, and communicate that effectively, the Faith's influence will increase and extend!

So as Professor Hong's book on John 3 becomes available to English-speaking readers worldwide, it should not be regarded as just another book to place on a stack of books that "should" be read "if we get around to it." It is priority reading for every church leader who is called to engage the church and the world with "the faith once delivered to the saints."

Furthermore, John Hong is the right person to offer this book to the World Church. He has researched and reflected upon, and preached and taught, the redemptive themes and meanings of John 3 for much of a lifetime. Many people have already experienced Second Birth and the Life of the Spirit through John's teaching and preaching vocation from his roots in John 3. With this book, the insights from John 3 will reach many more audiences than any one man could reach without the printed word.

George G. Hunter
Beeson Distinguished Professor of Evangelization
Asbury Theological Seminary
Wilmore, KY USA

Introduction

I received a phone call about two weeks after my arrival in Thailand as a missionary. The caller was a veteran American missionary who had been working in that country for more than 22 years. He invited me to speak at a conference, and at the same time apologized for giving me such short notice.

He said that the Christian Church in Thailand, composed of seven denominations, held a leadership conference every three years. The conference preparation committee had invited a famous Myanmar evangelist to be the main speaker, but he could not come because his government had refused to issue him a passport. The committee had wished to invite an Asian, and so extended an invitation to me.

I had spoken seven times to 120 leading pastors and 30 elders from throughout the country who had gathered in the city of Chiang Mai when an unforgettable event took place! My fifth message was based on the Gospel of John 3:1-16. I expounded on these verses, emphasizing regeneration and its significance. At the end of my message I extended an invitation to receive Christ, asking all those wishing to be born again to stand up.
I was awed to see more than 30 of the church leaders standing! They repented of their sins and accepted Jesus Christ as their

Savior. That event taught me some powerful lessons. First, the third chapter of John's gospel is a powerful portion of Scripture to use for the gospel proclamation. Second, some church leaders are not genuinely born again, even though they are known as Christian pastors. Third, God will use any Christian who is willing to help lead people to Christ.

After the conference, invitations for me to speak poured in from all around the country. Conference participants, when they returned to their respective places and shared what had happened there, encouraged their churches to invite me to come and speak. From that time on, John's third chapter has become the source of many of my evangelistic messages. Countless numbers of souls have been born again throughout the world through the Spirit's use of that portion of Scripture!
I wish to share this powerful Word of God with other preachers. The Lord has given me a special understanding of this portion of Scripture as I have prayerfully meditated upon it. Since my experience in Thailand, I have come to realize that John's third chapter is one of the Lord's wonderful scriptural gateways into the kingdom of God.

Now, at long last, I have put my meditations on John 3:1-16 into book form. I have found the content far from being perfect. However, it is comforting to know that no one can fathom all of the Word of God. It will continue to be a lifelong task! But there is one sure thing! This book is not solely the product of an academician's ivory tower. It is the product of "field work" with the Holy Spirit for the salvation of many souls.

Profound thanks should go to those who have written recommendation for this work. I give thanks to Dr. Robert Coleman and Dr. George Hunter who were my teachers while I was a student at Asbury Theological Seminary. Both of them are world-known distinguished professors and writers. Dr. Coleman was a distinguished professor at Gordon-Conwell Theological Seminary and Dr. George Hunter was a distinguished professor at the E. Stanley Jones School of World Mission and Evangelism at Asbury Theological Seminary.

My hope and prayer is that this book will be used by those who approach the Word of God deeply and evangelistically. I will be forever thankful if the Lord uses this book to bring many souls into his Kingdom. Is there any deeper joy than seeing souls, who are heading toward eternal destruction, turn entirely in the opposite direction and come to Christ to receive eternal life?

Above all, I am grateful to the Lord Jesus Christ who has called me to preach Christ crucified (I Corinthians 1:23). My praise goes to God who has used this portion of Scripture from John's Gospel to save many souls. Lastly, my deep thanks goes to the Holy Spirit who, whenever and wherever the third chapter of John's Gospel is proclaimed, convicts men and women, boys and girls, of sin, and ultimately brings them to salvation.

John Sungchul Hong
Asbury Theological Seminary

Chapter 1

There Was a Man

"Now *there was a man* of the Pharisees named Nicodemus, a member of the Jewish ruling council." John 3:1

1. The Introduction of Man

In the first chapter of the Gospel of John, Jesus the Son of Man is introduced (vv. 49-50). He was no ordinary man. The Apostle John describes him as One who was with God in the beginning (v. 2); One who created all of life (v. 4); One who had become flesh to make his dwelling among men (v.14); and One who would give all those who would receive him and believe in his name the right to become children of God...born of God, not man (vv. 9-13)! "There was a (another) man sent from God"; whose name was John (the Baptist). He announced that this man Jesus was "the Lamb of God, who would take away the sin of the world" (v. 29)!

By the end of chapter two, Jesus had called men to be his disciples, sought to reveal his religious authority, and had people believing in his name because of the miracles he had performed (v. 23). But He knew this would not be enough to fulfill the mission for which he had been sent, for He "knew what was in man"—sin. It would take more than belief that he was a miracle-worker to change man's nature (vv. 24-25). His Father had greater things in store for man—an everlasting relationship with God! And to have this relationship, man would have to change inwardly. Man needed his sins taken away in order to live with a holy God!

In chapter three of the Gospel John, we find Jesus being presented with the opportunity to tell "man" how this change could come about. "But there was a man who belongs to the Pharisees named Nicodemus, and is a member of the Jewish ruling council. He came to Jesus at night" (v. 1-2). It is through his conversation with the man Nicodemus that Jesus will tell "everyman" the Good News! The intention of God is quite clear. God wants to focus in on the change-of-heart necessary for "all men" (2:24). God wants it to be absolutely clear that He loves "man" more than any of His other created beings. The Book of Genesis (Genesis 1) made this focus on man very clear. We find that God first created a perfect environment for "man" to enjoy, and then created man...in his own image. He had personal conversations with man. He walked with man. He revealed his love to man. Later, when sin entered into man, He sought man's redemption by sending His Son—to die on the cross...for man! Jesus wanted Nicodemus—every man—to know the path he would need to take to make his redemption possible.

John 3 is often called the key to the whole message of the gospel, or more specifically, the key to the gateway to heaven. So, what exactly is this gospel? In a word, the gospel message is love—God's love for all men. It is a love that has within it the power to enable man to come and live with Him forever. This was God's "good news." Man may have a relationship with Him solely because He loves them!

2. The Ability of Man

The gospel is for man. For this reason, importance is placed on seeing all mankind from the perspective of Christ's gospel. What kind of being is "man?" Humans have many unique privileges and functions that make them distinct from animals. They can speak and remember. The fact that animals have limited ability to express themselves and to remember is true.

Research shows that some pigs can remember numbers. For example, if they are asked to answer two plus four, the pig can pick the number six among numbers on the floor. Some pigs can even subtract and multiply. To go a step further, some can even divide. However, these abilities are taught, not instinctive. They cannot calculate answers to such problems, nor can they teach such calculations to other pigs. However, their ability to do so is incomparable to that of human beings. The unsurpassed abilities to speak and to memorize are two very unique privileges God has given man.

Different from other species, humans can share ideas with one another. They can influence others by expressing their emotions and thoughts through music, writing, and creative art forms. The *"Mona Lisa"* of Leonardo da Vinci is an immortal work of art that expresses the beauty of human beings.

Man has been given the ability to many wonderful things such as computers, airplanes, and machinery. Man goes to the moon on spaceships and builds underwater cities. They explore deserts where they build "ideal" cities. All of these things amaze us.

In addition, human beings have the potential to receive and offer love. Love can exist between animals, but it seems to be merely a means of instinctual reproduction. However, many kinds of love exist among humans—romantic love of husband and wife, love of friends and family, and absolute love between God and human beings. It is safe to say that the topic of most movies and novels is love—or lack of love. Various kinds of love are demonstrations of the gift of creativeness given to man by the Divine.

A distinct type of demonstrative love found among humans is the kind that may be best seen in the home. Different from animal "families", human parents have children— ideally— as a result of their love for one another, and then spend the rest of their lives pouring love into those children. These parents strive to lovingly discipline and educate their children. They shed tears when their children suffer and show gladness when their children are happy and seem to be enjoying life. This process is ongoing. Loving families help to stabilize societies and countries.

3. The Limitation of Man

As roses, despite their beauty and fragrance, have thorns, human beings also have "thorns." These "thorns" often limit their enjoyment of life. Human beings frequently feel lonely in the midst of God's glorious environment, and attempt to overcome this feeling of loneliness in many ways. Many spend much their time on the internet. Others indulge in drugs or alcohol. Some may become addicted to their workplace or to involvement in sports. jump to other means such as gambling or unhealthy relationships to try to solve their loneliness are only temporary ways to help people forget about loneliness. The feeling of loneliness will reemerge over time. Often loneliness becomes a lifelong burden. Another "thorn" in man's experience is people seemingly having little or no sense of purpose in their lives. It is fair to say that they just exist, rather than live.

When night comes, they go to bed. When morning comes, they get up. Their lives consist of repeated meaningless sleep and meaningless awakenings. In most cases, people feel they are living in expectation of death, reluctantly heading toward death slowly, day by day. Often they do not even think of life or death. They continue to live as they always have. One day at a time.

How much time and energy does man put into searching for meaning and purpose in life? For many, very little is put into it. Some look for the meaning of life by pursuing monetary gain. Others pursue pleasure—at the peril of their lives. People put their lives on the line for religion, all kinds of religions. Physical and mental burn-out often results in man's desperate pursuit of life and its true meaning. They end up having chased the wind, empty of any meaningful purpose in life. The thorn of death itself is the ultimate "thorn," or limitation, in people's lives. Every human being is finite in that they are heading toward death as soon as they are born into this world. Death is inevitable. No one knows when it is near. No one knows how to avoid it. We all know, the order of birth does not correspond with the order of death.

Death approaches human beings regardless of time or place. For this reason, fear becomes another "thorn" to man. It exists in the deepest of the human heart. Man faces many kinds of fear while experiencing life: the fear of being left alone, the fear of losing one's health, the fear of future economic disaster, the fear of pain, the list goes on and on. We are often gripped with different degrees of fear---both imminent and distant.

4. The Needs of Man

In John 3:1, a man named Nicodemus, a prominent leader among the Jews, came to meet with Jesus during the night. To many of us, he seems to be almost perfect, at least in terms of academic and political standards. His needs appear to be few. He is highly respected by Israelites —a Pharisee and a member of the Jewish ruling council. When Nicodemus meets Jesus, a very important spiritual conversation begins. Within this conversation we discover four specific needs that this "man" Nicodemus has. They are everyman's needs.

First, Nicodemus is getting on in years. He asks in response to Jesus' words regarding his entering the kingdom of God, "Nicodemus, you must be born again"— "How can a man be born again when he is old"(3:3-4)? He has been an extraordinary person. But he has also become an old man, unable to avoid the passing of time. He is heading toward death. What is his need at this stage of his life? His need is to be certain he has eternal life with God. His accomplishments and relationships with men will soon come to an end.

He needs—he desires—his life to continue on with the God he has served.

Second, Nicodemus needs to be changed within—born again—in spite of his excellent personal qualifications and reputation with men (John 3:3,5). Soon, he will no longer be facing men. He will be facing God. Jesus tells him he must be born again. No one can enter the Kingdom of God unless he *is* born again. Nicodemus the Pharisee must die twice! Once, to sin, and experience the new birth; the other, to this life, and enter into the new life with Christ. If he died physically without having experienced this new birth, he would enter into a Godless eternity— according to the judgment of God. The need for Nicodemus to recognize this is urgent! He must meet with Jesus. He must be born again!

A third need is seen at the end of chapter two. Belief in his power to perform miracles and this believing in Jesus' name (reputation and character) would not be sufficient to satisfy man's deeper need. Jesus knew their hearts. Verses 24-25 says that Jesus would not entrust himself to man, for he knew all men...he knew what was in man's heart! What human beings know is much less than what they do not know. They did not know the condition of their own hearts. Christ knew the heart of Nicodemus for He knew the condition of the hearts of all men. Nicodemus needed to search for, and acknowledge, the condition of his heart before the second birth could be possible.

And Nicodemus" fourth need? He had to go beyond discovering the condition of his own heart. He had to come and surrender himself to Jesus, the Son of Man, the only one who had the power to change his heart. Only then would "he not perish but enter into eternal life" (John 3:16). As did Nicodemus, "everyman" needs to believe in Jesus and come to the One who has the power (and love!) to change a heart and transform a life. It is of necessity—to be born anew!

5. Table Tennis and a Queen

In conclusion, I would like to share the story of a young woman who possessed the abilities, limitations, and needs we have been thinking about. Name is Young-Ja Yang who is known as the queen of table tennis. She began playing table tennis when she was a third grader, and led her team to win a competition at the nation-wide elementary school ping-pong competition when she was a sixth- grader. She was so talented that she was selected as a national representative in her high school years. However, she later confessed that she possessed a mean character and that her heart needed to be changed. She shares below her testimony of how that took place.

> I had a mean spirit at the time. I lacked self-control. During practice or in games, whenever things didn't go well, I used to bite my paddle. While I was good during practice, the tension from the pressure of competition caused my face to turn red and often I would lose the game without a chance to play at my game level. The painful symptom of tennis elbow brought me back to church. I was unable even to bend or lift my arm, and the doctors warned me not to play ping-pong anymore. One day the mother of one of my veteran teammates suggested a solution. Why not go for prayer at a prayer mountain? At the prayer mountain a man was preaching. I became aware of the fact that I was a sinner, deserving death, but Jesus Christ had shed His blood on the cross for me. I decided to receive Jesus as my Savior. I sought God in a loud voice and prayed all night. When I came back to my quarters early the next morning, I couldn't believe it: My tennis elbow, that had dogged me for the last six years like a shadow, was completely healed.

After that time, she played ping-pong for the glory of God and the results were amazing! She won the team and doubles competition at the Canada Open and became a Triple Crown winner in the singles, doubles, and team competitions at the Seoul Open in 1982. She won the team competition at the Seoul Asian Competition in 1986 and the doubles competition at the New Deli International Competition that following year.

Later she won the doubles competition at both the Nikata Asian Competition and the Seoul Olympics in 1988. She was given the Chung-Yong Award, an award given to the athlete who contributed the most to Korean national development. These accomplishments in the field of professional tennis are those of a woman whose life was changed and heart transformed by the power of Jesus Christ. Her spiritual journey is an open invitation, for all who hear, to accept Jesus Christ as Savior and Lord.

Chapter 2

A Man of the Pharisees

"Now there was *a man of the Pharisees* named Nicodemus, a member of the Jewish ruling council." (John 3:1)

1. The Separated Ones

In John 3:1, we discover that Nicodemus was "a man of the Pharisees." What kind of people were these Pharisees—the "set-apart ones"? Pharisees attempted to live separated lives by strictly observing the laws of God, and refusing to live secular and mundane lives. The Apostle Paul testified in King Agrippa's court, that according to the strictest sect of the Jewish religion, he had lived as a Pharisee before committing his life to Christ. He describes his former religious life as one in which he had opposed the name of Jesus of Nazareth, personally putting many saints in prison and casting death votes against them (Acts 26:4-11).

It is estimated that, in Jesus time, no more than 6,000 Pharisees existed in Israel. Were few in number but they were the most highly respected group in that country. It was not easy for one to become a Pharisee. If people wanted to join this group, they had to take a vow, in front of three witnesses, to observe the Law for the rest of their lives. After having taken that vow, they had to make great and consistent effort to live holy lives and the laws of God. People respected them for, if nothing more, their passion for the Law.

The Pharisees held three major beliefs at that time. The first one was that there was only one God, who was passionate in his love for His people. The second one was that God had revealed to his people a two-fold law: One set of laws written down in the Pentateuch; the other orally transmitted from Moses to Joshua. The third belief was that if people followed the two-fold law faithfully, the resurrection of their bodies and eternal life for their souls were assured.

The Pharisees generated two institutions based on these beliefs. The first institution was the Great Court. The role of the Great Court was to legislate new oral laws when deemed necessary, abolish oral laws that were considered obsolete, and transmit established laws. The second institution was the synagogue. In the synagogue they would proclaim their beliefs, pray together, and read from the Pentateuch and the Prophets. Although the Pharisees studied the laws of God and observed the tradition of the elders with all their strength (Matthew 15:2), Jesus Christ rebuked them for being hypocritical (Matthew 23:15-36). Jesus severely criticized them for their application of the Law, obedience to the Law, and their interpretation of holiness found in the Law.

2. The Application of the Law

The Pharisees were deeply committed to obeying the laws of God regarding purification of body and spirit. In all facets of daily life, they attempted to live pure and holy lives. For example, to obey God's word of "Do not bring a load out of your house on the Sabbath" (Jeremiah 17:24), they defined the word load. The word load was defined as good as equal in weight to a dried fig, enough wine for mixing in a goblet, milk enough for one swallow, honey enough to put upon a wound, oil enough to anoint a small member, or water enough to moisten an eyesalve. By applying these definitions to their lives, they would separate themselves from other people. The Pharisees strictly separated themselves from Gentiles, Samaritans, and fellow Jews who did not study and interpret the laws as they did. They considered themselves to be more holy than other Jews and, certainly, those people-groups outside of Judaism. As a result, the Pharisees became a very exclusive religious group. They might have some relationship with other people, but they lacked any real spiritual interest in those who were not Pharisees.

The Pharisees took pride in being stricter in their beliefs than any other group of Jewish believers. Paul confessed, as we noted before, prior to his coming to Christ, that "according to the strictest sect of our religion, (he) lived as a Pharisee" (Acts 26:5, NIV). Since they observed the laws of God so rigidly, they were highly respected, but often feared, by other Jews. They were so intent on following the Law they disregarded the importance of the Prophets and the Psalms whose authors spoke so much of man having a love relationship with other human beings and with God. The core faith of Israel was to love God and love neighbors as they loved yourselves (Leviticus 19:18). Who were their neighbors? Were they people like themselves, knowledgeable of God's laws and living separated lives? No! Jesus said that a neighbor was like one who had "fallen into the hands of robbers" and needed others to love them and have mercy on them (Luke 10:29).

Pharisees wanted to avoid contamination. This calling of Christ to love neighbors would have required them to touch the unclean. This they would not do. They were called to separation, to holiness—their definition.

Another problem of the Pharisees was their lack of love. Christianity is the religion of love. If they memorized all the laws of God, but had not love, they were seen by Him as only resounding gongs or clanging cymbals (I Corinthians 13:1). Jesus loves the poor, the blind, the leper, the paralytic, the sinner, people with evil spirits, and children. He did not ask the Pharisee to merely observe the law but to love and help satisfy the needs of their neighbors. They seemed to disregard living out the spirit of the law.

A third problem the Pharisees had in applying the Law came from the fact that they were attempting to observe God's laws as they interpreted them and were trying to do so in their own strength. People cannot, in their own strength, observe even the Ten Commandments, however hard they try. Accomplishing the demands of God's law does not come from the resolution or effort of man, but from God's enabling power. For this reason, sinners need to come to Jesus for transformation and the gifts of the Holy Spirit. Only through the power of the Holy Spirit, can the requirements of the law be met.

3. The Problem of Obedience

The Pharisees were familiar with the Pentateuch and man's interpretation of it. They thought that knowing the Word of God was equivalent to knowing God. Based on their knowledge of the Scriptures, they considered themselves to be more righteous than other people. However, knowledge in itself cannot justify anyone. As mentioned before, they strictly observed the law, especially the laws of purification. But obedience based on an incorrect application of knowledge cannot justify the actions and thoughts of people.

What knowledge is the "very heart" of the Scriptures? What is to be obeyed? It is not what, it is who! Jesus Christ is the very heart of the Word of God! Jesus says, "You diligently study the Scriptures because you think that by them you possess eternal life. These are the Scriptures that testify about me" (John 5:39). The Bible focuses upon Jesus Christ, but the Pharisees refused to recognize Him. Instead, they focused on obedience to the Written Law, highlighting the biblical teachings concerning self-purification.

If they had accepted Jesus as their Savior, they would not only have been able to follow the laws of God and many of their traditions, but would have been able to worship Him and follow his commandments because only Jesus could provide them with external and internal purity. Only Jesus can transform sinners from the inside out. Only Jesus can enter into sinners' hearts and give them the power to faithfully observe the laws of God and life.

The Pharisees made great effort to study and obey the laws of God. However, no one can be made holy—justified—solely by observing the law outwardly. Through the law "we become conscious of inner sin" (Romans 3:20). Jesus claims that "unless your righteousness surpasses that of the Pharisee, you will certainly not enter the Kingdom of heaven" (Matthew 5:20). Jesus meant that no matter how the Pharisees seemed to be holy by observing the law outwardly, they could not enter the Kingdom. Then who can enter the kingdom of heaven, you ask? Those whose hearts are cleansed! In other words, people whose sins are forgiven by Jesus Christ and are born of the Holy Spirit may enter. The Pharisees highlighted only peripheral laws. They refused to highlight Jesus Christ, the "center-piece" of Jewish Scripture. The Apostle Paul, a Pharisee who had encountered Jesus Christ in the midst of his obedience to the peripheral laws, confessed that he no longer had confidence in the flesh (Philippians 3:3). No longer did he possess "a righteousness of (his) own that (came) from the law, but that which (was) through faith in Christ—the righteousness that comes from God and is by faith" (Philippians 3:9). When he came to Jesus, He needed to meet him in that way, too.

4. The Problem of Holiness

For the Pharisees, a holy life was of primary importance. They obeyed the Law, although often interpreting it according to the strict letter of the law, not its spirit! Tradition was also followed strictly in their attempt to live holy lives. They also separated themselves from those who did not obey the Law. They considered separated lives to be holy lives.

For example, regarding the sin of adultery, how would they deal with it when they confronted it in real life? How would they avoid this sin in their own lives? They believed that women were the real cause of adultery. So, when a woman entered their lives, they refused to initiate conversation with her. They would either leave or have her leave. If neither was possible, they would close their eyes and not look at her. As a result, some people ran into walls or other objects, making them bleed or bruise, in the effort to avoid contamination. One very orthodox sect actually called themselves the "Bruised and Bleeding."

Pharisees interpreted holiness as external conformity to the Law and tradition. But Jesus Christ considered it to be an internal conformity to the Spirit of God and a desire to do the will of God. For this reason, Jesus claimed that anyone who looked at a woman lustfully had already committed adultery with her in his heart (Matthew 5:28). One day some scribes and Pharisees brought a woman caught in adultery to Jesus Christ.

They were prepared to stone her to death. They decided to use this opportunity to trap Jesus and to kill him as well. They asked Jesus how he would deal with this woman. Jesus replied, "If anyone of you is without sin, let him be the first to throw a stone at her" (John 8:7, NIV). When the Pharisees heard what Jesus was saying to them, they began to go away one at a time, the older ones first, until only Jesus and the woman were left (John 8:9, NIV). Why did they leave? They left because they knew they were sinners who had already committed adultery in their own hearts. The Pharisees were ready to violate the sixth commandment (Do not murder), but keep the seventh commandment (Do not commit adultery). Externally they tried to conform to holiness, but internally they held hatred, jealousy, and murder in their hearts. True holiness came with man's internal conformity to the love and will of God.

Since the Pharisees pursued external holiness and not internal holiness, they ended up living lives which conflicted with the nature of God. They misunderstood the way of holiness. The harder they tried to attain holiness through their actions and outward experiences, the farther away they were in experiencing true holiness. Impure motivations, internal corruption, and moral depravity continued to live on in their hearts.

5. Several Lessons

Although Nicodemus, a Pharisee, possessed a strong religious passion, this passion came from within himself. He appeared to be holy outwardly, but was a sinner like everyone else in his heart. He followed religiously the traditions cherished by his fellow Pharisees, but often forgot the basic ideas found in the Law. We can learn several lessons from Nicodemus and other Pharisees.

The first lesson to learn concerns the significance of having good relationships with other people. Even though we have a lot of knowledge about the Bible, we can be Pharisees by failing to establish sound personal relationships. Establishing sound relationships with other people means that we love other people as God does. Loving relationship are made so much easier when we accept Jesus Christ as our Savior. He gives us the will and the power to do so.

Another lesson is related to the Pharisees' misleading concept of holiness. Holiness does not merely mean to observe the Sabbath and to wash hands before a meal. Although external observance of the laws of God certainly is not, it cannot make people holy. Holiness comes from the transformation of one's inner being. This transformation takes place when the Holy Spirit dwells in our hearts and minds. It is then that external changes can take place.

A third lesson we can learn has to do with obedience. Real obedience does not mean the literal conformity to laws and traditions as the Pharisees thought. It does not mean to follow a certain leader blindly. Real obedience is to follow the commandments of Jesus Christ, who died on the cross for us and was resurrected on the third day. To have true obedience, we need to come to the cross of Jesus Christ, confess that we are sinners, accept Jesus Christ as our Savior, and allow the Holy Spirit to do his work in us.

A Korean pastor, Tae-Woong Lee, a former Catholic who suffered from guilt in spite of his externally holy life, is a good illustration of this third lesson.

I learned Roman Catholicism through missionary priests, but I lived without having any relationship with the living God. I honestly couldn't believe God existed. I enjoyed mass for it allowed me to forget and escape reality. It enabled me to dream and to immerse myself in a solemn and pious atmosphere. If anything, Catholicism reminded me I was a sinner each time I went to confession. When I committed a sin that I felt was too secretive to confess, my guilty conscience tormented me and caused me to fall into deeper depression. Soon I gave up trying and vegetated each day, wanting only to survive. I was hopeless, not knowing what to do about my sin. But then I remembered—Jesus Christ had died on the cross and His death resolved all our sins! My sin! —I could be forgiven, once and for all! This was something unbelievable but it was true. I couldn't resist it any longer. I decided to accept it by faith.

Since that time, Lee, as an evangelist, has led numerous people to Christ, and trained many missionaries. He has been greatly used of God. The life of a young man, who appeared to be holy on the outside, had been totally changed—both the inner and out nature—by Jesus Christ. You can experience it as well. Just come to Jesus Christ!

Chapter 3

A Member of the Jewish Ruling Council

"Now there was a man of the Pharisees named Nicodemus, a member of the Jewish ruling council." (John 3:1)

The Jew Named Nicodemus

He is high and powerful Pharisee. Nicodemus has the Sanhedrin status, member of the Jewish ruling council. He had been chosen for the highest position we can assume as a Jew. He is a true and faithful follower of Judaism, the highest caliber.

However, Nicodemus the Jew was more than this. He had been born in the land of David, the Southern Kingdom. When Israel divided into two separate kingdoms, southern Judea secured legitimacy by keeping priests, the tabernacle, and the bloodline of King David. Nicodemus was a southern Jew, who was proud of the fact that they had separated from both pagan Gentiles and traitorous Samaritans of the Northern Kingdom.

Lastly, Nicodemus objected to the religious teachings of a new Jewish sect led by Jesus. He not only refused to believe the teachings of Jesus, but also participated in the persecution of Jesus' followers.

2. A Member of Jewish Ruling Council

Membership on the Jewish ruling council signified that Nicodemus was a very prominent and highly respected leader of Judaism. He occupied a very powerful and outstanding position in both political and religious life.

The Sanhedrin consisted of seventy-one of Judaism's finest: the high priest, a chairman, twenty four chief priests, twenty four elders, and twenty-two scribes. This ruling council had the power to deal with religious, civil, and criminal cases. It had the power to sentence people to death, although execution required the permission of the Roman governor. In only a few cases would permission be rejected. It had unimaginable power, including powers of legislation, jurisdiction, and administration. It was the overseer of Jewish religious life: supervising the priesthood, discussing the interpretation of the Law, regulating ritual, and arranging the religious calendar.

Nicodemus was a member of this powerful Sanhedrin. This fact already demonstrates that he is a very excellent leader because its member had to meet several qualifications: Above all, he must be well versed with Judaic traditions and rabbinic literature. In addition, "The applicant had to be morally and physically blameless. He had to be middle-aged, tall, good looking, wealthy, learned both in the divine law and diverse branches of profane science such as medicine, mathematics, astrology, magic, idolatry, etc." He must be humble, thoughtful, fearful of committing sins, and respected by other people.

As a leader in the Sanhedrin Nicodemus was considered to be—in the eyes of his fellow-man—an almost perfect person . He was regarded as flawless in his religious, social, and family life. But despite all this, Nicodemus knew within his heart that he was missing something—a personal relationship with God. Otherwise, he would not have come to Jesus as he did.

3. The Name Nicodemus

Nicodemus was highly qualified as a leader, and his reputation reflected his excellence. The name "Nicodemus" implied a special standing. Since he had a Greek name, his name was accepted in both local Jewish and Greek culture; the latter being the very center of world culture at that time.

A name is very meaningful to Jews, even today. In the Old Testament, God called Abram out of the land of the Chaldeans where he lived comfortably (Genesis 12:1-3). He led a nomadic life, moving from place to place. Despite his wandering, he had hope that God would make his family into a great nation. God changed his name from Abram to Abraham in the process of fulfilling His covenant. The name "Abraham" meant a father of many nations, and he actually became the father of many nations.

We can find a similar case in the New Testament, taking the example of Simon, brother of Andrew. One day, Andrew brought him to Jesus, and Jesus changed his name when they met for the first time (John 1:42). The name Jesus gave him was Cephas, in Aramaic, and Peter, in Greek, both of which meant "rock." Jesus said that Simon Peter would play a very vital role in the building of God's Church on earth (Matthew 16:18).

What is the meaning of the name Nicodemus? Nicodemus is a compound word formed from the two words, "nikao"(νικαω: to win) and "demos"(δημος: people). A "winner of people." His life corresponded to his name and he "won" the reputation of being a highly respected Pharisee and a learned member of the Sanhedrin that ruled over the Jews.

He was so highly reputed that Jesus recognized him on the spot and called him "Israel's teacher" (John 3:10). He had authoritative knowledge of the laws of God around which the life and thought of Israel revolved. He was "a winner" of people in terms of wisely applying the laws of God and the Old Testament. On the top of that, he politically became "a winner" as people appreciated his wisdom as a leader in the Sanhedrin.

4. The Problem of Nicodemus

It would not have been easy to find a better qualified leader in terms of religion, morality, and politics. In fact, Jesus refers to Nicodemus as "Israel's teacher." However, he had a problem! His understanding of the true knowledge and spirit of the Law was incomplete. Nicodemus was not yet ready to enter the kingdom of God. Jesus directly asked him, "You are Israel's teacher and do you not know these things?" (John 3:10). But it was not his lack of knowledge and understanding that Jesus was speaking of. Jesus spoke of the need for Nicodemus to be "born again" in order to enter the kingdom of God. Jesus clearly declared "I tell you the truth, no one can enter the Kingdom of God unless he is born of water and the Spirit" (John 3:5). Jesus highlighted the urgency of being born-again three times (3:3, 5, 7), but Nicodemus was unable to understand the need for this kind of spiritual experience.

Why didn't he understand Jesus about being born-again? This concept was found in the Old Testament? First of all, he was a Pharisee. Pharisees highlighted the Pentateuch over the teachings of the Prophets. The prophet Ezekiel spoke to the house of Israel, "rid yourselves of all the offenses you have committed, and get a new heart and a new spirit. Why will you die, O house of Israel? For I take no pleasure in the death of anyone" (Ezekiel 18:31-32). Going a step further, Ezekiel also claimed, "I (God) will give you a new heart and put a new spirit in you; I will remove from you your heart of stone and give you a heart of flesh. I will put my Spirit in you and move you to follow my decrees and be careful to keep my laws" (Ezekiel 36:26-27). If Nicodemus had paid attention to these teachings, and had cast away his prejudices, he would have been better able to understand the meaning of Jesus' words that one had to be "born of water and the Spirit."

Nicodemus had difficulty understanding Jesus about being born-again for another reason. He probably did not see the need to change his lifestyle since he considered himself already living an exemplary holy life. Why did he need a new challenge in his life? Even though Nicodemus considered himself to be a winner in this life, Jesus was saying he would be a loser in eternal life, if he did not give up some of his present beliefs. No one enters the Kingdom of God unless he is born again.

A third reason Nicodemus had difficulty understanding Jesus was because he had never experienced being born-again. We cannot fully know the truth of being born-again with our heads alone. When we experience being born-again in our lives, we can more fully understand the meaning of a new birth. In that sense, knowledge and experience go hand in hand in Christianity. We cannot enter the Kingdom of God by knowledge alone.

5. Giants of Faith

Nicodemus held a strong passion for religion, had become a learned scholar of the Pentateuch, and was an excellent political and social leader. However, he did not know the most important thing about how to enter the kingdom of God. The truth was that "one cannot enter the kingdom of God unless he is born of water and the Spirit." He was putting his "confidence in the flesh", as the former Pharisee Paul confessed in his letter to the Philippians (3:4), rather than "in the Spirit." All his achievements in life, as were Paul's, would be worth nothing, if he was not able to enter the Kingdom.

As Nicodemus must be born again, we too must be born again. It may be useful for us to hear the testimony of Dr. Robert E. Coleman who faithfully attended a Methodist Church and had been thoroughly religious since his childhood.

> At the age of twelve, I went through the customary confirmation class, after which I took the vows of Church membership. In making that commitment, I professed to repent of sin and believe on Christ. I was sincere, yet, tragically, there was no comprehension of the Gospel. Despite my spiritual ignorance, my outward behavior generally measured up to the respectable expectations of society. I did not drink, smoke, curse or engage in sexual promiscuity. I took my Bible with me wherever I went— and sometimes read it. Moreover, before bed at night, I would usually say my prayers. What was even more obvious, I seldom missed worship on Sunday morning. From the stand-

point of religious performance, I was clearly ahead of most students. I do not remember the words that flowed from my mouth that night, but I know there came forth an honest confession of my sin. There that night, kneeling on the floor between the study desks in that class room, I opened my soul to the saving grace of God.

After his conversion experience, Coleman served as a pastor, and later became a professor of evangelism. He has played a key role in the lives of numerous evangelists and disciples. You may be passionately involved in church life today but have not experienced being born again. Many have done this. But hear the words of Jesus, "You must be born again!"

Chapter 4

Knowing

> Now there was a man of the Pharisees named Nicodemus, a member of the Jewish ruling council. He came to Jesus at night and said, 'Rabbi, *we know* you are a teacher who has come from God. For no one could perform the miraculous signs you are doing if God were not with him.'"
> (John 3:1-2)

1. Searching For the Truth

John 3 begins with the story of Nicodemus coming to Jesus at night. From a human perspective he is considered to be an excellent person. He is a Pharisee, a teacher of Israel who teaches the Scriptures to the people, and a member of the Jewish ruling council which has political power. To many he is highly regarded as a very significant and influential person, but he comes to Jesus, yes, a noted religious teacher, but a carpenter's son—a vocation regarded by men as being of little significance. And he does so, as we have said, at night. Why? Why nighttime?

Nicodemus is a person who is searching for truth. But it appears that he does so in secret, not wanting to reveal his identity to other people. Perhaps he comes to Jesus at night because he risks embarrassment if it is discovered that he, an important member of the Jewish ruling council, is on a spiritual mission to discover spiritual truth from a lowly carpenter.

Nicodemus also might have considered that he would not have enough time to talk with Jesus during the daytime because Jesus would be surrounded by people. Rabbis at that time considered nights to be good times for discussing and studying religious laws without interruption. Choosing nighttime to have a deep conversation with Jesus, without being disturbed, revealed that he was serious in his search for truth.

2. A Searcher

One characteristic of Nicodemus was his passion to study the laws and traditions and to apply them to their everyday lives. Pharisees took pride in possessing their knowledge, and were eager to show it off in front of people. Nicodemus attempts to display his own knowledge when he meets with Jesus. His first words to Jesus highlight this knowledge, saying, "Rabbi, we know you are a teacher who has come from God."

What does Nicodemus know? He knows that Jesus is a man who has come from God. does not mean that Jesus is the Son of God, but that he was sent by God for a special reason. Nicodemus begins by calling Jesus "Rabbi", although Jesus is probably much younger than he is. If Jesus was just a carpenter, he would not have been able to perform miracles. He acknowledges that Jesus is a special teacher who has received a special calling from God. Nicodemus comes to Jesus—this insightful miracle-worker— hoping that he can receive the truth he is searching for.

He is not the only one who acknowledges the fact that Jesus is someone special, a rabbi, perhaps, sent from God. Nicodemus does not say that "I know you are a teacher from God." Rather, he implies that many people also acknowledge that fact, by saying that "we you are a teacher from God." However, he is the only one serious enough and courageous enough to come to Jesus seeking truth.

Nicodemus is also a humble man. If he was not, he would never have come to Jesus, the lowly carpenter. As mentioned before, he is an excellent person in terms of education, family, morality, and social position. Humble men, however knowledgeable, realizing they do not possess all truth, search for it.

Nicodemus came to Jesus at night because he was searching for the truth. He was a brave man, for the streets at night were dark, with little, if any, light. Danger lurked on the streets. However, Nicodemus walked through these dark streets to visit Jesus because of his passion for pursuing the truth. Jesus proclaimed that "men loved darkness instead of light...but whoever lived by the truth would come into the light" (John 3:19, 21). Jesus must have had Nicodemus in mind.

3. The Verbs "To Know"

Nicodemus said that he knew that Jesus was a teacher who had come from God. Greek has eight verbs that help give an in-depth meaning of the word "knowing." Two words seem to stand out above all the rest.

The first word is "ginosko" (γινώσκω). This verb was used by the Greeks to describe a relationship between two people. When two people get to know each other, they begin to respect each other and a personal relationship between them develops. They experience many thoughts and emotions together. This verb is found in Matthew 1:25, "But he had no union with her until she gave birth to a son." Having "union with" (γινώσκω)—a man and a woman "knowing" one another! Becoming as one! This verb implies that such an intimate relationship cannot be accomplished solely by human effort. Nicodemus was very knowledgeable in the Law and religious traditions, had a noble personality, and was very passionate in regard to his religion. However, he himself could not develop a deep, intimate, personal relationship with God. (This relationship might well have been what Nicodemus was looking for and why he came to Jesus!) It would only come through the supernatural work of the Holy Spirit. The Holy Spirit begins this work in human hearts when people accept Jesus Christ as their Savior.

The second verb for "know" is the Greek word "oida"(οἶδα). This verb features knowledge that is acquired by observation. When Paul urges Thessalonians to imitate himself, he states that "For you yourselves know how you ought to follow our example"(2 Thessalonians 3:7a). Thessalonians knew that they ought to follow his example because they had listened to his teaching and observed his life and ministry.

People become quite familiar with this concept of "knowing." We come to know (οἶδα) about many things through the newspaper. We live in a time when floods of information can be known through the internet. We know.... We know.... We know.... However, this kind of knowledge does not come from having a personal relationship, but only through seeing and hearing about things, and by possessing intellectual power.

4. Oida, To Know

The use of knowing in John 3:2 focuses upon the word οἶδα, not γινώσκω. When we compare the usages of the two verbs, the reason becomes clearer. First, γινώσκω focuses on knowing through personal relationship, but οἶδα emphasizes knowing only through acquisition of knowledge. For example, my wife and I know each other through personal relationship (γινώσκω), but I do not know the U.S. President Barack Obama through personal relationship. I have never met him personally. Nevertheless, I know him through television, newspaper, and conversations about him (οἶδα). Nicodemus knows Jesus in this much less intimate sense. Later, we find he has come to know Jesus (ginosis) intimately!

Secondly, γινώσκω features a knowing that grows deeper as time goes on. It is not the kind of knowing that comes through a one-time experience. For example, I married my wife thirty some years ago. I did not know her completely when I married her. After I pledged to marry her, I courted her for six months. Even after more than thirty years of marriage, we are still in the process of getting to know each other. This kind of knowing is γινώσκω. In contrast, οἶδα requires just the one-time acquisition of certain knowledge. I learned the multiplication table when I was a third grader. I now have a deeper understanding of math than I did at that time, but I do not need to delve any further into knowledge of the multiplication table. A one-time acquisition of knowing the multiplication table was enough for me!. Returning to my knowing my wife, courtship was not enough. A wedding ceremony was not enough. This kind of "knowing" is only οἶδα.

Thirdly, γινώσκω indicates a knowing that highlights the unification of two persons, their becoming as one. οἶδα signifies only an acquisition of certain knowledge. I married my wife and we became one, as the Bible taught us. We are still in the process of knowing each other, but we are unified and getting to know each other in a deeper way. This is γινώσκω. Knowing (oida) about President Barack Obama does not mean that he and I are united in thought and forming a deep relationship. Nicodemus is in search of a relationship much more deeper and intimate than oida.

5. Right Knowing

Nicodemus came to Jesus and said that he knew Jesus. However, his knowing was merely intellectual. Jesus said that was not enough. He needed to be born again. We may be just like Nicodemus. We can know about Jesus through sermons, the Bible, and conversations, but this knowledge about Jesus cannot bring about a personal relationship with Him. To know γινώσκω Jesus, we must be born of water and the Holy Spirit. We must come to know Jesus through the work of the Holy Spirit within our hearts. It is only then that our minds and ways of life can be transformed. We must be born again. We must be in search of ginosis!

Rev. Soon-Young Hong gave his personal testimony about his change from knowing Jesus intellectually to knowing him personally. He was the chief of chaplains in the Republic of Korea Army and was known as a living saint. He now serves as pastor of the Shin Duk Evangelical Holiness Church. His personal journey from οἶδα to γινώσκω had its beginning during his turbulent later-childhood years. He had been befriended by a Christian who had given him a job in her carpenter's shop, fed him, and taken him to church.

> I liked the days I went to church because I didn't have to work on those days. I also enjoyed taking notes on the pastor's sermons, especially the parts that touched my heart. Often I used notes that I had taken on the pastor's sermons and shared them with my friends at evening school. I attended church earnestly because it was fun. After high school graduation I went on to seminary. During my second year in seminary there was a revival meeting. I was blessed during these meetings I learned so much about Jesus. I didn't know how to thank Jesus for what He had done on the cross, for His death and resurrection. I had all this knowledge about Him—and it was wonderful! It was obvious that my mind became set on God at that time. Yet I was not satisfied. The seminary had emphasized persuasiveness and the ability to explain concepts. I continued on in my religious education. I became a military chaplain. I became well-versed in classical Chinese literature. I read a good deal of psychology, philosophy and other literature. But my sermons were no different from character admonitions or ethics and morality lectures. I was like Peter with his empty nets, and my empty nets could not be filled with the empty praises of people. I longed for a radical conversion experience like that of Paul or Luther.
>
> I thank God for transforming my life in a way (unlike Paul's or Luther's) that I was able to handle and in a way that was edifying. I started to grow gradually and change slowly.

You know much about Jesus. Do you want to know about Him *and* have a growing and intimate relationship with Him? Rev. Soon-Young Hong experienced that transformation—going from *oida* to *gnosis*. You can, too.

Chapter 5

A Teacher from God

"Now there was a man of the Pharisees named Nicodemus, a member of the Jewish ruling council. He came to Jesus at night and said, "Rabbi, we know you are *a teacher who has come from God*. For no one could perform the miraculous signs you are doing if God were not with him."(John 3:1-2)

1. Drawn to Jesus

As a result of his education, Nicodemus is well-versed in the Old Testament, especially the Pentateuch. His education shines brilliantly when he is appointed a member of the Sanhedrin. But Nicodemus has been drawn to Jesus! Shouldn't his position and religious education be enough to satisfy him? Why is this happening? Why is he being drawn to this man—this Galilean?

Early in his ministry, Jesus had been considered by many religious leaders to be just a young, ignorant, unlearned man. One day when Jesus was teaching the people, the Jews asked one another, "How did this man get such learning without having studied?"(John 7:15). The fact that Jesus did not attend school publicly was well-known to the Jewish leaders and had been circulating among the people. It hadn't appeared that he would have too much to offer.

However, the Jews became increasingly aware of Jesus. His teaching contained wisdom that touched people's hearts. His teachings "came true"(Deuteronomy 18:22)! In addition, Jesus challenged many of the traditions that had been passed down to them. Nicodemus wanted to know more of this man and his teaching. For whatever reason Nicodemus had for coming to Jesus, God was going to use this moment! He had a message to give to the world and He would do it through this nighttime encounter!

2. The Origin of Jesus

Was Jesus really speaking of "heavenly things" (John 3:12-13)? Had he really "come from God?" Jesus certainly resulted in good things happening, contrary to the results of the Pharisees' teaching. Nicodemus was drawn to Jesus, amazed by this man's teaching and wanting to make an impact on people too.

Nicodemus was not only amazed by Jesus, but also confessed to Jesus personally that he believed him to be a miracle-worker who had "come from God." Jesus had not learned his wisdom from man. Nicodemus had wisdom, but Jesus' teaching changed lives. People were being healed! Lives were being transformed! His teaching was also changing the mind of Nicodemus, and hopefully, his heart as well! Why was it making such an impact on lives? Where did his teaching come from? From God Himself? It indeed seemed so! Nicodemus believed so. Nicodemus realized the divine origin of Jesus' teaching and came to inquire more of him. Nicodemus was Israel's teacher. As a true teacher, he acknowledged his own limitations and the special impact of Jesus. Otherwise, there would have been no reason for him to visit Jesus and have a secret, possibly dangerous, conversation with him at night.

Jesus spoke to the Jews in the temple later on— "My teaching is not my own. It comes from him who sent me. If anyone chooses to do God's will, he will find out whether my teaching comes from God or whether I speak on my own"(John 7:16-17). Were these words ones might have shared with Nicodemus? Jesus was more than a mere "carpenter's son." [Nicodemus, you are on a journey to find this out!] Jesus told Nicodemus in John 3:16-17—whether Nicodemus understood the depth of this claim or not at this time might be questionable—"God sent his Son (me) into the world." Nicodemus had realized the divine origin of Jesus and, by coming to Jesus now, was learning so much more!

This happens today as well! Many people still consider Jesus as that which comes from a great teacher but no more. They need only to absorb its content and engage in a "conversation" with Jesus Christ.

3. The Power of His Teaching

The second reason for Nicodemus calling Jesus a teacher come from God was because of the power he had seen—or had been told about—displayed in the many miracles that had taken place during Jesus' short time of public ministry (John 2:23 and 3:2). Matthew records that Jesus had gone throughout Galilee teaching, preaching, and healing every disease and sickness among the people. News about him spread all over Syria (4:23-24)! Jesus drove out evil spirits, and calmed the storms of nature by his words! Three cases of reviving the dead occurred during his three year ministry (Matthew 9:23-25; Luke 7:11-17; John 11:43-44). This power to do good could only have come from God!

All teachers, including Nicodemus, convey knowledge and personality to people. Some teachers pass down mere knowledge. Jesus does more. His knowledge, character, and power are revealed in his actions and his teachings. Transmitting only knowledge (a responsibility of teachers) and influence (as good as that might be) still cannot produce the power to transform lives.

However, Jesus has come from God. His teaching has the power to bring about transformation. His words are powerful. God forgives. God saves. God rescues people from difficulties (problems and sin). God consoles. God's words give hope to those who have no hope. These are the words of Jesus...the One who has come from God.

The power in Jesus transforms lives. Lives become different—inside and out. Peter, a rough Galilean fisherman, would never have experienced such dramatic change, if Jesus' words had not had the power to change him. He became not only one of Jesus' disciples, but also a leader who established churches and performed miracles after Jesus' ascension into heaven. Peter, like Jesus, was considered to be an unlearned person. But he was selected by God to write two books (letters) of the Bible that have been very influential in people's lives (I and II Peter). His transformation is a strong example of the power of Jesus - changing teaching.

Nicodemus himself is an example of the power Jesus had to change a life. Why would such a well-known scholar of the Jewish world come to Jesus, a lowly carpenter? What could Nicodemus possibly learn from Jesus? He learned from this teacher about the necessity of transformation, of change, of a new birth. We have evidence of his experiencing this transformation later on in the Book of John. We find him opposing his own colleagues, putting in a supportive word for Jesus when the Jewish ruling council was voting to kill him (John 7:51). We find him having the courage to openly help bury Jesus on the day of Jesus' death on the cross (John 19:39-40). There is enough here to strongly suggest that Nicodemus had been changed. Changed from that of a secret believer of Jesus to that of a public follower of the One sent from God!

Jesus' teaching was not just a simple transmission of knowledge. His teaching was accompanied by corresponding evidence to back up his words. Deeds went hand-in-hand with his teaching. Without Jesus having the power to support his claims, nobody could have received Jesus as the Messiah. Since Jesus had come from God, his teaching was accompanied with God's power.

4. The Good Fruit from Jesus

It is safe to say, too, that there may have been another reason why Nicodemus, in his apparently short time of making discoveries about this young teacher, believed Jesus to be from God.

He had seen or heard about the miracles performed but also the God-like changes in man that came about as a result of them. Jesus produced inner fruit! And it has continued to do so. History is filled with examples! Men and women have changed inwardly, turning sinner into saint.

Saul, the Pharisee, systematically persecuted Christians in his attempt to destroy Christianity. His heart? One filled with a sinful, self-nature—hatred, jealousy, fits of rage, selfish ambition, pride, and the like. But his heart was changed, and he, re-named Paul, became a leading follower of Christ. His heart bore new fruit—love, joy, peace, faithfulness...the fruit of the Spirit (Galatians 5:19-23).

The story of John Newton is very well-known. He was a vicious slave merchant who took black people in Africa and sold them in the United Kingdom or in the United States. One day, he was transformed by Jesus' teaching regarding the need for spiritual re-birth. He, too, was changed from sinner to saint! When he became a pastor, he wrote the words of the great hymn, *Amazing Grace*, reflecting the grace of Jesus who had brought such a dramatic change in his life!

We cannot count the number of people who have sacrificed their lives to serve the poor or the uneducated. The life of Henry Gerhart Appenzeller is a prominent example. He was a missionary to Korea a century ago. Many Korean people were transformed spiritually and became national leaders who contributed to the development of Korea because of his sacrificial life. Appenzeller, a fruit-bearer! One transformed by Jesus.

Not all influential people in the Church have been men! Jesus' teaching has also borne fruit in the lives of many women. Throughout history, men have often treated women as inferior beings. Not so in the Church! The prestige of women has soared wherever the teachings of Jesus are allowed to penetrate. Women have taken advantage of new opportunities to develop their potential, and excellent women leaders have influenced all walks of life. Susanna Wesley was considered by many as "the most capable woman in England" at the turn of the 17th century. As a theological thinker, she had no superior in her day. Suzanna was the mother of nineteen children of whom nine survived. She taught them six hours a day, six days a week! Two of her more-noted children—John and Charles Wesley! Suzanna Wesley's life in Christ bore fruit...abundant fruit!

Countless others—men and women, boys and girls—have had their hearts and lives changed by the life-changing power of the Lord Jesus Christ.

Jesus' teachings have also helped to transform entire nations. History reveals the impact Jesus' teachings have made on social, economic, and political institutions of such countries as The United States, Germany...our own Korea. Germanic tribes warred among themselves and threatened neighboring areas during the Early Middle Ages. Eventually they united and the German area was transformed into a powerfully united, modern and highly influential nation. Jesus' teachings played a very important role in this creation, as it slowly but powerfully penetrated the hearts of the German people. Strong men and women everywhere, attracted to the life and work and principles of Jesus have become fruit-bearers—theologians, musicians, philosophers, scientists, business-people, and political leaders—helping to stabilize and civilize their nations.

Jesus' teachings have also had a powerful and positive effect upon family life. Huge differences can be seen between families that cherish Jesus and those who do not. Love, not hatred, is present in families that value his teachings. There is an unconditional love displayed between husband and wife, brothers and sisters. Undoubtedly, Jesus' teachings have produced abundant fruit.

5. Two Opposite Families

Nicodemus was coming to Jesus seeking truth. Was Jesus, who was amazing people with his teaching and performing miracles, the Messiah? His teachings were leading many people to believe that Jesus was the Messiah for whom the Israelites were looking. Nicodemus to discover who Jesus is was going to become a turning point for him. His view of life, and he himself, would never be the same again. Jesus was a teacher who had come from God. If he had not come from God, his powerful teaching would never have produced such results.

A comparison study of two families reveal the importance of accepting Jesus and his teaching. The U.S. government has carefully traced the troublesome family line of the Jukes. The lives of approximately 1,200 descendents of the Juke Family were traced and the following statistical data emerged as a result of the research.

Some 400 of these were physically self-wrecked, 310 professional paupers, 130 convicted criminals, 60 habitual thieves and pick-pockets, and 7 murderers; while out of the whole 1,200 only 20 ever learned a trade, and of these half of them owed it to prison discipline.

Another family, the descendants of Jonathan Edwards, who took the lead in the First Great Awakening in New England in the 1700's, was quite the opposite.

The lives of more than 400 Edward Family members have been traced. They include 14 college presidents, and 100 professionals, 100 of them have been ministers of the Gospel, missionaries, and theological teachers. More than 100 of them were lawyers and judges; 60 have been doctors, and many more became authors of high rank, or editors of journals.

The Edward's family reveals the good fruit which can come from Jesus! Such a difference between the two families! This difference ought to encourage—and convince—us to accept Jesus as our Savior, to become part of His family. Such fruit! Such good fruit!

Chapter 6

The Miraculous Signs

"Now there was a man of the Pharisees named Nicodemus, a member of the Jewish ruling council. He came to Jesus at night and said, 'Rabbi, we know you are a teacher who has come from God. For no one could perform *the miraculous signs* you are doing if God were not with him.'" (John 3:1-2)

1. An Extraordinary Teacher

Nicodemus was almost a perfect man according to the religious standard of Judaism two-thousand years ago. He was a Pharisee who possessed an extraordinary religious passion. His academic success was demonstrated through Jesus' recognition of him as Israel's teacher (John 3:10). As for political success, he was a popular member of the Jewish ruling council which consisted of seventy-one of the finest religious people Judaism could find. Nicodemus was an extraordinary man in every respect.

He was a good man—but he must have felt that spiritually he was lacking something. He came to visit Jesus determined to have Jesus help him find out what it was. Jesus was different from any of the other religious teachers in Israel. To Nicodemus, Jesus' teachings and the miracles which had followed, provided strong proof that this teacher had been sent by God!

He was convinced that Jesus was no ordinary teacher. God would speak to him through this man!

There were others who felt the same way about Jesus, but they were fearful. Many powerful religious leaders were aggressively opposed to Jesus and had accused him of blasphemy. Nicodemus came to Jesus at night.

2. The Miraculous Signs

Nicodemus came to Jesus for another reason—Jesus' miracles that accompanied his teachings. Nicodemus indicated that these miracles were further proof that Jesus was a teacher who had come from God. He confessed before Jesus that he believed that Jesus was not only the kind of teacher who transmitted knowledge but who backed up his words with power—power that came from God (John 3:2)!

Miraculous signs appealed to many people in Jesus' days, just as they do to people today. In the Gospel of John, three kinds of people showed interest in the miraculous signs performed by Jesus: Jewish spiritual and political leaders, many common people, and Nicodemus.

The Jewish leaders had asked Jesus about the signs, demanding, "What (other) miraculous sign can you show us to prove your authority to do all this" (John 2:18)? Jesus' reply was unexpected...and threatening! Jewish leaders had expected the miraculous signs such as the healing of the paralytic, the healing of people who were blind, and the feeding of the hungry. But when Jesus spoke of destroying the temple and raising it up again in three days (John 2:19), that was too much!. Jesus was referring to his crucifixion and resurrection—the signs that he would later perform—but they did not understand (John 2:20-22). Instead, they were furious at him!

To the common people, Jesus' miraculous signs were certainly ones that amazed them! "Many people saw the miraculous signs he was doing and believed in his name" (John 2:23b). However, their belief was not based on God's Word or the redemptive ministry of Jesus, but only on the miraculous signs he was doing. Therefore, Jesus "would not entrust himself to them, for he knew (what was in) all men" (John 2:24).

Nicodemus, too, was interested in the miraculous signs Jesus performed, but he did not demand that he do more of them, as the Jewish leaders had. In addition, his interest was not based on the miraculous signs of Jesus, like many people of today are interest in. He was searching for spiritual truth. Truth that would, he hoped, transform his life and his heart. Jesus knew in his heart what he needed (as he did everyman!). He taught him a much more important truth than that contained in any sign; the truth of needing to be born-again. Miraculous signs were not the truth in themselves but were deeply drawing Nicodemus to the truth. Signs confirmed that Jesus' wIranords were true, and that this young teacher had much more to say to him which he needed to hear. Attracted to this Man of truth, Nicodemus, as well as many other sincere people, would experience being born again.

3. The Miraculous Signs and Word

As we have said, the miraculous signs that Jesus performed had led Nicodemus to visit him. Jesus' words, along with the signs, had given Jesus credibility. He seemed to always back up his claims with a show of miraculous power. Imagine if Jesus had taught the following truths without the support of miraculous signs: "I am the bread of life" (John 6:35, 48); "I am the light of the world" (John 9:5); "I am the resurrection and the life" (John 11:25). Who would have believed him? Far from believing the truth, people would have stoned Jesus to death for blasphemy.

Jesus declared, "I am the bread of life," reminding the crowds of the miracle Moses had performed in the desert. The Israelites had become hungry during their long travel across the desert. God had promised to care for them after their deliverance from Egypt so He provided them with bread, manna, and quail to eat, telling them, "At twilight you will eat meat, and in the morning you will be filled with bread. Then you will know that I am the Lord your God" (Exodus 16:12). When Jesus declared "I am the bread of life," he was proclaiming that he was the God Who provides. Jesus fed thousands of people with only a little boy's five small barley loaves and two small fish (John 6:11). He not only told people that he was the bread of life, but he demonstrated it. Remember the two disciples going to Emmaus? They testified about Jesus saying, "He was a prophet, powerful in word—and deed—before God and all the people" (Luke 24:19).

When Jesus said he was "the light of the world," he was declaring that he was God. It was God who had created light when "the earth was formless and empty, darkness being over the surface of the deep" (Genesis 1:3). Jesus was bringing new light from God into the world. He would become the Revealer of all things good. The Guide into all truth. He would illuminate the world and its people with this revealing, guiding, light. The prophet Isaiah declared, "the Lord will be your everlasting light, and your God will be your glory" (Isaiah 60:19).

Why would the Jews want to punish Jesus for this announcement? He had already demonstrated it. Jesus met a blind man from birth who had lived in the darkness for forty years. He had taken him out of darkness into beautiful healing light! Healed his eyes right in front of his disciples (John 9:7)! Jesus gave the man his sight, as he had proclaimed—"I am the light of the world."

Jesus had also proclaimed, "I am the resurrection and the life"(John 11:25). This could not be! Not unless he was claiming that he was God! One day, the king of Aram sent Naaman to the king of Israel, asking to cure him of his leprosy. Tearing his robe, the king of Israel said, "Am I God? Can I kill and bring back to life" (2Kings 5:7)? Aram could not cure Naaman. But God later did! Jesus brought Lazarus, who had been dead for four days (John 11:43), back to life! Was Jesus God? Yes! Jesus claimed himself to be God and it was confirmed by wonderful signs.

4. The Meaning of the Miraculous Signs

Nicodemus came to Jesus because of his teaching and the miraculous signs he had performed. He was convinced that Jesus was a teacher sent from God. He was also convinced that he could learn truth from such a great teacher. Nicodemus was a man who searched for truth with a courageous and humble spirit. He was courageous because he came to Jesus as a member of the opposing Sanhedrin; he was humble because he, a well-known teacher of the Law, sought truth from Jesus, a lowly carpenter's son.

Jesus welcomed Nicodemus, for he saw his sincere heart, and took this opportunity to share the core truth of Christianity. The most important teaching of Jesus is that man must be born-again. No other teaching or miraculous sign could change the purpose and direction of Nicodemus' life. Miraculous signs can make people believe in Jesus, who performs them, but signs in themselves cannot make people born-again.

Although Nicodemus is an excellent man in terms of religion, political influence, and academic ability, he cannot enter the kingdom of God unless he is born again. Although Nicodemus is humble and courageous in searching for the truth, all his sincerity would amount to powerless human effort. All of people's extrinsic excellence may lead them to heaven, but they cannot enter into heaven—not without experiencing an inner transformation.

Jesus did not want to waste time with Nicodemus by beating around the bush. So he got straight to the point: "No one can see the kingdom of God unless he is born again" (John 3:3). Jesus knew that Nicodemus could not enter the kingdom of God through his own efforts and accomplishments, however excellent and perfect they might be. Nicodemus must be born again. This second birth could come about only by his putting his trust in Jesus the Son of God.

Miraculous signs become more and more relevant as Jesus' power brings about internal change in those who believe in him. If there is no power to back up what Jesus says, no one will believe in him and obey his teachings. Even with his displays of power, there are many who reject Jesus! Miraculous signs have helped many people acknowledge Jesus as a wise teacher, but reject him as One who was sent from God.

5. The Individual and the Church

Two miraculous signs are considered to be the most important ones in Christianity. The first is the transformation that takes place in the heart of an individual. How can a personal life be transformed in a moment of time? Through extensive reading and studying of good literature? Absolutely not! Through philosophy and religion? Again, absolutely not! Nothing in the world can transform people in a moment, but there is a Person who can! He is Jesus Christ who died on the cross to forgive sin and who was resurrected on the third day in order to raise a person from death unto life! If you accept Jesus in your heart, you will be changed in a moment! Every sin forgiven and the Holy Spirit living in your heart! The second-birth is truly a miracle! A sign that can be seen by men!

The second miracle is the growth of the Church. From its very beginning, the Church has been under attack. People have made every attempt to destroy it. Many churches have fallen due to political oppression. Many Christians have shed their blood because of religious persecution. However, the more the Church has been persecuted, the more it has expanded and thrived. This miracle continues on today!

The early Christians numbered one hundred and twenty at Pentecost, the time of birth of the Church. The Lord added to the Church daily. The number quickly grew to 3,000 and then 5,000 before too long (Acts 2:41, 4:4). The number grew to fifty million in 1000 A.D., and became two hundred and fifteen million in the 1700s. The number exploded entering the 20th . It became five hundred million in the 1900s; one billion three hundred million in 1980; one billion eight hundred million in 1990; and two billion two hundred million by the middle of 2006!

Nothing is comparable to these two miracles in the history of the world! Are you willing to take part in them? The miracle of new birth? The miracle of entering into a growing universal church? Nicodemus made that decision, and millions upon millions of other people did as well. Will you plunge into this gigantic spiritual wave which began when His Son came into the world to prepare man for the kingdom of heaven?

Chapter 7

The Miraculous Signs (2)

"Now there was a man of the Pharisees named Nicodemus, a member of the Jewish ruling council. He came to Jesus at night and said, 'Rabbi, we know you are a teacher who has come from God. For no one could perform *the miraculous signs* you are doing if God were not with him.'" (John 3:1-2).

1. Man's Desire for Satisfaction

From the human perspective, the visit of Nicodemus to Jesus should never have taken place. Considering the prestigious status of Nicodemus, it was a very humbling task for him to come to Jesus. Realistically, would anyone of high social, religious, and political position dare pay Jesus a visit? As far as we know there was only one—Nicodemus.

As mentioned previously, Nicodemus visited Jesus for two reasons: Jesus' teaching and his miraculous signs. His miraculous signs had attracted many Jews to him. They would often ask Jesus to do miraculous signs to satisfy their thirst for physical displays of power. On several occasion, Jesus saw their physical hunger and satisfied their need for bread. However, once fed, they lost interest in him. Jesus described the attitude of the Jews in the following way: "you are looking for me, not because you saw miraculous signs but because you ate the loaves and had your fill" (John 6:26). Satisfied with their physical needs being met, they had little concern for Jesus meeting their spiritual needs.

2. A Brief History of the Israelites

After King Solomon died, Israel was divided into two kingdoms. The northern kingdom, Israel, consisted of ten tribes and the southern kingdom of Judah, consisted of the tribes of Judah and Benjamin (1 Kings 12:20). Israel was able to build a strong nation in the land of Canaanites, but tragedy began with the division of Israel.

The northern kingdom began to worship idols, forgetting the God of Israel. Far from fearing God, they made two golden calves as their gods. In addition, they appointed priests from among all kinds of people, even though they were not Levites. They also instituted their own religious festivals (1 Kings 12:28-32). These sinful acts directly challenged the legitimacy of the religion which God had instituted in the book of Leviticus.

These acts led to an inevitable consequence. In 722 B.C., 200 years after its birth, the northern kingdom was destroyed by a brutal Assyrian Empire (2 Kings 17:6). Many Jews went into Captivity. The southern kingdom feared God much more than the northern kingdom did. However, they did not learn the lesson from this conquest, and started to worship idols, imitating the northern kingdom.

Although the life of the southern kingdom was longer than that of the northern by 120 years, Judah went the way of Israel. The southern kingdom fell in 606 B.C. to Babylonian invaders from the north (2 Kings 25:21) led by Nebuchadnezzar—one of the mightiest monarchs of all time. Again, many Jews were deported to the invader's homeland. The remaining Jews lived in horrible circumstances, enduring severe oppression and persecutions from other foreign nations.

After the fall of Babylon (called Iraq today), they were ruled by Medo-Persia (today's Iran). After the collapse of Medo-Persia in 332 B.C., the hooves of Greek war-horses, led by Alexander the Great, trampled over them. As Greece became weak, the land of Judah became the battle-ground between northern Syria and southern Egypt. History repeated itself when the land of Palestine became annexed to the Roman Empire in 63 A.D.

The Jews suffered from the rule of the Roman Empire, which was the strongest one they had ever faced. The Jews were troubled with starvation and many kinds of disease. On top of that, their wealth was taken by the Romans under the pretext of taxation. They felt that God had made the "sky above them like iron and the ground beneath them like bronze" (Leviticus 26:19).

3. The Hope of the Jews

The Jews suffered from extreme hardship, poverty and disease due to the oppression and persecution by the above empires. From the human perspective, their life was characterized by despair and they were void of any hope in their lives. The only hope they had was for God to intervene in their painful situation. Hope of God's intervention was found in God's covenant to them. A long time ago, God had promised Moses, "The Lord your God will raise up for you a prophet like me from among your own brothers. You must listen to him" (Deuteronomy 18:15).

A prophet like Moses! was a powerful promise. Moses was the one who had delivered the Israelites from the bondage of Egypt after 430 years. The Israelites held to the hope that just as Moses had delivered them and built up the nation of Israel, this promised prophet would destroy the Roman Empire by the strokes of "the ten plagues" and thus rebuild the nation. However, the awaited prophet should offer proof that what he would proclaim in the name of the Lord would come true. In other words, he should perform miraculous signs. Jews at the time of Jesus were waiting for "the prophet" and frequently talked of Jesus being this prophet. They had even asked John the Baptist, "Are you the Prophet?" (John 1:21, 25). When Jesus healed the man crippled from birth, Peter and John proclaimed that Jesus was the prophet (Acts 3:22, 23). Many people began to believe that Jesus was the one they were looking for because they had seen the miraculous signs he had performed (John 4:19, 7:40, 9:17). After Jesus healed the blind man and raised Lazarus from the dead many more were convinced that he was the prophet who had been promised.

They went even further and suggested that Jesus was their long-awaited king—the one who would deliver them from Roman bondage. "After the people saw the miraculous sign that Jesus did, they began to say, 'Surely this is the prophet who has come into the world'—they intended to come and make him king by force" (John 6:14-15)!

The reason why so many miraculous signs were recorded in the Gospel of John was because God wanted to introduce (through the witness of John) His Son Jesus as "the prophet," not only to Israel but to the world.

4. The Desire of Human Beings

Many Jews acknowledged Jesus to be the Prophet sent from God; their understanding of Jesus was correct as far as it went. They had suffered from long-term persecution for at least 600 years, enduring many kinds of humiliation. One way to resolve their deep-rooted enmity was to destroy the Romans through the power of the Prophet and enslave them as revenge for the oppression the Israelites had suffered. What an honorable reversal that would be!

However, the Israelites totally neglected one important thing. They wanted to get back their honor, but they had forgotten why they had lost their country. First, they had given up their relationship with God to worship pagan idols. Secondly, they had abandoned relationships with other people through their moral corruption. As a result, they were forsaken by God, exiled to a godless world. But God, in spite of their sins and faults, had not totally abandoned the Jews. God would frequently send a sign to remind them of His presence and His love and grace.

Daniel and his friends were good examples of God's abundant grace. God gifted them. His presence in the midst of a fiery furnace had rescued Daniel and his three friends! Daniel, alone in a hungry lions' den, came out of it alive to continue his distinguished leadership of the Jews in exile! Even Nebuchadnezzar honored him with positions of authority.

Both the Greek and Egyptian Empires, 332 B.C. -198 B.C., had shown consideration for the Jews, with this time period being referred to by some historians as one of relative "peace and happiness."

At the end of Malachi's life, however, God had become silent. No word, no signs. The Jews sat in spiritual darkness for 400 years.

It was not until the time of the incarnation of Jesus that God reappeared to the Jews. Jesus began to amaze them with his teachings and miraculous signs. People began to wonder—was Jesus the one promised of God who would change their world? Was he the Prophet?

People must have had lumps in their throats, thinking this might possibly be true. Crowds attempted to make Jesus king after he had fed more than five thousand people with five loaves and two fish!

Another attempt to make him king occurred soon after Jesus' resurrection of Lazarus. When Jesus entered Jerusalem, many people took palm branches and shouted, "Hosanna! Blessed is he who comes in the name of the Lord! Blessed is the king of Israel" (John 12:13)! The miraculous sign of raising Lazarus from the dead, along with all the other miracles they had seen before that event, convinced them to give an enthusiastic welcome to King Jesus (John 12:18).

The Jews wanted glory. They had been humiliated for hundreds of years. God wanted them to have something different—a restored relationship with Him. The only way into this relationship led to two of the greatest of all signs—the death and resurrection of Jesus.

5. Nicodemus and a Korean Novelist

Nicodemus was drawn to Jesus because of the teaching and signs Jesus performed. However, there was a difference between Nicodemus and the other Jews. Nicodemus did not ask for more miraculous signs. He did not attempt to persuade him to become king either. Instead, Nicodemus wanted to make sure that Jesus was the one sent from God. He also had a spiritual need. God was with Jesus. Nicodemus wanted God to be with him too. Jesus saw the heart of Nicodemus and gave this Pharisee opportunity to experience spiritual new birth.

We might have several motivations for coming to Jesus—loneliness, fear of death, friendship, wealth and health from God, the expectation of signs...many other motives. All these things contribute to the drawing of us to Jesus Christ. However, they should not be our last train station, our last stop before meeting God. Jesus challenged the depth of Nicodemus religious position by stating, "No one (not even Pharisees) can see the kingdom of God unless he is born again." Why did Jesus tell him about being born-again? The reason is quite simple. If Nicodemus was not born again, he would not be forgiven of sin, nor would he have peace of mind in his present life. Nor would he would be able to enter God's kingdom in his future life. We are all like Nicodemus. We must be born-again. .

Yun-Hee Jung, a Korean novelist, was divorced two times and involved in a serious car accident, and experienced a very close call with death. In her own words:

> My body was filled with gloomy ash colors of death as I lay on the hospital bed. The surgical incision on my right side was a foot long. A water-like secretion seeped out from it. Burning with thirst, but oozing secretions, in spiritual darkness and physical decay, without strength left to even despair, I was suspended in virtual death. Such a powerless situation is not much different from complete despair. I had no desire to live and no reason to fear death. Yet I became paralyzed in morbid fear. One morning about ten days after the surgery, I heard the sound of the cart coming down the corridor. When I shut my ears and closed my eyes, a thought of Jesus flashed across my

mind—of Him in that final moment on the cross, his side pierced, pouring out blood and water. "O Jesus, my wretched condition of this day is the consequences of my sin. O Lord, thank you for allowing me to see you through this accident. Thank you for helping me to remember the one who poured water from His side, wounded by a spear, in order to save me."

Chapter 8

The Miraculous Signs (3)

"Now there was a man of the Pharisees named Nicodemus, a member of the Jewish ruling council. He came to Jesus at night and said, 'Rabbi, we know you are a teacher who has come from God. For no one could perform the miraculous signs you are doing if God were not with him.'" (John 3:1-2).

1. An Excellent Teacher

Nicodemus, Jesus declared, was "Israel's teacher" (John 3:10) and taught the Law to the Israelites very diligently. He had sat under the teachings of some of the finest Jewish teachers. Though he was an excellent teacher, it was only knowledge that he transmitted to other people.

Jesus was a different kind of teacher. He had never attended formal schools where the Law was taught. However, whenever Jesus opened his mouth and began to teach, people were amazed and influenced by his life and his words. One day, after Jesus had finished a lengthy teaching on a mountainside, "the crowds were amazed at his teaching, because he taught as one who had authority, and not as their teachers of the law" (Matthew 7:28). His teachings were often accompanied by miraculous signs. The signs were used to introduce the Jews to the One who would come from heaven—the One whom God had promised to send to them. But these signs caused two kinds of responses from the Jews, both positive and negative.

2. The Miraculous Signs: Negative Response

Jesus performed many miraculous signs. In fact, the Apostle John left the following testimony: "Jesus did many other things as well. If every one of them were written down, I suppose that even the whole world would not have room for the books that would be written" (John 21:25). John selected seven of these signs to introduce Jesus to the people of Israel.

Jesus (1) changed water into wine (John 2:1-11); (2) healed the royal official's son (John 4:43-54); (3) healed the one who had been an invalid for thirty eight years (John 5:2-9a); (4) fed the five thousand (John 6:1-11); (5) walked on the water (John 6:16-21); (6) healed a man born blind (John 9:1-7); and (7) raised Lazarus from the dead (John 11:42-44).

When the Israelites saw these miraculous signs, their responses were not always friendly. Some people turned them into opportunities to publicly turn against Jesus. Two signs, in particular, the healing of an invalid and the healing of a blind man, caused the Jewish religious leadership to respond negatively. Another, the raising of Lazarus, produced a mixed response.

When Jesus healed the person disabled (an invalid) for thirty-eight years, the Jewish leadership began to persecute him because he had healed on a Sabbath day (John 5:16). At that time, not only had Jesus violated the Sabbath, he had even called God his Father. The leaders also had difficulty in acknowledging that Jesus had cured the man's long-lasting disease. Jesus healed a man born blind, but the Pharisees rejected that miraculous sign as well. Some of the man's neighbors questioned whether the man who had sight was truly their neighbor—perhaps a case of mistaken identity!?

Another sign, one of the greatest of them all, drew a mixed response from the people. Jesus raised his friend Lazarus from the dead! Many who had come to visit and comfort Mary and Martha, Lazarus' sisters, reacted by putting their faith in Jesus, but the enraged chief priests plotted to kill him (John 11:45, 53)!

Many common people believed in Jesus because of the changes brought about through his miracles. Most of the Jewish leadership refused to believe—because of their religious tradition!

3. The Miraculous Signs: Active Responses

Four of the seven miraculous signs Jesus performed—changing water into wine, healing the royal official's son, feeding the five thousand, and walking on the water— resulted in positive responses from the people.

The first of these miraculous signs, changing water into wine, Jesus performed at Cana of Galilee. This sign demonstrated his love for people and revealed his own glory, and his Father's power. As a result, the disciples put their faith in Jesus (John 2:11). The term "faith" here refers to the disciples becoming more and more determined to accept—and follow— Jesus as the Messiah.

Later Jesus revisited Cana. There he met a distressed royal official whose son was close to death in Capernaum. While still in Cana, Jesus told the father that his son was healed! No journey to Capernaum was even started! The royal official and his entire household came to believe in Jesus (John 4:53).

The feeding of thousands of people who were hungry, with a young boy's lunch of five loaves of bread and two small fish, resulted in people being so impressed "Surely he is the Prophet!" that they wanted to make him king by force, believing him to be the promised Prophet who could deliver them from bondage to the Romans (John 6:14-15). Jesus slipped quietly away from them.

The fourth positive response to a sign came when Jesus walked on water. One day the disciples got into a boat and set off across the Sea of Galilee to Capernaum, Miles from shore, they became fearful when a strong wind suddenly came up and put them in danger of drowning. Jesus was not with them at this time. He had left them earlier to spend some time alone in prayer. Jesus suddenly appeared, walking on the water! The disciples, terrified by what Jesus was doing, but encouraged by Jesus' words to no longer be afraid, took him into the boat. The wind died down. They immediately reached the shore where they were heading (John 6:20-21)! Their responses? One of relief, joy, new courage, and an increased confidence in Jesus. Mathew 14:33 also records this positive response, and more. After arriving on shore, with their renewed faith in Jesus, the disciples worshiped, crying out to him, "Truly you are the Son of God!" This was the first time the disciples had acknowledged the divinity of Jesus through a miraculous sign.

4. The Teacher Jesus...and More

Jesus revealed his true identity through these seven miraculous signs. Many people acknowledged him to be the teacher who had come from God. Nicodemus, too, had done so, as we saw earlier in John 3:2. But there was more! Jesus laid down a new and essential teaching—man must be born-again! The hearer, Nicodemus, represented everyman in this need. He listened, and so must all men. He later responded. Again—so must all men!

Jesus was regarded by many as a holy man. How could he have come from God, unless he was holy too? It would have been impossible for one unholy to produce such powerful teachings and power-filled signs. The man blind from birth, when pressured about where his healer was from, voiced this belief when he said, in John 9:31-33, "He opened my eyes. We know that God does not listen to sinners. He listens to the godly (holy) man who does His will.... If this man were not from God, he could do nothing."

Jesus was also regarded as the prophet whom Moses, centuries ago, had been told would come. The people who had been miraculously fed by Jesus recognized that. After the people saw the miraculous sign that Jesus had done, they began to think. Surely this is the Prophet who is to come into the world (John 6:14). Later, people who had been listening to Jesus teachings concerning his oneness with the Father (divinity) and their need to come to him for eternal life exclaimed, "Surely this man is the Prophet" and "He is the Christ" (John 7:40).

Their own Scriptures contained a description of this man. Isaiah described the ministry of the Messiah: He will come to save you. Then will the eyes of the blind be opened and the ears of the deaf unstopped. The lame will leap for joy and the mute tongue will shout for joy....Gladness and joy will overtake them and sorrow and sighing will be no more" (Isaiah 35). The miraculous signs about which John writes were seen as the fulfillment of this Messianic prophecy. Believing Jesus to be more than a holy man, many people asked the question, When the Christ comes, will he do more miraculous signs than this man? (John 7:31).

Others believed that Jesus, who had amazed even the religious leaders with his teachings and had performed many miraculous signs, was not only a holy man, teacher, prophet, and Messiah, but, more importantly, the Son of God. In fact, Jesus himself, indirectly, announced, after he had healed the man who had been an invalid for thirty eight years, My father is always at his work to this very day, and I, too, am working (John 5:17).

Many Jewish leaders would not accept this announcement. On the contrary, the announcement became an opportunity for them to plot to take the life of Jesus (John 5:17-19). Surprisingly, their own interpretation of his announcement had indeed been accurate. He was calling God his own Father, making himself equal with God" (John 5:18).

5. His Identity Revealed

The purpose of Jesus' many other miraculous signs was clear—to reveal his true identity. Why did he need to reveal his identity? Because he wanted his Father's will to be done: people to believe in him so that they could have a personal relationship with God. John wrote at the end of his gospel, "Jesus did many other miraculous signs in the presence of his disciples, which are not recorded in this book. But these are written that you may believe that Jesus is the Christ, the Son of God, and that by believing you may have life in his name" (John 20:20-31).

"That which is written" teaches us as well. Miraculous signs demand a decision. Watching for miraculous signs to occur, and accepting the teachings of Jesus, will not be enough. Our responses to the miraculous signs that came later—his life, his death, and his resurrection—decide our own eternal destiny. Many people in Jesus' time did not believe in him. Neither have people since that time.

John shares sadly in the 12th chapter that "When he had finished speaking, Jesus left and hid himself from them. Even after Jesus had done all these miraculous signs in their presence, they still would not believe in him. This was to fulfill the words of Isaiah the prophet, 'Who has believed our message...?'" It still happens today! Our own eternal destiny depends upon our belief in Jesus, his word, his actions, and our response. What Jesus asked of Nicodemus, he asks of us, "Are you born again of water and the Spirit?"

Chapter 9

Born-Again

"In reply Jesus declared, 'I tell you the truth, no one can see the kingdom of God unless he is *born again.*'" (John 3:3).

1. The Beginning of the Conversation

Nicodemus came to Jesus at night and began to talk, "Rabbi, we know you are a teacher who has come from God. For no one could perform the miraculous signs you are doing if God were not with him" (John 3:2). Nicodemus' intentions were to praise Jesus. Many people had seen Jesus perform miraculous signs, and his teachings obviously had struck a chord with them. However, as a religious leader, it must have been difficult for Nicodemus to call the unknown Jesus a teacher who had come from God. A man was only entitled to be called rabbi after he had graduated from a rabbinical school and was at least forty years old. Nevertheless, Nicodemus called the younger Jesus,

"Rabbi." And the young rabbi initiated a theological dialogue that had the potential of changing, radically, this Pharisee's life! He must be born again (John 3:3)! It must have been like plunging a dagger into Nicodemus' heart! So unexpected! He, a man of his status...needing to be born again!?

2. The Meaning of the Second Birth

Why did Jesus say to Nicodemus, one who was regarded as one of excellence in terms of morality, religion, and education, that he must be born again? If Jesus had been talking to a woman who had been caught in adultery about the necessity of being born-again, this might be understandable. If Jesus had told the criminals, who hung on the crosses alongside Jesus at the crucifixion, to be born again; or the demon-possessed man; or Judas Iscariot, this would not leave us with any question as to its necessity. However, the need for Nicodemus to be "born-again" did not seem to be appropriate in this case. There must have been a deeper meaning for Jesus to tell Nicodemus he must be born again. But there wasn't!

The term born-again means being "born from above." "Born from above" means the opposite of being "born from below." Being "born from *above*" implies born from *heaven*—born of *God*. On the contrary, "born from *below*" connotes being born from *the earth* or born of *man*. At the root, the terms "from above" or "from below" signify origin or belonging.

"Born from above" means that the power to experience this rebirth comes from heaven or God. People who are born from above are in the world, but not of the world. Their citizenship is in heaven. Their actions therefore—will be heavenly ones! For example, people who are born-again bless and pray for those who persecute them, rather than hate them. Those who are "born from below" belong to this world. They are in the world, and, of the world. Their nature is of human descent, not of God. Their actions therefore— will be worldly. Being born-again does not mean gradually improving oneself through continuous effort of your own—becoming a good person by your own power. It is a supernatural work of God.

3. People Must Be Born Again

Human beings cannot stand before God blameless with their earthly self-improvement records raised high! Again, the meaning of born-again is quite clear. You must be born *from above*, or born *of God*. Knowing the meaning of these words, we can easily understand why Jesus told Nicodemus he needed to be "born-again." Although he excelled in academic ability, religious life, and political power, and was highly respected by the Israelites, he had achieved all those accomplishments through his own power. Despite his great achievements, he was still a man who lived on this earth trying to get into God's kingdom by his own efforts! A relationship with God was necessary! To enjoy this eternal relationship he had to be born again—not enabled to do so by his own power, but enabled by the power of God. If such a good person as Nicodemus, had to be born again, how much more must we all be born again? "No one can see the kingdom of God unless he is born again (NIV)."

We want to pay attention to those first two words "no one" in the above verse. These words draw our attention because they were so unexpected. The chapter began as a private conversation between Nicodemus and Jesus. Since it appeared to be a private conversation between Jesus and Nicodemus, it would seem that Jesus' more appropriate reply would have been "*you (Nicodemus)* cannot see the kingdom of God, unless *you* are born again." Instead, he draws the whole world into this most important teaching.

Why did Jesus change the reader's focus from the man Nicodemus to all men? From "you" to "no one?" This seems to be a very impersonal way to converse with one who has come to speak with you. This sudden and deliberate change by Jesus was not due to any ignorance on his part of social graces. He intentionally changed the wording because he wanted to leave a message that would not only be applicable to Nicodemus. Must the man Nicodemus be born again? O Yes! But so must all men, if they are to enter God's Kingdom! God's redemptive plan was to be offered to all mankind!

Another reason why Jesus changed the wording was because of what had happened to Adam, the first man. Originally, God had formed man (given birth to) from the dust of the ground and the Holy Spirit had blown the breath of life into his nostrils (Genesis 2:7). The first man, Adam, had had a deep relationship with God. He, for the moment, had God's love all to himself. However, Adam neglected God's serious warning (Genesis 2:17) and yielded (with the help of his good wife!) to Satan's temptation to disobey God and eat from the tree of the knowledge of good and evil (Genesis 3:6).

God had said that the penalty for doing so would be death. Adam died spiritually when he ate the fruit of the tree! The Spirit of God left him. Since the first Adam, everyone has been spiritually dead—a state in which man is without the existence of the Holy Spirit in him (Romans 5:12) because of sin—disobedience. God gave man the invitation to "do it over again." Every descendant of Adam must spiritually experience a new birth. A new birth, this time by the power of "the holy breath" of God!

4. The Premise of Born-Again

As mentioned before, the first Adam, as well as his descendants, died spiritually. In other words, the Holy Spirit no longer dwelt in them. Without the Holy Spirit, people feel emptiness, and loneliness, a spirit of alienation from God deep down at the bottom of their heart. They feel in bondage to this life. This is not all! They sense a spiritual deadness, the fear of death often dominating their thoughts (Hebrews 2:15). Physical death means that the soul, which is alive, leaves the body, which is now dead. There is no more opportunity for a person to make choices that will allow him or her to enjoy life with God in heaven. When all the dead are resurrected, they will be judged according to the choices they have made during their lives here on earth. The result of this judgment will be eternal hell for those who have not chosen to be born-again of God; eternal life with God if they have. For this reason, all people must be born again. The rest of their lives will be spent in unrest if they do not.

As we have said, the meaning of being born-again is to be born from above. Everyone born on earth must be born again; in other words, they must be born from God. Since I was born in the Hong family, my last name is Hong. Likewise, if you want to be a part of the God's family, you need to be born into God's family—Christian. Born again! The Holy Spirit residing in your heart and mind!

How can you be spiritually born again and have the Holy Spirit come into your life? You must acknowledge two things: First, you must *admit that you are a sinner*. You commit sin because the Holy Spirit's presence and power is not in you. You fall short of who God is and fall short of what He wants you to be. You must confess that you yourself can do nothing to be born-again. Your own good deeds, effort, and intentions amount to nothing! Secondly, you must admit that you need to *know Jesus personally*. Why? The reason is very simple. God loves you and desires to have a relationship with you. Jesus Christ is the one who came from heaven to make it possible for you to have life with God. He is the spiritual bridge for people to cross over into new life! He died on the cross and was raised again, making it possible through his power, for you to be born again—this time by the seed of His Spirit! Lastly, if you want to be born from above, you must *come to him*. Admit your sins and receive Jesus Christ as your Savior. Ask him to forgive your past life. Ask him into your life.

Then, by the Holy Spirit and his power finally living in you, you will be enabled to develop and maintain an intimate relationship with Jesus. The relationship will continue to grow as you read God's Word and pray to Him every day. Other ways to help you maintain that intimate relationship will be by faithfully attending worship services, having fellowship with other Christians, and seeking ways to serve Him.

5. The Story of Chuck Colson

Born-Again is the title of a book written by Chuck Colson. His book has deeply touched the hearts of many Christians. Colson was a professor who taught law at a university and was later appointed special counsel for President Richard Nixon. When he was in his forties, he had every glory that a man could have. As an adviser and special counsel for the president, he had wealth, honor, and political power. He held his head high.

However, he was later involved in a major political scandal called Watergate and appeared before the judges concerning his part in it. The glory of yesterday turned into the disgrace of today. In desperate agony, he visited Tom Philips, a close friend, saying "I cannot understand why these things happened to me." Philips answered, "Chuck, these things will be beneficial." Colson responded, "Do not say that. How could they be beneficial?" Philips added, "I will lend you a book that is worth reading." He lent Colson *Mere Christianity,* written by C. S. Lewis, a well-known scholar of English literature at Oxford University, England. Lewis had been an agnostic, holding the view that the existence of God cannot be known. The life and thoughts of Lewis were totally transformed when he met Jesus. After being born-again, he produced many Christian books, including *Mere Christianity.*

Colson took this book and went with his wife to a small motel in a remote country place. He spent several days with her, talking, walking, thinking of his life, and reading the whole book, but his problem was not yet solved. He visited Philips again. While having supper together, they naturally talked about the book. Philips shared about the limitation of human beings and of spiritual death. More importantly, he told about God's love through Jesus Christ and added that Colson could also be born again, if he believed in Jesus and accepted him as his Savior.

Even though Colson was not able to fully understand it, tears suddenly began to run down his face on his way home at midnight. Because of the tears, he was no longer able to drive, so he pulled over to the shoulder of the road. While the car's engine was running, he cried out, admitted that he was a sinner, and asked Jesus to be his Savior. God answered his prayer and met him at that moment. He was born again.

Later, after hearing the testimony of Colson, Philips took him to a meeting of Christian members of the United States Congress in Washington D.C., where Christian Republicans and Democrats got together. Harold Hughes was a leader of the Senate who had dealt with the Watergate scandal and was a political opponent of Colson. Hughes asked Colson what brought him to the meeting. Philips informed him that Colson had accepted Jesus and was born-again. Hughes approached Colson. When Colson grasped his hand, Hughes hugged him, offering his congratulations. After Colson was convicted for the role he played in the Watergate scandal, he was put into prison.

While in prison, he cried out to God, shouting and complaining that he was in jail, even though he was born again. He didn't understand why this was happening. Still struggling with this thought, he got along with all kinds of prisoners, among them many African-Americans. After four months in jail, he received a call from Senator Hughes. He consoled Colson by saying that if he could; he would be in jail in place of Colson. Colson was deeply moved by his words. Hughes, a political opponent, volunteering to be in jail instead of Colson! Colson's attitude began to change after that and he began to help other prisoners with their legal issues.

After being released from prison, Colson started the Prison Fellowship Organization to help prisoners. A big problem is that many people get involved in crime again after their release from prison. The vicious circle of crime keeps repeating itself. Through the Prison Fellowship, prisoners are invited to a retreat for week—with permission from the government. During the retreat, the Prison Fellowship provides room and board and evangelizes them, encouraging them to be born again. After people are released from prison, Prison Fellowship helps them to find jobs. Through this ministry, Colson has become a very influential Christian leader in the U.S.A.

Jesus said to Nicodemus, "I tell you the truth, no one can see the kingdom of God unless he is born again." This is the most important truth in Christianity. No one can become a Christian, unless he is born again. People can become members of local churches. However, they cannot see or enter the kingdom of God, unless they are born again. You can have that assurance, too!

Chapter 10

The Background of Born-Again

"In reply Jesus declared, 'I tell you the truth, no one can see the kingdom of God unless he is *born again.*'" (John 3:3).

1. The First Man

Everyone must be born again. Jesus spoke very directly to the Pharisee Nicodemus of the urgent necessity for everyone to personally experience a second birth—a spiritual one. Jesus had told him, "I tell you the truth, no one can enter the kingdom of God unless he is born again." Nicodemus, as a teacher of Israel, should not have been surprised when Jesus told him, 'You must be born again'(John 3:7), but he was. He questioned Jesus as to how it would be possible for a man to enter "a second time into his mother's womb to be born" (John 3:4).

In this encounter with Nicodemus, Jesus was not only speaking of this Pharisee's need to be born again but the need for all men to be born a second time (John 3:3,5), a point we made earlier. For a better understanding of this need for all men to be born again we need to go back to when it all began...to the time of the first man Adam. His story will provide background for us to better understanding this obscure (to Nicodemus) concept of spiritual rebirth. His story is the story of every man. Three major themes: (1) God's creation, (2) pride in the human heart, and (3) spiritual death will be looked at.

2. God's Creation

God created the heavens and the earth. Soon Adam—the first man— was created in God's own image. God blessed him and said to him, "Be fruitful and increase in number" (Genesis 1:26-28). God's plan for Adam was for him to have a three-fold relationship. The primary relationship was to be with God himself. Adam had been created to enjoy a deep and intimate spiritual relationship with God. In this relationship, he would experience the love of God and enjoy breathing, thinking, acting and speaking out for the glory of God. The second relationship was to be one of fellowship with another human being. God created a help-mate, woman—to live intimately with Adam. Together they would enjoy their Creator, all that He had created for them, and would populate the earth with more of their kind...the descendants of Adam. The third relationship involved the environment that God had created. Adam and Eve were to subdue and care for nature...the environment God had made for them to enjoy (Genesis 1:28; 2:8-10,15).

God created Adam and Eve in His own image. God is spirit (invisible). He does not have a physical body (John 4:24). But man was a physical creature. Therefore, our description of man being "created in God's own image" will focus on the characteristics of the spiritual rather than physical nature. The spiritual nature of Adam's (and Eve's) is seen in Genesis 2:7, "God formed the man from the dust of the ground and breathed into his nostrils the breath of life, and the man became a living being." Adam, receiving God's breath of life, the Spirit, became an immortal creature enjoying life with his Creator and the rest of creation. As God was eternal, so was man—in the beginning!

In addition to immortality, Adam was a rational and holy creature. He could discern light from darkness, righteousness from sin, and good from evil. But he had been given free-will as well. He (Adam), the first man, was given the freedom to do or not do God's will. God desired to have a personal relationship with Adam, but He would not force Adam to obey Him. God was free; Adam was free!

Maintaining such a spiritual relationship with God depended upon Adam's desire to have one. The power of choice was a wonderful gift from his Creator, but with it came much responsibility. "The Lord God commanded the man, you must not eat from the tree of the knowledge of good and evil, for when you eat of it you will surely die" (Genesis 2:16-17). Both the prohibition and warning given to Adam (and Eve) were expressions of God's love. God's love was seen in the prohibition (Genesis 2:16). God knew the trouble they would get into by possessing this knowledge and, therefore, because of His love neither for them—not wanting His loved ones to be hurt nor to die— He told them very clearly not to eat the fruit from that tree!

Secondly, an infinite God set the absolute standard for good and evil. If He allowed finite man—limited in knowledge and having the inability/unwillingness to see harmful consequences of certain actions taken—to discern good and evil, disobedience leading to chaos and destruction would eventually follow. His enemy's power would see to that! God's love for Adam would not want that to happen!

Thirdly, freedom outside of God would not be true freedom, but would result in man abusing his own freedom. Adam's freedom would lead him into slavery, not into freedom. He would become a slave to sin, as would all others after him. God's love for man has no room for slavery of this kind!

Finally, if Adam had his own standard of good and evil, he would be like God. God is the ultimate judge of good and evil. When human beings discern good and evil based upon their own finite standards, they are responsible for the results of such discernment. Adam's assertion to reign as another god would have disastrous consequences, and God knew it. God is a jealous God ("You shall have no other gods besides me" (Exodus 20:3). He is jealous because He loves man and does not enjoy watching his children get hurt.

3. The Pride of Human Beings

The second chapter of Genesis gives us the context out of which the necessity for man's being born-again can be seen. Man has been created—from the dust of the ground. The heavens and earth have been formed and a beautiful environment for man has been made. God told Adam that he could eat freely from all the fruit-bearing trees he found in the Garden of Eden. There was one exception: eating from the tree of the knowledge of good and evil. Violation of this prohibition would lead to death (Genesis 2:16-17). We assume that God, who created Adam and designed the Garden of Eden for him to tend and keep, desired to give him the best of everything! Adam's continued enjoyment of this relationship with his Creator would be dependent upon his willingness to obey Him. Genesis 3 begins with this relationship between God and Adam being threatened. And soon the relationship is broken. The cunning serpent, Satan, God's adversary, asks Eve a question: "Did God really say, 'You must not eat from any tree in the garden'?" Although God offered Adam the freedom to eat any fruit except the fruit from the tree of the knowledge of good and evil, the serpent emphasized the prohibition. The serpent changed the image of God from that of a caring and personal "Lord God" to a very impersonal and, perhaps, indifferent "God." Eve's answer draws our attention. She makes two changes in her response to the serpent's question. The word "surely" is dropped from God's warning and the word "touch" is added to it. Is this exclusion and inclusion of these words significant? It appears to be so.

Certainly casualness in referring to God's command appears. The word "surely," which Eve excluded in her answer, was more than unwise! It suggested doubt, and appeared to be an intentional attempt to take away the certainty and credibility of God's word. She also inserted the word "touch." For whatever reason, Eve told the serpent, "God said, 'you (man) must not

The Background of Born-Again 71

even touch it, or you (man) will die.'" Is she suggesting that in her mind God is exaggerating just a little bit to make a point? Although the warning of God through Moses: "Do not add to what I command you and do not subtract from it, but keep the commands of the Lord your God that I give you" (Deuteronomy 4:2), has, obviously, not yet been given, the need for Adam and Eve to accept God's commands and prohibitions was certainly, and fearfully, understood.

The serpent responded quickly to this golden opportunity to exploit Eve's own doubt. He directly attacked her "seed of doubt," by saying to her, "you will not surely die" (Genesis 3:4). This word of Satan (Jesus called him "the father of lies" in John 8:44) was the first lie recorded in the Bible. This lie was a frontal attack on the love and credibility of God. Uncertainty in the mind of Eve led to doubt, which led to distrust, which led to disobedience, which caused a deadly rupture in the intimate relationship between God and man.

Next, the serpent told Eve "when you eat of it (this fruit) your eyes will be opened" (Genesis 3:5a). The serpent focused on emphasizing a positive result (to man) of his eating the fruit of knowledge of good and evil, rather than on the negative result. Man would acquire a new level of perception about himself! "You will be like God, knowing good and evil" (Genesis 3:5b). This was the serpent's way of tempting man to elevate the already high status he had attained to that of a god. Man's status would be raised! No longer would man need to be under the reign of God—for he "was like" God! Today's secular humanism gave birth at this moment. Man could decide to judge good and evil themselves, carve out their own destiny, and, eventually, resolve the problem of eternity by themselves. Satan's declaration was the height of pride and an expression of self-idolatry. The evil desire to do whatever they wanted to do—to go their own way—was aroused, and a natural violation of God's commands and prohibitions took place. Man, with God's gift of freewill, chose to follow the way of disobedience. Adam and Eve's disobedience of God's command brought about the emergence of moral autonomy in man's mind, an autonomy that would result in their making their own decisions without having to look to God for guidance. Concluding that she no longer needed to depend on God or trust His word, Eve made her decision. Looking at the tree from this new perspective, she looked at the fruit as a source of enjoyment, no longer something to be forbidden. Since the fruit of the tree was "good for food, pleasing to the eye, and desirable for gaining wisdom," Eve, and then Adam, ate of it (Genesis 3:6). Together, they disregarded God's prohibition. This was first act of disobedience recorded in the Bible.

4. Spiritual Death

As God had warned against eating the forbidden fruit and Adam had disregarded His warning, Adam experienced spiritual death. His spiritual death meant separation—separation from God. The Spirit of God, who had personally dwelled in him, left him because of his sin of disobedience. Since then, every human being is born into spiritual death. The Apostle Paul expressed the entrance of spiritual death in the following manner: "Therefore, just as sin entered the world through one man, and death through sin, and in this way death came to all men, because all sinned...." (Romans 5:12).

What are people like who are spiritually dead in their transgressions and sins? As Paul described them, they "follow the ways of this world and of the ruler of the kingdom of the air, the spirit who is now at work in those who are disobedient. Gratifying the cravings of (their) sinful nature and following its desires and thoughts (Ephesians 2:2-3)." Man has no power to resist these cravings. Spiritual death is certain. When "the ruler of the kingdom of the air" throws out the bait—the ways and temptations of this world—man, with his sinful nature, craves it and swallows it, selling out their consciences with little hesitation. People are easily tempted.

Man, with this sinful nature, does not worship God but idols. Some people worship idols made of stone or wood. Others make and worship idols in more cunning ways. Misusing reason and abusing the gift of freewill given by God, they worship idols made out of their own selfishness. The final result of idol worship is the serving of oneself, pursuing their own desires for money, power, and sex.

People who are spiritually dead no longer are able (willing?) to share loving fellowship with other people. They tend to take advantage of their neighbors because of their own selfishness, rather than sacrificing themselves for the sake of their neighbors. People deceive their neighbors, and their friendships last only as long as these neighbors continue to be useful and can be manipulated. For this reason, many people repeatedly disorient themselves, thus experiencing the gradual destruction of personality and degenerating into very isolated people.

People who are spiritually dead tend to abuse the resources of the earth, using them only for themselves, rather than being stewards of earth's resources for the glory of God and the enjoyment of their neighbors. They destroy large forests, disgorge industrial sewage into the rivers, and pollute the air in many ways. They hunt and destroy animals in excessive numbers for their own selfish profit. The wonder and beauty of God's various ecosystems are often threatened and some destroyed.

As a result of man's abuse of the natural environment God has created, "injured" nature begins to counter-attack. Disease, floods, air and water pollution, and many other things do damage to man and come as a result of man's "sins" against nature.

Christians certainly must share the gospel message with people willfully abusing our environment. There is much in God's Word which, if applied, can help to bring about nature's healing.

But this is not the real reason for sharing the gospel. People who are spiritually dead will one day experience physical death as well. Their souls/spirits will be separated from their bodies and they will have to meet God. The Bible clearly proclaims, "Just as man is destined to die once, and after that to face judgment" (Hebrew 9:27). He will judge them according to the eternal decisions they have made. God created man as eternal beings. He delights in thinking that they might enjoy life together—forever! But there are many who reject His ways and have chosen their own. They are responsible for the choices and decisions they have made. The Bible states: "each person will be judged according to what he had done" (Revelation 20:13; see Romans 2:6).

People who do not seek the God who loves them will be eternally separated from Him. The Bible clearly declares that separation from God in this life is not the end: "But the cowardly, the unbelieving, the vile, the murderers, the sexually immoral, those who practice magic arts, the idolaters and all liars—their place will be in the fiery lake of burning sulfur. This is the second death" (Revelation 21:8). On that day, God's warning of "you will surely die" will be eternally fulfilled.

People who cling to their own ways are spiritually dead and face an eternal death. They must be born again! Christians have a responsibility to do all they can to reach out to them with the gospel message—God has come! For them! They must be saved from their disobedience and sin. They must be revived from spiritual death. They have taken a wrong path. Their paths must be made straight! Christians must rescue people who are on paths leading to an eternal life without God by sharing the good news of the gospel with them.

5. An Invitation

All people, including Nicodemus, must be born again. The reason is clear. All people after Adam and Eve begin their lives without a personal relationship with God. They do not have the Spirit of God. They are separated from God. When this short life ends, no one will escape God's righteous judgment. He or she will either be doomed to eternal punishment in hell or blessed to have eternal freedom and enjoyment with Him. Everyone's destiny is dependent upon experiencing a spiritual re-birth. The only way to change one's destiny is to ask to be born again, to ask that they be born from God. The Spirit of God will come and dwell in their hearts, making them new people. They will then belong to heaven, not to earth. Setting their hearts on things above them will grow spiritually as people of heaven not earth (Colossians 3:1). They need to belong to heaven—and enjoy a new life in God now, here on earth.

Are you born again by the Holy Spirit? In other words, are you born from above? Are you born of God? Does the Spirit of God dwell in you? Are you searching for the things above, though you still live in this world? If you are not born again, pray to God with your face bowed before Him. Confess to Him that you are a sinner, and receive into your heart Jesus Christ as your Savior.

Chapter 11

The Kingdom of God

"In reply Jesus declared, 'I tell you the truth, no one can see *the kingdom of God* unless he is born again.'" (John 3:3)

1. Spiritual Blindness

According to John 3:3, all human beings, including Nicodemus, must be born again. Why must they? The reason is very clear. As mentioned before, the Spirit of God does not dwell in their hearts at the time of birth. Without the Spirit of God working in them they have no spiritual fellowship with God. Relational links with God have been totally severed because of sin.

People who cut themselves off from fellowship with God are spiritually blind. They cannot see spiritual things with their physical eyes and they cannot hear spiritual things with their physical ears (Isaiah 43:8). They are blind in terms of spirituality. They doubt the existence of God. The Apostle Paul explains, in his letter to the Romans, "their thinking became futile and their foolish hearts were darkened...they became fools. They exchanged the truth of God for a lie. They are without excuse"

(Romans 1:20-25). They committed the sin of pride by making themselves substitutes for God. They trusted in their own power and wisdom. They trusted in their own ways, not the ways of God. People with this heart condition are not born-again and, therefore, cannot see the kingdom of God.

2. The Reign of God

What is this kingdom of God? How can man see it? What does it mean to not be able to see the kingdom? The kingdom of God means the reign of God or the rule of God, begun and maintained by His power. Surely this world is not the kingdom of God. Man, in his disobedience and sin, somewhat unknowingly, walks in obedience to the devil (Ephesians 2:1-3). The Reign of God exists in those who believe. When we believe and receive Jesus Christ, we are born again and enter into God's kingdom, a kingdom where new life reigns—a life of "righteousness, peace, and joy in the Holy Spirit." The Holy Spirit comes into our lives to begin his rule over us. We walk in obedience to the Holy Spirit who has displaced the "ruler of the kingdom of the air." The kingdom of God expands when the number of people who are born again increases.

The Apostle Paul explains the kingdom of God in the following manner: "For the kingdom of God is not a matter of eating and drinking, but of righteousness, peace and joy in the Holy Spirit, because anyone who serves Christ in this way is pleasing to God and approved by men" (Romans 14:17-18). Eating and drinking are absolutely essential to the survival of man, but they are purely physical acts. Righteousness, peace, and joy—absolutely essential—come from the spiritual acts of God.

Eating and drinking" give us pleasure, but that pleasure is only temporary. On the contrary, the pleasures of the kingdom of God are spiritual and eternal. People enjoy "righteousness, peace, and joy," when God rules over their inner world. When people enjoy these things, they live abundant lives. They overcome circumstances of whatever sort and enjoy a spirit of "righteousness, peace, and joy" through the power of the Holy Spirit.

Valetta Steel Crumley enjoys the "righteousness, peace, and joy" given by God to the fullest. She tells in her book, *Another Valley, Another Victory, Another Love*, about losing her husband to cancer. Before long she also lost her three children one by one. She became very despondent, but experienced tremendous help from the Holy Spirit during her hardships. She helped other unhappy wives, and they formed small fellowship groups to support each other. These small groups became bigger and bigger to the extent that more than ten thousand women got together once a week, sharing love, comfort, and fellowship with one another. The testimony of Crumley touched many lonely women. She finally began a ministry in Taiwan. While engaged in this ministry, she was raped. However, she continued to experience "righteousness, peace, and joy" because the Spirit of God reigned within her. Her life continues to influence others for Christ! She is living in the Kingdom!

3. Righteousness, Peace, and Joy

The kingdom of God is a matter of "righteousness, peace, and joy." In other words, when the Spirit of God rules over us, we enjoy "righteousness, peace, and joy" in our hearts. What is this righteousness we can have? Righteousness involves having the capacity—through word, thought, and deed—to live a godly life.

Without help from the Holy Spirit, righteous thinking, words, and deeds are not possible. People must be born again to live righteous lives. When we are born again, all our sins are forgiven and taken away. There is then room for the Holy Spirit to reside. He begins his work of righteousness in us. The most important of all experiences in Christianity, man being born-again from above—becoming right in the mind of God—becomes a spiritual necessity.

The kingdom of God is also a matter of peace. We enjoy peace when the Holy Spirit comes into our hearts. We enjoy this peace in three areas of our lives. First, we enjoy peace when we maintain a right relationship with God. If our relationship with God is broken, our peace is also broken. Second, we enjoy peace when we maintain right relationships with other people. This kind of peace can be enjoyed best in a faith community. When our relationship with other people is rather uncomfortable, we lose our peace. Third, we need to maintain a right relationship with nature. When we treasure and take good care of nature, peace comes to us. However, if we abuse nature, nature will abuse us too. In addition, our bodies are also a part of nature. When we do not take care of them, we lose peace. When we lose our health, we cannot enjoy peace. People who are ruled by God enjoy peace by taking good care of the nature.

Joy is also experienced in the kingdom of God. When we live righteously, and enjoy peace in our hearts, joy will naturally spring from our lives. For this reason, many claim that joy is the ultimate sign of God reigning on our lives. In the kingdom of God here on earth, we live joyful lives through the guidance and enablement of the Holy Spirit, regardless of our circumstances. Our joy springs from supernatural origin. Even people who are not born again can have joy. They have joy when they buy new clothes or when the baseball team they like wins the championship. However, this kind of joy is only temporary, worldly, and carnal.

People who enjoy "righteousness, peace and joy" please God and have the approval of others, according to Romans 14:18. They contribute to the expansion of the kingdom of God. People, through their own power, cannot enjoy this "righteousness, peace and joy," nor can they please God.

4. Seeing

People who are not born again can neither she nor enter the kingdom of God; the Scriptures claim that "flesh and blood cannot inherit the kingdom of God, nor does the perishable inherit the imperishable" (1 Corinthians 15:50). How then can we see and enter the kingdom of God? Jesus gives us a succinct answer to this very important question: "No one can see the kingdom of God unless he is born again." And to become born again requires that one gives his heart and soul to God by believing in Jesus Christ.

Seeing" the kingdom does not mean people see with physical eyes; we cannot see "righteousness, peace, and joy", but we can see the beautiful results which spring from each. There are two words in the Greek language that help us understand the exact meaning of seeing. One word helps us to know what it does NOT mean. That is the word "blepo"(βλεπω), which identifies seeing as one of the human five senses—to see. The word that does help us is "eidon"(ειδον) which means perceiving, experiencing, or participating. This is the word used in the Gospel of John passage. Put simply, people who are not born again cannot experience or participate in the kingdom of God. Even perceiving the kingdom is difficult.

What do you "see" when you attend worship services? If you see only the building, artifacts, and people, you are only seeing with your physical eyes. However, if you participate in praise and worship, and experience "righteousness, peace and joy" among the Christians, in word and in deed, you are seeing the kingdom of God—in action! You have entered the kingdom!

It is also exciting to note that seeing does not indicate experiencing the kingdom of God only in the distant future, but experiencing it in the present. Living in the Kingdom, we can experience "righteousness, peace and joy" in all of our relationships (with God and man), even when undergoing the hardships and sufferings of this present world. We have entered into a spiritual Kingdom which will one day be a physical one as well, loved and led by God Himself. This "entering into" the kingdom is the amazing experience "seen" by all those who have been born again.

5. Corrie Ten Boom

Corrie Ten Boom was a woman who enjoyed "righteousness, peace and joy" in the midst of unspeakable sufferings. She was sent to a concentration camp with her sister because they hid Jews during the World War II. Hunger, cold, manual labor, hard surroundings, and loss did not take away her peace and joy.

Although her sister died due to the harsh circumstances, Corrie walked with God "in the Kingdom."

After World War II was over, she shared the gospel with the Germans who had harshly persecuted her and her sister because she knew that Jesus had also died for them on the cross. One day, she came across a German soldier who had abused them in a concentration camp. She discovered that hatred was spurting from her heart. At that moment, she seemed to hear Jesus, saying that He also had died on the cross for the guard.

Her hatred soon turned to pity and love. She shared Jesus' love with him. Guided by Jesus, she went to the United States. Her testimony touched the hearts of many Christians in the United States and her encouraging message strengthened many lives. She was known to many Christians as a warrior of faith. "The righteousness, peace and joy" that came from Jesus made it all possible.

Chapter 12

Nicodemus' Second Question

>"'How can a man be born when he is old?' Nicodemus asked. *'Surely he cannot enter a second time* into his mother's womb to be born!'" (John 3:4).

1. Wrong Knowledge

One night Nicodemus came to Jesus and said, "Rabbi, we know you are a teacher who has come from God. For no one could perform the miraculous signs you are doing if God were not with him." These words to Jesus revealed that Nicodemus had stored up a lot of knowledge about him. In fact, the words "we know" reveal to us that many of the Jewish teachers possessed knowledge about Jesus. What did they know? What did Nicodemus know? They knew three things. First, they knew that Jesus performed miraculous signs. Second, the miraculous signs could be done only by a teacher who had great power. Third, therefore, Jesus was a teacher who had come from God, the Source of this power. Nicodemus was well known as Israel's teacher (John 3:10). He was well-versed in the Pentateuch as a Pharisee. He had studied the Mishna, a Jewish commentary on the Pentateuch. As a result, he had become Israel's teacher who taught the Law to many Jews. Sadly, however, in spite of all his broad knowledge, he did not have a personal relationship with God.

2. The Limitation of Knowledge

Nicodemus did not know the real Jesus. He thought that Jesus was one of many teachers who had come from God. In the history of Israel, there had been many teachers who had come from God and who had taught them about God. They sometimes performed miraculous signs to prove that their teachings were of God. However, Jesus Christ was not only one of many teachers who had come from God. Jesus was teaching about God and doing many miraculous signs to support his teachings as did the previous teachers. However, Jesus came not only to teach but, more importantly, to reveal who God was. Most of all, Jesus was the Son of God, who had come to reveal God's moral character and His will for man.

The two most important moral characteristics of God Jesus spoke of were holiness and love. In fact, Jesus had come to demonstrate, by His own life, these characteristics. How did he show them? Through his own life, death, and resurrection! Jesus was tempted in every way, like all men, but yet he was without sin (Hebrew 4:15). At the same time, he came to people who were sick, hungry, and demon-possessed, and showered God's abundant love upon them.

The ultimate demonstration of Jesus' revelation of God's holiness and love was seen by his death on the cross. In his death, he showed that he was different from all other teachers. No one is without sin before the holiness of God, and every sin must be judged by God. However, taking the place of all sinners, Jesus, the Teacher, satisfied God's holiness through his death on the cross. Jesus' death on the cross also dramatized God's lavish love for all men. Jesus not only took on himself the sin of all people, but he also paved the way for man to be forgiven. Jesus, in laying down his body and shedding his blood on the cross, demonstrated the ultimate love of God.

However, Nicodemus did not know these things. These things were yet to come. Although he was conversant with the Law, he was not familiar with the gospel—the "other" news! He did not fully realize who Jesus Christ was; the full demonstration of God's holiness and love. He did not know, for his own knowledge could take him only so far. It would not be enough. His soul was still apart from God—but it would not be for long.

3. The Limitation of Understanding

Jesus showed great compassion to Nicodemus who approached him that day. Eighteen of the most important words Nicodemus would ever hear came from the lips of Jesus, "I tell you the truth, no one can see the kingdom of God unless he is born again"(John 3:3). Absolutely no one! These words would change this Pharisee's life forever! Jesus told Nicodemus directly that he could not experience the kingdom of God through his own actions and knowledge—as great as they were.

Nicodemus was unable to understand Jesus' reply, "You must be born from above." This was deep spiritual truth and his mind and heart could not grasp it. He revealed the shallowness of his own spiritual knowledge by asking Jesus, "How can a man be born when he is old? *Surely he cannot enter a second time* into his mother's womb to be born!"

Remember, this second birth cannot be accomplished through human effort. Nicodemus' reply to Jesus was either one of frustration, or, perhaps, sarcasm at the absurdity of the thought. He saw another birth as a human impossibility. And it was! It could only come about through a divine miracle. If it could be accomplished through human effort—and it definitely could not be—Nicodemus would certainly have been a man who deserved to be born again, due to all his accomplishments and credits.

Jesus used the words "born-again" in the sense of being "born from above"—an accomplishment of God—Nicodemus interpreted it to mean being "born a second time"—an accomplishment of man. When Jesus spoke of it as a spiritual rebirth, Nicodemus understood it as a physical rebirth. He could not understand the difference between spiritual and physical rebirths.

People who have no spiritual relationship with God consider His truth to be foolishness, as Paul stated: "The man without the Spirit does not accept the things that come from the Spirit of God, for they are foolishness to him" (1 Corinthians 2:14). The man without the Spirit in this verse refers to people who are not born again.

You, too, may still not understand Jesus words, "No one can see the kingdom of God unless he is born again". You may, as well, feel this to be sheer foolishness. If you do not wish to understand, you cannot live in God's kingdom. You must be born from above (of God). Ask Him to help you have even a mustard seed of understand!

4. Misunderstanding

In many cases, misunderstandings take place among people because of their limited knowledge and comprehension. Misunderstanding Jesus' words regarding having to be born-again, Nicodemus asked Jesus the following question: "How can a man be born when he is old? Surely he cannot enter a second time into his mother's womb to be born."

In Jesus' time, Jews "traveled over land and sea to win a single convert" (Matthew 23:15). Through human efforts and words of persuasion, Gentiles had been converted to Judaism. They were accepted into Judaism, like a newly-born baby. It appears that confusion, perhaps even anger, might have existed in Nicodemus' mind, when Jesus told him, Israel's teacher, a Pharisee, and a member of the Jewish ruling council, about being born-again. By Jesus saying that "no one can see the kingdom of God unless he is born again" was Jesus treating him like an inferior? Even worse, like a sinner?

When Moravian Christians asked John Wesley, "Are you born again?" he could have been perplexed, or even angry at them. After all, Wesley was a pastor, a seminary professor, and a missionary. Instead, Wesley saw the compassionate concern of the Moravians and later received that new birth they had spoken of. To Nicodemus, who enjoyed as much social and religious position as John Wesley, perhaps more, Jesus' words emphasizing the necessity of his being born-again. This might have made him feel that he would lose face. For this reason, Nicodemus answered in a brusque manner, "How can a man be born when he is old? Surely he cannot enter a second time into his mother's womb to be born."

Jesus' words that "no one can see the kingdom of God unless he is born again" might have also made Nicodemus feel that he would have to reject the accomplishments of his past life. All the deeds, efforts, study, prayers, hopes, doubts, and fears of his past had all come together to create his present identity! Born again!? Do away with his present identity? His reputation? He must have misunderstood the words of Jesus!

For some people, ridding themselves of all past actions and status and starting all over again would be a blessing. Take for example, a criminal who has served several terms in prison. If he or she could delete all the criminal records of the past and have a fresh new start, this would be a blessing to him or her. However, Nicodemus was in a different situation. He was not a criminal. He was a pious Pharisee, a highly respected member of Jewish ruling council, and a very knowledgeable teacher of Israel! His present prestigious status stood as a memorial to the hard effort, discipline, and many accomplishments of his past life.

If Nicodemus took the words of Jesus in this way, his reply to Jesus' words was understandable. His answer could have been interpreted: "Jesus, how can I deny my birth—my past and my present life? This is totally impossible for me to do! It would be like an old man entering a second time into his mother's womb. For me to deny my honorable past life and be born again is impossible." This must all be just one great big misunderstanding!

5. Continuous Change

Nicodemus revealed not only his misunderstanding but also the limitations of his knowledge and understanding. Nonetheless, a commendable attitude still remained. Even though Nicodemus did not immediately understand Jesus' word about being born-again, he did not stop in his pursuit of Jesus' teachings.

He did not react to the feeling of the moment. Although he did not immediately understand the meaning of being born-again, he did not mock Jesus' words. He did not regard Jesus as being inferior to him in terms of his social and religious position in the Jewish world. Instead, he apparently listened carefully to Jesus, who was younger than he, and sought to understand the meaning of Jesus' words. Searching for the truth was too important for him to leave his pursuit of Jesus. Later in the Gospel of John, we find further actions were taken by Nicodemus that lead us to believe that he, indeed, became a born-again follower of Jesus Christ (John 7:50-52 and 19:38-42). What about you? Will Nicodemus's spiritual journey be your spiritual journey too?

Chapter 13

Nicodemus' Second Question (2)

"'How can a man be born when he is old?' Nicodemus asked. 'Surely he cannot enter a second time into his mother's womb to be born!'" (John 3:4).

1. True Knowledge

True knowledge plays an important role in entering the Christian world. Without sufficient knowledge and the understanding of what God wants us to do with it, no one can receive Jesus. Again, this knowledge does not mean simply gathering information. True knowledge includes knowing about the will of God, which goes far beyond the intellectual aspect of knowledge and then doing it. In other words, true knowledge is that which is useful in bringing about the transformation of the heart as well as change in the behavior of men. Transformation and change come through faith. We know the truth; therefore, we act upon it...stepping out by faith into the truth of God.

However, Nicodemus had not gathered this kind of knowledge. Even though he was "Israel's teacher" and proud of both his secular and religious knowledge, he did not possess the kind of knowledge that, when he acted upon it, would transform his spiritual relationship with God, and his social relationship with other humans. Paul describes Jewish religious teachers like Nicodemus as being, "zealous for God, but their zeal (was) not based on knowledge" (Romans 10:2).

Why did Israel's religious leaders, in their zealous pursuit of godliness, fail in their attempt to live true lives of righteousness? The reason is very simple! They failed to do so because they sought to live by their own sense of righteousness. Paul said in Romans 10:3, "Since they did not know the righteousness that comes from God and sought to establish their own, they did not submit to God's righteousness." As a result, they had no personal relationship with God. This tragedy happens in present-day religious circles too. Many want to establish their own sense of righteousness, and, therefore, live an unhealthy religious life based on works, not faith.

2. Church Membership

Many people "know" a born-again experience that is dependent on church membership. Often they are born into Christian families who habitually attend worship services. From birth they follow their parents religiously! Their "born-again experience" evolves over the years as they make contact with parents, various Bible teachers, pastors, and other respectable friends. They become accustomed to their church's religious rituals and events. They acquire Christian terminology, manners, and life-style. Knowledge of things "Christian" lead them to enter into church membership.

Others begin attending church when they are adults. Some of them have come to church services because of hardships they have been experiencing: financial difficulties, health problems, the loss of loved ones, etc. They were perhaps invited by good church people to enter into an environment where they can find help and stability. Although such people are not used to the vocabulary terms and rituals of the church, they make every effort to adapt themselves to the traditions of the church. They often become church members gradually adjusting to life in the church. Since they begin their church experiences late in life, they attempt to compensate for their lost time by participating enthusiastically. They not only adjust themselves to a new society (the church) and learn a new language (a religious one) but they frequently achieve recognition as church leaders.

Regardless of the many good experiences these people have in the church; if they do not respond to the truth that Nicodemus was confronted with, that "You must be born again," they remain outside of the kingdom of God. Even though they are church members, they are still in spiritual darkness. They have no personal relationship with Jesus, although they have heard about God the Father, Jesus Christ, and the Holy Spirit. They are what we call nominal Christians. They carry the name Christian, but they are not Christian in a born-again experience.

They attend church, but do not receive Jesus Christ. the Bible clearly declares that people cannot become Christians by "natural descent, nor of human decision or a husband's will" (John 1:12-13). They "must be born of God." Sadly, we find many nominal Christians in today's churches. They cannot experience the kingdom of God, unless they are born again. These nominal church-goers are just like Nicodemus and the Jews, attending their synagogues regularly and doing good works, but never entering into a personal relationship with Jesus.

3. Baptism

Baptism, too, is a very important ceremony in the life of a church. Millions of people take baptism classes. In many cases, baptism is a very moving experience, and those baptized are warmly welcomed into church fellowship. However, a trap can be found here! Many baptized church members believe that they are born again because they have been baptized. Baptism is part of the Great Commission given by Jesus before he ascended to heaven—"Go throughout the world and make disciples...baptizing them...and teaching them...." (Matthew 28:19-20). It is considered one of the two holy sacraments (Baptism and the Eucharist) in many Protestant traditions.

However, if people believe they are born again because of their baptism, they mislead themselves. They are baptized because they have been born again! The apostle Paul describes the experience of baptism very beautifully in Romans 6:3-5a: "Don't you know that all of us who were baptized into Christ Jesus were baptized into his death? We were therefore buried with him through baptism into death in order that, just as Christ was raised from the dead...we too may live a new life. If we have been united with him (Christ)...."

When are we united with Jesus Christ? At the time of baptism? Of course not! When we are born again, we are united with Jesus Christ. Old things (our wills and our ways) have passed away; all things have become new. Being united with Christ means denying the old way of life. At the time of baptism? Of course not! It happens when we are born again. Being united with Jesus Christ in an active sense and denying the old ways of life in a passive sense does not come from baptism with water, but from being born-again, by being baptized with the Holy Spirit (1 Corinthians 12:13). For this reason, baptism with water should be exclusive for born-again Christians. The Apostle Peter claims that baptism with water is not a ceremony performed to get rid of sin, but a symbol of obedience to the will of God. In his own words about baptism: It is "the pledge of a good conscience toward God (1 Peter 3:21).

4. Office

When one is given a leading position in a local church it reveals that that person is highly recognized in the church. A church member can be appointed to an office only if a person meets at least two qualifications; first, the church member must be faithful to that church; second, the person must be considered gifted for the office.

The local church needs people who can serve in various ways. Men's groups or women's groups need leaders in order to function well. Church boards and committees also need leaders. Youth groups and young adult groups require faithful leaders. A well-structured local church needs many kinds of officers in order to meet the needs of people.

Often, because of the many needs of the church congregation and its community, the local church may unintentionally, but carelessly, appoint unqualified people to certain leadership positions.

Many of those appointed believe that they are Christians because they have been appointed to a certain office. This is wrong assurance, based on wrong knowledge. Christians are not born-again because of their office in a church. This approach is analogous to putting the cart before the horse. Even to a horse, this is ridiculous! To serve the local church faithfully can be a meaningful experience, but the experience and assurance of being born-again is the essential experience. Nicodemus had a noble office, but he was not born again.

Many people like Nicodemus exist in South Korea's churches, as they do in other countries. The name of God is blasphemed and the churches are criticized by society because of the leaders who are not born again (Romans 2:24-25). Nicodemus was not born-again, but he was a teacher of Israel. Likewise, there might be Korean theologians who are not born again. Nicodemus was not born-again, but he was a Pharisee. Likewise, there might be pastors who are not born-again.

Even, as Nicodemus was a leading member of the Jewish ruling council, there might even be leading (famous) pastors who are not born again, but have authority and power over South Korea's churches. If pastors who are not born again minister to a congregation, its members probably will not hear of their needing to be born-again either. The Bible says "If a blind man leads a blind man, both will fall into a pit" (Matthew 15:14).

5. An Historical Example

A person who is a faithful church member or has been baptized or receives a leadership position in a church amounts to only a "resounding gong or a clanging cymbal" unless he or she is born-again (1 Corinthians 13:1). Jesus' words to Nicodemus are still true today. Jesus tells him that "no one can see the kingdom of God, unless he is born-again."

Take the example of John Wesley. He was a pastor, a theologian, and a missionary. He had been appointed to noble offices in the church. However, he was not born again because of any of these positions he held. He was passionate in serving other people, but he was not born again because of this compassion. Nor did his giftedness make him born-again.

One day John Wesley had his heart "strangely warmed." He believed Jesus Christ to be the One who had taken away his own sins and doubts. He had a personal relationship with Jesus Christ at last. He had experienced being born again. Later, he influenced many others to be born-again when he preached about the transformation he had experienced. His transformed life, as well as the transformed lives of numerous others, eventually changed English society and, by extension, made an impact on American society as well. Are you born again? Or are you still relying on church membership, baptism, or church office instead of the second-birth to bring you into the Kingdom of God?

Chapter 14

The Secret of New Birth

"Jesus answered, 'I tell you the truth, no one can enter the kingdom of God unless he is born of water and the Spirit'" (John 3:5).

1. An Additional Explanation

Jesus replied quickly to the absurd but frank response of Nicodemus who had misunderstood the truth of being born-again. Nicodemus, confused by Jesus' words suggesting, to him, a second physical-birth, had asked, "How can a man be born when he is old?" Jesus used different words this time to help describe this essential born-again experience: the words, "born of water and the Spirit" and "no one can enter kingdom." He is determined for Nicodemus to understand this most essential of spiritual truths! Jesus loved Nicodemus and was determined that he be born again! He saw how close Nicodemus was to the kingdom and wanted to make every effort he possibly could to give him a better understanding of this truth.

Jesus used these three words to help his new teacher-friend understand the truth of spiritual rebirth: water, the Spirit, and enter. With the help of these very simple and familiar words,

Jesus hoped to open, even further, Nicodemus' mind, and, more importantly, his heart. His desire was to take the mystery out of the concept of the new birth and turn it into a reality for Nicodemus. These words could very well hold the secret to a better understanding of what he had previously told Nicodemus. Jesus prayed that they would; for again, no one can enter the kingdom of God unless he is born-again.

2. Water

Why does Jesus say that no one can enter the kingdom of God unless he/she is born of water? What is it about water that is so vital to the understanding of someone entering into the kingdom of God? Although water has multiple functions, one of its most important functions is cleansing.

In the Old Testament, God commanded the Jews to go through numerous purification ceremonies to cleanse themselves before entering into His presence or the presence of other human beings. Whenever lepers, physically and lawfully unclean, were cured, they were required to wash their bodies and clothes with water before they could come back to live among people (Leviticus 14:8-9). Priests needed to be cleansed with water before their ordination (Leviticus 8:6). When priests became unclean while performing their ceremonial duties, they needed to wash their bodies and clothes afterwards. Without this cleansing everything they touched would be considered unclean, including themselves and God's sanctuary. For this reason, priests cleansed themselves with water. If they did not do this, they remained unclean and, they too were "cut off from the community" (Numbers 19:20).

Based on these Old Testament teachings, which Nicodemus surely would have known, Jesus' use of the words "born of water" would make his statement more easily understood. Every human being becomes unclean because of sin. Sin must be washed away. Even though our outer appearance can be cleansed by washing with water, our inner beings are still unclean and stained by all sorts of sin. The Bible describes the sinful nature of the inner man as containing "a guilty conscience" (Hebrew 10:22). Jeremiah says that "The heart is deceitful above all things and beyond cure" (17:9).

How can a deceitful heart beyond cure be cleansed, and a guilty conscience be purified? Needless to say, they both need to be washed with water—holy water! The author of Hebrews states, "let us draw near to God with a sincere heart in full assurance of faith, having our hearts sprinkled to cleanse us from a guilty conscience and having our bodies washed with pure water" (Hebrew 10:22). In other words, when we realize that we are sinners, sin must be cleansed with spiritual water in order to approach God. Cleansed with spiritual water... cleansed by the work of the Holy Spirit! Deceit and guilt in the human heart taken away, for without the forgiveness of sin by the Spirit of God no one can enter His kingdom. Nicodemus had to be "born of water."

3. Repentance

All sinners must be cleansed from sin. However, a crucial factor should not be ignored in the process of cleansing—repentance. Repentance is the recognition of one's sins and the turning away from them. How can a person expect to be cleansed without first confessing that he/she is unclean, and then asking God to make it happen?

The first person to mention repentance in relation to water was John the Baptist. According to Luke, "He [John] went into all the country around the Jordan, preaching a baptism of repentance for the forgiveness of sins" (Luke 3:3). John required baptism with water as a symbol of repentance. Therefore, the most important part of John's baptism was repentance by all those who would come to God in faith. Many came to be baptized by John in the Jordan River.

Jesus' explanatory words to Nicodemus regarding being "born of water" meant that he, Nicodemus, as well, needed to be cleansed of sin. Sin would not be washed away by water alone. People must admit having sin in their lives and desire to turn away from it completely. The will to do so is to be repentant, and people will experience an inner transformation as a result of that repentance.

After being filled with the Holy Spirit on the day of Pentecost, Peter preached that God had made Jesus both Lord and Christ. Jews were cut to the heart when they heard the words, "Repent and be baptized, every one of you, in the name of Jesus Christ for the forgiveness of your sins. And you will receive the gift of the Holy Spirit" (Acts 2:38).

According to Peter's sermon, people must repent to receive forgiveness of sins and be born-again. He preached that people who receive the baptism of repentance will receive the following two gifts: forgiveness of sins and the indwelling presence of the Holy Spirit. Were these gifts to be exclusively given to Jews? Absolutely not! Gentiles, too, can experience forgiveness of sins and be born-again, if they are willing to repent (Acts 2:39). Therefore, Jesus' word to Nicodemus about being born of water and the Spirit is applicable to all human beings, not only the Jews. We all must be born of water. In other words, we all must repent of our sins and be cleansed with water, the water of the Holy Spirit.

4. Blood

When Jesus told Nicodemus to be born of water, water signified cleansing through repentance. Is it true that if people really repent, they will cleanse themselves from all sin? Of course not! Human beings must honestly repent, but only God can cleanse someone of sin. Only God can forgive sin. Being born-again includes two works: the work of man--repentance of sin, and the work of God--forgiveness of sin.

In the conversation with Nicodemus, Jesus used the word water to help Nicodemus better understand the relationship between these two important concepts—repentance and forgiveness. Nicodemus, as is every man, was a sinner. He must be washed with water. He must be made clean—through repentance.

But we need the blood of Jesus Christ for the forgiveness of sins; "without the shedding of blood there is no forgiveness"

(Hebrew 9:22). When we are forgiven through the blood of Jesus Christ, we receive the Holy Spirit and are born again. For this reason, Jesus told Nicodemus to be born of water, meaning *the blood* of Jesus. Through the blood of Jesus, Nicodemus can be cleansed and born again.

The Apostle John understands the relationship of the three-- water, blood, and the Holy Spirit. He writes, for there are three that testify: the Spirit, the water and the blood; and the three are in agreement (1 John 5:7-8). Why are they in agreement? The reason is simple! Water emphasizes cleansing and people are cleansed by the blood of Jesus Christ. The Holy Spirit emphasizes God's gift that is given to people who are cleansed, the experience of being born-again.

Therefore, the process of being born-again has both passive and active aspects to it. For the passive aspect, man is a sinner (dirty!) and is in need of being cleansed. People grapple with feelings of guilt and condemnation. To remove the sins, people need to be washed with water. Being washed with water involves both the work of man and God. People need to repent of their sins and then God will forgive their sins through the blood of Jesus Christ.

After the problem of sin and condemnation is resolved in a passive way, God gives people the Holy Spirit as a gift. As a result, they are born again of water and the Holy Spirit. Water works as a connective link between the problem of sin and being born-again. In addition, water connotes repentance and blood. Because of the precious blood of Jesus Christ, every sinner, including Nicodemus, can experience forgiveness and being born again.

5. The Power of Repentance

One day I interpreted for an American who was preaching in a small Korean church of about thirty people. He preached a sermon on repentance. After the sermon, he invited people to respond with the following words: "If anybody recognizes that he or she is a sinner before God and people and wants to sincerely abandon sin, please come forward."

I thought of how shameful it was to accept an invitation to come forward! I did not think anyone would respond, because one characteristic of Korean culture is saving face. Contrary to my expectation, eight people came forward. I was very surprised. They all stood in a row and a woman who stood at the end of line suddenly dropped down onto the floor and began to wail with many tears.

After the prayer, I had a conversation with the woman and asked why she had been wailing. She told the following story: her daughter, an eleventh grader, attended the church, but she had persecuted her daughter very much, trying to prevent her from attending. However, her daughter continued to attend, urging her mother to go with her. The daughter invited her that day because a well-known preacher from America was scheduled to preach. The woman accepted the invitation because she wanted to see the American. While she listened to the sermon, she realized how sinful she was. She confessed that she was sorry for persecuting her daughter and opposing God, and realized she was a sinner. That night her life was transformed by the blood of Jesus Christ. He washed away her sins. She was born again of water and the Spirit.

Chapter 15

The Secret of New Birth (2)

"Jesus answered, 'I tell you the truth, no one can enter the kingdom of God unless he is born of water and the Spirit'" (John 3:5).

1. Two Elements of the Born-Again Experience

There are both passive and active elements involved in being born-again. People need to resolve the problem of sin and the consequences of sins they have committed. They have struggled with the sinful nature from the very moment of birth, but have found they cannot solve the problem of sin by their own actions and power. God knows they are powerless and is not willing to abandon them in this predicament. He calls to them, comes to them, and invites them to be cleansed from their sins.

God seeks human beings before they seek Him. People who recognize God's preeminent grace and come to Him will be cleansed from their sin and freed from a guilty conscience by Jesus Christ. He has already died for them on the cross. He has shed his own blood and died to pay the price for all the sins they committed.

Therefore, the blood of Jesus Christ on the cross completely cleanses those who admit that they are sinners and turn from their sinful lives to God. Jesus' words born of water is an invitation from a loving God to repent and be cleansed by the power of the blood of Jesus Christ shed on a cross.

Besides the passive element, there is an active element in this experience of being born-again. This active element is seen in the transforming power of the Holy Spirit. God's gift to people who repent of their sins and are cleansed by the blood of Jesus Christ is the gift of the Holy Spirit who comes into their hearts. The new birth is a wonderful, mysterious, and grace-filled work of God!

2. The Holy Spirit

Why is the Holy Spirit given to people as a gift? The reason is simple. Being washed with water is nothing more than external purification. Even the forgiveness of sins through repentance is no more than external because the sinful nature of people has not changed. However, being born-again indicates that a new nature has come and entered into man.

The Bible stresses this truth in the following way: "His [Jesus'] divine power has given us everything we need for life and godliness" (2 Peter 1:3). When people are born again, God gives everything we need for a godly life. For this reason, people who are born again have free and godly lives as well as eternal life. This godliness does not come from external discipline but from the transformation of the inner being and the internal discipline generated by the Holy Spirit.

Furthermore, the Apostle Peter describes the divine power within man as "divine nature" (2 Peter 1:4). How can human nature be transformed into divine nature? This is possible because of the indwelling of the Holy Spirit. Nicodemus, who came to Jesus, was almost perfect in terms of morality and religious life. However, the reason why he had to be born again came from the fact that his inner being—his heart had not yet been changed.

Many people misunderstand the meaning of being born-again by thinking it means a reformed life. Of course, the reformation of one's life is important, but reformation itself cannot change the inner being, or human nature. Take the clock for example. If a spring of the clock is broken, wiping the glass or replacing it cannot make the clock go back to normal operation. Only replacing the spring with a new one can make a difference.

Human beings are the same. Cleansing or decorating the human appearance is useless because the root of the problem is sin springing from the inner being. All the "reforming" (changing) of one's physical appearance is useless until divine changes take place in the inner being. Living good moral and transformational lives draw people's attention, but there still remains the total impossibility of dealing with the problem of the heart. It is "deceitful above all things and beyond cure." We ourselves cannot resolve the problem of the corruption of the deceitful heart.

For this reason, being a religious person is no satisfaction. Many people are still chained to sin and the law in spite of all their religious efforts. People must be reborn by the Holy Spirit. Only the Holy Spirit can come into their lives and change their evil nature into a divine nature. They literally become "new creatures."

3. Faith

As mentioned before, being born of water includes repentance, but faith is required to be born of the Holy Spirit. Repentance and faith go hand in hand. Repentance that is not accompanied by faith is not real. Inversely, faith that is not accompanied by repentance is not real. Repentance and faith are two sides of the same coin.

Therefore, faith is required to be born of the Holy Spirit. Peter clearly explains the relationship between faith and being born-again. First, he declares that sinners are born again on the basis of the blood of Jesus Christ (an objective fact) (1 Peter 1:18-19). Second, people are born again on the basis of faith (a subjective fact) (1 Peter 1:21). Third, people are born again through hearing the words of truth (1 Peter 1:23).

Faith is an indispensable ingredient for the experience of being born-again. Sinners are cleansed from their own sin through true repentance and the blood Jesus shed on the cross for them. In other words, they are born again of water. One thing left in the experience of being born-again is to be born of the Holy Spirit. People need to receive God's gift, the Holy Spirit, through faith.

When they reach out in faith to receive the Holy Spirit, the Spirit reaches into them and they are transformed. If the Holy Spirit is not involved in their lives, their experience of being born of water, repentance and Jesus' blood, is a limited one. Although they are cleansed from all the sins they have committed in the past, they will be hopelessly weak in their struggle against temptations they will face in the future. They must have the power of the Holy Spirit to help them.

Jesus loves Nicodemus very much. His words to him are an invitation of love, encouraging him to enjoy a new way of life: of which will make it possible for him to enter into the Father's kingdom. "No one can enter the kingdom of God, unless he is born of water and the Spirit." Needless to say, Nicodemus' new life, through the indwelling power of the Holy Spirit, will not only assure him of heaven but will make of him a changed man inwardly—one like Jesus

4. Transformation

According to Jesus Christ, when people are born of water and the Holy Spirit, their lives change. When the problem of sin is settled and people become clean vessels, the Holy Spirit indwells the cleansed hearts and lives. Likewise, when the Holy Spirit actively works and indwells their lives, their lives inevitably change. This change happens not by reformation—efforts of their own—but by the presence and power of the Holy Spirit.

People who are born of water and the Holy Spirit experience a change of personality.

As internal change deepens, their external lives also begin to change. Most of all, there thinking changes from seeking self-centered interests to pursuing God's glory. As the fundamental thinking pattern changes to pursue the glory of God, all the areas of their lives begin to change, including their ways of speaking and deeds.

These changes brought about by the Holy Spirit have no other explanation except that God is at work. No other factors such as resolution, efforts, good deeds, charity, or religion can change lives in a moment. However, life is transformed overnight by the indwelling of the Holy Spirit. People enjoy peace with God internally, and begin to overcome sins externally. One step further, they now desire to share God's love with people who do not know Jesus Christ.

One's purpose in life has been changed by the work of the Holy Spirit. People who had been endlessly running around trying to find purpose in life find it. Once unable to shake off feelings of emptiness and loneliness, they now have the most vital relationship with God! They are now eternally different people. Satisfaction springs up from the bottom of their hearts because they have a new purpose for their lives, the glory of God.

Since people have a clear purpose for life, their ways of lives become different. Before they were born again, they used any means they could to accomplish their goals without hesitation. Now, they are different! Since now their goal is to glorify God, they begin to choose appropriate ways to attain this goal.

The people who are born of water and the Holy Spirit experience changes of purpose and ways of life, but sometimes these changes cause trouble in this world. Living lives of godliness among people who are not interested in doing so often causes heartache. However, this life on earth is not the end. The final destination—the kingdom of God— will be amazing. One day, when they leave this world, God will not only welcome them, but also reward them for their lives of righteousness.

5. Two Aspects of History

People who are born of water and the Holy Spirit inevitably see their own personal history divided into two time periods: pre-born-again and born-again. The first time period was one of deepening sin—outside the kingdom of God—and the other, a period of deepening spiritual transformation. and growth in joy, peace and righteousness—inside the kingdom! These two periods of life sharply contrasted with one another. All because of the amazing defining and maintaining work of the Holy Spirit at conversion and beyond. When Jesus was speaking to Nicodemus regarding this need for him to experience yet another birth, he knew of the eternal blessing that would come, not only to this teacher of Israel, but to all men—in all the ages to come! Are you born of water and the Holy Spirit? If you are not born again, will you receive Jesus Christ into your heart today? Into your life? Like Nicodemus apparently did.

Chapter 16

The Secret of New Birth (3)

"Jesus answered, 'I tell you the truth, no one can enter the kingdom of God unless he is born of water and the Spirit'" (John 3:5).

1. New History

Nicodemus, thoroughly steeped in Jewish thought and tradition, heard a secret hidden deep in Jesus' words, "no one can enter the kingdom unless he is born of water and the Spirit," a threat to basic Judaism. We know that various religious laws and decrees had been traditionally observed and passed down in Israel. Nicodemus had spent almost his entire life consumed in teaching and protecting them. The very existence of Israel's religious identity was being challenged by Jesus' words!

The phrase "born of water and the Spirit" threatened all the religious traditions and histories of Israel. They would have to begin anew. Jesus' words would end all traditional ways of religious life, all attempts to observe the laws, all kinds of sacrifices, and all the religious life revolving around the temple in Jerusalem.

The reason is simple! They were being told that all the time and effort taken to observe the laws was not important! Jesus was talking about the transformation of souls, not the observation of laws, bringing people into the Kingdom of God. Washing with water according to ceremonial law would not cleanse people's hearts. They would need internal transformation. This would only happen when they were "born of water and the Spirit." By being told, by this young unlearned Galilean teacher, that one had to experience an inner rebirth, a way of religious life which had been going on for millenniums was being threatened! Nicodemus' whole life spent attempting to follow the Law had been a waste!

2. The Pictures of Human Beings

The OT frequently describes the heart of man. In the first three chapters of Genesis, Adam and Eve are depicted as obedient followers of God, created in His perfect image, living in a perfectly-created environment, and enjoying an intimate relationship with their Creator. As the first couple, they were privileged to share perfect love with each other and with God. They were free to enjoy life! The only thing God had told them not to do was to eat the fruit of the tree of the knowledge of good and evil (2:17). Later, early in chapter 3, we find Satan tempting them to do so, and their giving in to the temptation! Why did they disobey God and spoil such a wonderful life with Him? Why did they commit sin? What was their problem? It was found deep in their hearts. The problem of Adam and Eve was their arrogance and pride. Their hearts were never satisfied. They had no needs, but they always wanted more, expected higher things, things that were beyond their reach as man. They had a want—they wanted just a little bit more "to be like God!" They sinned, and as a result, they lost the privilege of living in a perfect environment, sharing perfect love with each other. This also happens today. Many people, living in the United States where an almost perfect (compared to most countries) environment exists, still have problems and conflicts due to sin that need to be resolved.

The Israelites who experienced the Exodus, present us with another picture to help us understand the nature of man's heart. They had suffered from slavery in Egypt for 430 years, but finally experienced freedom from this oppression. Egypt was struck down with ten plagues that demonstrated the unprecedented and mighty power of God. Afterward, God led the Israelites into the promised land of Canaan, further demonstrating His power and love for them. What about the lives of the Israelites who experienced such love and mighty power of God? Did they then live clean and perfect lives after all that? No! The Israelites blamed God for the troubles they had during the journey to Canaan. They turned to worshiping idols instead of God. The list of acts of disobedience committed by the Israelites was endless. Why? Even though they had experienced deliverance from Egyptian bondage, they inevitably committed sin because there had been no change in their inner nature—in their hearts!

The life of Solomon gives us a third picture of the heart of man?\what man without God was really like. With the exceptional wisdom God had given him, Solomon ruled Israel for many years. His country flourished and his influence expanded to other neighboring countries. Solomon temple and his royal palace became magnificent monuments of architecture in his day. Leaders of many countries came to Israel to see his temple and palace and to seek his wisdom. Did Solomon live a clean life? No! Abusing the wisdom he had been given, he had many concubines and worshiped idols. His sins changed the history of Israel. Why? Solomon's heart had not been cleansed of his sins. Even though Solomon enjoyed perfect wisdom externally, he had a sinful nature. He sought for inner joy and peace through his own efforts and accomplishments. He pursued after many things he thought would bring satisfaction in life, but all became "utterly meaningless" to him (Ecclesiastes 2:10-11)! He did not pursue the heart of God!

3. The Old Covenant

Why do people fail to live clean lives in spite of God's gifts to them? Why do people still live sinful lives even while experiencing God's almighty power? Why do seemingly-privileged people commit sins? As mentioned before, people have sinful natures. Without being born of water and the Holy Spirit, people cannot live clean and holy lives, regardless of all the good things God provides in their lives.

We find God's promise of this new life in the Old Testament. In Jeremiah, "'The time is coming,' declares the LORD, 'when I will make a new covenant with the house of Israel and with the house of Judah. It will not be like the covenant I made with their forefathers when I took them by the hand to lead them out of Egypt, because they broke my covenant, though I was a husband to them,' declares the LORD" (Jeremiah 31:31-32). God's Word told of the introduction of a new covenant which would come into the world at an appointed time.

The new covenant prophecy which Jeremiah mentioned brings to mind the Israel's old covenant. Before we learn about the new covenant, reviewing the old covenant is necessary. As we know, God delivered the Israelites from centuries of slavery in Egypt through the leadership of Moses and Aaron. While the liberation and freedom they had experienced was fresh in their memory, God told them why He had led them out of Egypt.

First, God led the Israelites out to show them himself and to call them to become holy people as He was holy (Leviticus 19:2). If they would do so, God would be present among them and dwell with them (Exodus 25:8). Second, based on their holy lives, they would then desire to share God's redemptive love with others. As a result, the whole world would be filled with holy people who feared God (Exodus 19:4-6).

For these two reasons, God made a covenant with the Israelites at Mount Sinai. The Israelites were required to observe the Ten Commandments and laws, and then they could become a holy nation. This is the old covenant. God made the covenant through the laws; chapters of Exodus 20-24, Leviticus 26, and Deuteronomy 28-30 record the old covenant.

However, the Israelites failed to keep this covenant. They broke the covenant, as married couples break their marriage covenant today. Failure came when they attempted to keep the covenant by external means only. Their inner beings remained totally unaffected. External effort without internal transformation came to nothing.

4. The New Covenant

However, God did not abandon the Israelites. God loved them, as a faithful husband loves his wife. God gave them a new covenant to replace the one they had broken. As the old covenant was given to the people of Israel through Moses, the new covenant is promised them through the prophet Jeremiah. God declared, "I will make a new covenant with the house of Israel and with the house of Judah."

What are the contents of this new covenant? According to Jeremiah, "'This is the covenant I will make with the house of Israel after that time,' declares the LORD. 'I will put my law in their minds and write it on their hearts. I will be their God, and they will be my people. No longer will a man teach his neighbor, or a man his brother, saying 'know the LORD,' because they will all know me from the least of them to the greatest,' declares the LORD. 'For I will forgive their wickedness and will remember their sins no more'" (Jeremiah 31:33-34).

The new covenant presupposes the old one. The old covenant asked people to be holy people, like God, through external effort. The new covenant asks people to be holy people through the transformation of their hearts. This will be wonderful news to the Israelites who feel they have violated the laws and, therefore, have been abandoned by God.

The new covenant contains three important points. First, "I will put my law in their minds and write it on their hearts." This first point indicates transformation of the heart. Second, "no longer will a man teach his neighbor, or a man his brother, saying, 'Know the Lord,' for they will all know me...." This emphasizes the changed relationship of people with their community—their love for others.

Third, "I will forgive their wickedness and remember their sins no more." This highlights a changed relationship with God due to his forgiveness of their sins.

In this new covenant, the transformation of man's inner being becomes key to their having a true relationship with God. Their broken relationship with God will change into a relationship of restoration and fellowship.

Since the Israelites experience a transformation of the inner being and possess a renewed relationship with God, they come to know the indwelling God. How do they come into this deep relationship with God? God forgives their sins. They have personally asked him to put his law in their minds and for him to write it on their hearts (31:33)! Under the old covenant, they were bound by guilt, but now their sins are forgiven, to the extent that God does not even remember their previous sins (31:34).

5. God's Power

To be "born of water and the Spirit" would require Nicodemus to give up everything he held dear and to stop teaching much of what he had been taught. In spite of his efforts and deeds, he was still in darkness. Despite his excellent knowledge and learning, he was under the bondage of basic principles and the laws of this world (Colossians 2:20). Even with his noble status and high social position, his life remained unfulfilled. The religious life he had cherished the most was not able to produce the transformation of his inner being. Jesus is telling him that what he really needs now is not the deadness of the old covenant but the life of the new covenant. He can be born again, through no effort of his own. It would be completely by the "effort" of God.

The covenant that "I will put my law in their minds and write it on their hearts, I will be their God, and they will be my people" can only be possible through God's grace. God no longer wants to have a perfunctory religious relationship with Nicodemus; He wants an intimate relationship with him.

God wants to come into people's hearts through the Holy Spirit. He wants to enjoy intimate and inseparable relationships through the indwelling of the Holy Spirit. Nicodemus can be one of the first to begin this level of relationship with God. In that new relationship he can call God Father through the work of the Holy Spirit. However, this relationship cannot be generated in the heart of Nicodemus unless he allows God to work within him—"by water and the Spirit."

A relationship with God through the indwelling of the Holy Spirit is totally different from having a relationship through law. A relationship with God based on laws is only maintained when the laws are strictly observed. However, it is impossible for Nicodemus to perfectly keep the laws. He does not have the power to do so himself. Now, to him, God is not the God of love. On the contrary, God is a fearful God who judges and reproaches people. Only the work of God can change this relationship of fear into a relationship of love, the love of Father to son.

How can Nicodemus be relieved of his feeling of condemnation? The more he attempts to observe the laws, the more he is discouraged by feelings of guilt. There is no way of solving the problem by himself. However, God will declare Nicodemus forgiven of sin through the new covenant. When he receives God's declaration, he will be set free! This is totally the work of God. Yes! The new covenant is entirely the work of God.

6. A Story of a Seminarian

Many people have been born of water and the Holy Spirit by the work of God, because God loves people who still do not know the true meaning of their lives. The closer God approaches people, the farther, it seems, they go away from God. He extends His hands of invitation toward them, calling them with a loving voice, and as they respond to him, He causes them to be born-again. That is the work of God.

There was a female seminarian in South Korea who enthusiastically worked for a local church and studied very hard. She entered Seoul Theological Seminary with enthusiasm and dedication to God. Her life began to change, as did many of the other students. She faithfully attended early morning-prayer meetings and all-night prayer services. Participation in these ways was considered as the sign of a true seminarian. At that time, I taught a class in Theological English at that seminary as a lay person and she visited me. After she told me this and that, then she asked me the following question: "Do you really believe in the existence of God?" Do you really believe that Jesus is the Son of God and died on the cross for us?" Answering positively to these questions, I asked her the same questions, feeling that further discussion of these questions was needed. She answered these questions negatively. On the spot, I explained having an intimate relationship with God, the internal transformation of people through the Holy Spirit, and Jesus' redemptive death for her. Suddenly shedding tears, she not only confessed that she was a sinner, but she also received Jesus as her Savior. God really changed her. She graduated from the seminary and became a witness of the gospel, evangelizing people in many places in South Korea. Do not ask me how she experienced such a dramatic change in such a flash of time. God worked within her heart with water and the Holy Spirit. Abandoning all external efforts, she experienced the work of the Holy Spirit in her heart. She was really born again!

Chapter 17

The Secret of New Birth (4)

"Jesus answered, 'I tell you the truth, no one can enter the kingdom of God unless he isborn of water and the Spirit'" (John 3:5).

1. The Promise

No matter how excellent man may be in terms of morality and religious life, they cannot be born again by their own efforts and power, nor by observing the law. Being born of water and the Holy Spirit is the mysterious work of God. God not only urges people to be born again, his Spirit actively "enters into man and creates new creatures in Christ" (II Corinthians 5:17)! Leon Morris describes this mystery in the following way:

> Jesus makes it clear that no man can ever fit himself for the kingdom. Rather he must be completely renewed, born anew, by the power of the Spirit. These solemn words forever exclude the possibility of salvation by human merit. Man's nature is so gripped by sin that an activity of the very Spirit of God is a necessity if he is to become a citizen of God's kingdom.

Man cannot resolve the problem of sin. For this reason, God not only urges people to be born again, but promises to provide the power to become born-again. To study this promise further, we need to go back again to the Old Testament.

2. Background of the Promise

We previously studied the new covenant promised by Jeremiah. Let's briefly look again at some of the background of this new covenant. The Israelites had forsaken God, the very one who had delivered them from bondage in Egypt. They had alienated themselves from Him. They abandoned God to worship other gods, forsaking the God who had delivered them from bondage and led them into the land of Canaan. They had personally seen Him at work on this long journey, revealing his great power and love to them many times, but to them it was not enough. They became impatient and turned to idols.

Idols take on various forms. There are idols made out of silver or gold, wood or stone ...interestingly enough, almost anything from God's own creation! Regardless of the various forms of idol worship, the essence of worship is man himself. People pray for themselves in front of idols they have made for themselves. They worship these man-made idols because they want their own needs met. They do not want God to tell them what they need. After all, idol worship is an act of self-service, people turning their backs on God and chooses a life of their own.

Jeremiah urged the Israelites to return to God and to forsake idol worship, but they did not listen to him. Finally, God proclaimed judgment upon them and sent them into slavery once again in Babylon (Jeremiah 16:11-13; 20:6). Disregarding this solemn warning, the Israelites did not abandon their idols, but even worshiped them more passionately than ever before.

Even then, God desired to show mercy once again upon the Israelites. The promised new covenant which Jeremiah announced would be a demonstration of God's mercy. No new law would be given for them to try to observe. God promised restoration, by his power, not their strength, and because of his mercy, not their manipulation. Much of this promised covenant is seen in Jeremiah 30-31: He introduced the covenant with the words, "I (the Lord God) will discipline you but only with justice; I will not let you go entirely unpunished ....But I will restore you to health and heal your wounds" (30:11d, 17a). Later, in 31:33-34, God says, "This is the covenant...I will put my law in their minds and write in on their hearts. I will be their God and they will be my people...."

3. Water

The prophet Ezekiel was one of the captives who were taken into Babylon. Ezekiel began to proclaim a message similar to that of Jeremiah. He claimed that the fundamental reason for the destruction of Israel was idol worship. Idol worship was practiced even in the temple where God dwelt (Ezekiel 8:5-13). God had not said that he would restore the relationship with the Israelites and their country through the observance of laws. Observing the law would not bring about the cleansing of their hearts or prevent them from worshiping idols. What they needed was not law, but a spiritual new birth, a birth which would come by being "born of water and the Holy Spirit."

In Ezekiel 36:22-25, much of Ezekiel's new covenant appears:

> Therefore say to the house of Israel, 'This is what the Sovereign Lord says: 'It is not for your sake, O house of Israel, that I am going to do these things, but for the sake of my holy name, which you have profaned among the nations where you have gone. I will show the holiness of my great name, which has been profaned among the nations, the name you have profaned among them. Then the nations will know that I am the LORD, declares the Sovereign LORD, when I show myself holy through you before their eyes. For I will take you out of the nations; I will gather you from all the countries and bring you back into your own land. I will sprinkle clean water on you, and you will be clean; I will cleanse you from all your impurities and from all your idols.'

According to Ezekiel, the new covenant totally reflected the grace and mercy of God. God did not offer Israel the new covenant based on their good works or accomplishments. God would give them the new covenant in order to sanctify His own name, which had fallen in disrepute among the Gentiles, especially the Babylonians, due to Israel's disobedience and disregard for his honor. The covenant was God's covenant, one hundred percent, and only God could see it come to pass. He alone would "rebuild" and "replant" them..."then they will know that I am the Lord" (Ezekiel 36:36, 38)! New covenant that God promised them would bring the Israelites back to their land and purify them with *clean water*. What would they be cleansed from? God would cleanse them from all the impurities brought on by their idolatry. The prophet Ezekiel purposely added the word clean to the water for two main reasons.

First, the Israelites needed clean water, not "dirty" water, to cleanse themselves from all the impurities and idols they had come in contact with. God's clean water contrasted with the "dirtiness" of their sins. Second, clean water was not normal water, but special water, purified personally by God. God had instructed the Israelites about how to make special water of cleansing to cleanse people who had become unclean (Numbers 19:1-9).

Needless to say, only God could purify the people with the clean water in the new covenant found in Ezekiel. God promised to wash the Israelites from all their impurities and idols with clean water. Although they were taken into Babylon because of their sins, God promised to completely remove the sins of their past with clean water. Once sin is removed through obedience to God's word, they can be born again of the Holy Spirit.

4. The Holy Spirit

When we look at Ezekiel 36:26-28, we can better appreciate the words of Jesus who taught people to be born of water and the Holy Spirit.

> I will give you a new heart and put a new spirit in you; I will remove the heart of stone out of your flesh and give you a heart of flesh. And I will put my Spirit in you and move you to follow my decrees and be careful to keep my laws. You will live in the land I gave your forefathers; you will be my people, and I will be your God.

God gave the Israelites in Babylon the following advice: "If a righteous man turns from his righteousness and does evil, he will die for it. And if a wicked man turns away from his wickedness and does what is just and right, he will live by doing so" (Ezekiel 33:18-19). This admonishment is a word of grace. Although the Israelites had turned away from righteousness and become Babylonian exiles, they were being given an opportunity to return to the land the Lord had promised their forefathers, and, more importantly, to once again have a relationship with God.

The condition for their restoration was very simple. They were admonished to admit their sinfulness and repent of their sins. In so doing, God would do two things for them. First, He would cleanse them from their sins. Secondly, God would put a new spirit within them. When they repented and lamented of their sins in Babylon—where they were humiliated and degraded—God would wash away their sins and give them a new spirit.

Why is this new spirit mentioned in the new covenant? First, the Israelites would be empowered to live new lives only by the power of the Holy Spirit. Second, they would be the recipients of grace, not law. A new dispensation would fall upon them. Thus far they were found to be sinners under the heavy weight of the law. With the Spirit given, they would no longer suffer under the law but would be free to enter into a life of grace. God will turn a man's heart of stone into a heart of flesh through an internal transformation performed by the Holy Spirit. This new heart is expressed as a heart of flesh because it will be active, not passive open to God's love and mercy and sensitive to God's Word. In addition, this heart will be sensitive to the guidance of the Holy Spirit and obeying it. Moreover, the heart of flesh is one which is open to Israel's neighbors and their needs. Ezekiel speaks of "My (God's) Spirit" (36:27), emphasizing that this power of transformation comes from God's Spirit. Only through the work of the Holy Spirit, can the Israelites become holy people, enabled to observe God's laws and decrees faithfully. When they obey the Word of God, they become God's people and God becomes their God. In other words, they begin to reflect God, living holy lives as His children.

5. Fruit

Now we understand Jesus' words, "born of water and the Spirit," in a deeper and more significant way. Jesus' words are the continuation of the new covenant that had been offered to the Israelites. The Israelites had lost their country because of their sin and idol worship. They had been offered a new covenant by Jeremiah and Ezekiel but had continued to disregard it all these years! They were still outside the kingdom of God! God still wanted them "in."

As a teacher of Israel, Nicodemus should have known about these things, but he was still bound to a law impossible for him to faithfully observe, just as his forefathers had been unable to do. Still depending on his own power, knowledge, and social status, he lived in a condition much like that of Israel's in Babylon—exiled, away from God. Jesus' words contained the new covenant God had promised in the Old Testament: "no one can enter the kingdom of God unless he is born of water and the Spirit."

According to the last part of the new covenant of Ezekiel (Ezekiel 36:29-31), blessings would come from being faithful to the new covenant.

> I will save you from all your uncleanness. I will call for the grain and make it plentiful and will not bring famine upon you. I will increase the fruit of the trees and the crops of the field, so that you will no longer suffer disgrace among the nations because of famine. Then you will remember your evil ways and wicked deeds, and you will loathe yourselves for your sins and detestable practices.

The new covenant promised the following blessings: the salvation of daily life, the salvation of daily needs, and the salvation of spiritual life. First, I will save you from all your uncleanness indicates the salvation of daily life. The people who are born of water and the Spirit would be able to resist evil habits and temptations in their daily lives. Second, I will call for the grain and make it plentiful signifies the salvation of daily needs. The daily needs of the Israelites, who no longer reaped the prosperity of their former country, would be provided by God. Third, you will loathe yourselves for your sins and detestable practices refer to the salvation of spiritual life. Even though people are born of water and the Spirit, they still struggle with the sinfulness or corruption of their hearts. However, they will enter into a new level of spiritual life through this struggle! This three-fold promise of blessing will become a stepping stone to the new birth a new spiritual life.

When Jesus told Nicodemus that "no one can enter the kingdom of God unless he is born of water and the Spirit," he was actually calling for Nicodemus to give up all his previous religious life, a two-faced life, a life chained to laws, and a life that depended on self achievement. Jesus' word was an invitation to blessing, the blessing of a new life characterized by freedom and power of the Holy Spirit. The invitation of Jesus also comes to us. Are you born of water and the Holy Spirit? Do you wish to be blessed with "new life?"

Chapter 18

The Kingdom of God (2)

"Jesus answered, 'I tell you the truth, no one can enter the kingdom of God unless he is born of water and the Spirit'" (John 3:5).

1. Double Meaning

Jesus Christ introduced the kingdom of God to Nicodemus, but the kingdom of God has a double meaning. We find the expression of the kingdom of God in John 3:3,5, but it has different emphases in terms of time and meaning. Verse 3 describes the kingdom people enjoy in the present, but verse 5 emphasizes the kingdom of God in the future. The kingdom of God in verse 3 focuses on present spiritual blessings here on earth, but in verse 5 the kingdom is eschatological and its spiritual blessings to be seen in the future—in heaven.

The kingdom of God in the present emphasizes that they are ruled by God, but still live in this world. They can enjoy the fruits of "righteousness, peace and joy in the Holy Spirit" in any situation they face. However, living in this earthly kingdom of God— limited by body, time, and space— is just the beginning. People who are born of water and the Spirit must wait for the final fulfillment of the kingdom of God. The kingdom of God, that man entered into at the time of his new birth, will be the environment within which the Holy Spirit continues to prepare God's "new creatures in Christ" for the new heavenly Kingdom!

2. Characteristics of the Kingdom of God

When Jesus told Nicodemus to see and enter the kingdom of God by being born-again, that kingdom included both the present and the future. The kingdom of God that he would enter into at the moment of being born of water and the Spirit would be fulfilled at the end of the world. In other words, the kingdom of God has already begun, but is not yet fulfilled, powerfully moving toward its final fulfillment. The kingdom of God is totally different from the kingdoms of this world. How different is it?

Most of all, the kingdom of God is spiritual. Kingdoms of this world hunger for land. For this reason, endless territorial disputes occur around the world. However, the kingdom of God has a spiritual nature, not a geopolitical nature. Since kingdoms of this world are controlled by politicians, they are involved in endless political activities and strife. However, in the kingdom of God, the Lord is involved in endless spiritual love and peace.

Teaching that the kingdom of God, in both the world and heaven, is spiritual also connotes the presence of an inherent spiritual power. Why? The reason is simple! Spiritual power comes from the presence of the Holy Spirit who works in the lives of people born of water and the Spirit. Since the kingdom of God comes through the Holy Spirit, it has spiritual power from its very inception. Because of this spiritual power, the kingdom of God is ever expanding as it proceeds to its fulfillment.

People from nations all over the world become citizens of the kingdom of God. The kingdom of God cannot be expanded through man's use of military power or violence. In fact, no dictator's conquest by violence has ever won over the hearts of people. However, since the kingdom of God consists of people who are changed from within, born of water and the Spirit, people from all nations can come into this kingdom. The Holy Spirit approaches everyone—regardless of appearance, ethnic origin, or language.

The Holy Spirit sends out witnesses to share the gospel message throughout the world. People who respond to the gospel message and are born of water and the Spirit become members of the kingdom of God. The Apostle John describes the fulfilled kingdom of God as a great gathering of people who have been born again: After this I looked and there before me was a great multitude that no one could count, from every nation, tribe, people and language, standing before the throne and in front of the lamb (Revelation 7:9).

Lastly, the kingdom of God expands gradually. Jesus mentions the gradual expansion of the kingdom of God: Jerusalem first, then, all Judea, and then Samaria and to the ends of the earth (Acts 1:8). The boundary of the kingdom of God are expanded by people who are born again and filled with the Holy Spirit witnessing to those who have not yet seen and believed. All born-again Christians are called to contribute to this expansion of the kingdom of God.

3. The Visa of Heaven

Jesus clearly states how to get a visa to the kingdom of God by saying that "no one can enter the kingdom of God unless he is born of water and the Spirit." According to this word of Jesus, the visa to the kingdom of God is not through religious or moral works and aspirations. People can get any this-world visa through their knowledge, wealth, accomplishment, and application in this world; but these things do not allow one entrance into the kingdom of God. You can enter into the kingdom of "the ruler of the air", yes, but not into God's kingdom!

Can people enter the kingdom of God with a religious visa? Of course not! No matter how deeply they are devoted to religious life, they cannot enter the kingdom of God on the strength of their religious life. A Buddhist monk in South Korea for several years disciplined himself and never lay down while sleeping, and all he had with him at the time of his death was a ragged robe and several ballpoint pens. The monk demonstrated his respectful and sacrificial dedication to his religious life, but all his effort failed to get him into the kingdom of God.

Can people get the visa to the kingdom of God by their dedication to Christianity? No! No matter how deeply they may be devoted to church life such as attending worship, giving offerings, and serving other people, they cannot enter the kingdom of God through showing dedication to the church. John Wesley is one of the most striking examples of this. His father was a pastor, and he, John, was a pastor too. In addition, he was a professor at a seminary and a missionary. He believed that if he passionately preached the gospel message to the Indians in America, God would lead him to heaven. However, all his efforts at that time were merely his own religious deeds and he was not able to get his visa to enter the kingdom of God.

Can living a morally clean life guarantee the visa to the kingdom of God? No! The practical problem of ethical people is that they often break the very ethical code they espouse. Their morally clean life can draw people's attention and praise, but they know within themselves they have not been cleansed. They enjoy people's praise outwardly, but they feel a sense of guilt inwardly. People cannot get the visa to the kingdom of God by living a morally clean life.

Who, then, can get a visa to enter the kingdom of God? Only people who are born of water and the Spirit! By "water and the Holy Spirit" is the only means possible of receiving God's visa. As mentioned before, water indicates the experience of purification from sins. People must be cleansed from all the sins they have committed. In addition, people must be cleansed by the power of the Spirit, becoming a new creation in Jesus Christ (2 Corinthians 5:17). All those who have had their sins forgiven and have become new creations through the indwelling of the Holy Spirit, regardless of their religious, moral, and social status in this world, are the ones qualified to enter the kingdom of God. The Holy Spirit within a person is their visa into the kingdom of God.

4. No-Visa Entry

No-visa entry is now possible between South Korea and the United States, but several years ago Koreans were not able to enter the U.S.A. without a proper visa. The only way to enter the U.S.A. without a visa was to enter illegally. Koreans without visas became illegal immigrants. God's kingdom would be similar. Illegal entry into the U.S.A. is still possible, but it is impossible in the case of God's kingdom. Therefore, no visa means no entry into God's kingdom.

What people do not get the visa to enter God's kingdom? Every human being! Adam and Eve did not get the visa because the Holy Spirit left them when they committed sin by disobeying God. They became spiritually dead. However, that was not the end of the tragedy. No descendant of Adam and Eve ever gets a visa because all are born spiritual dead (Romans 5:12).

Everyone walks toward death. People who are spiritually dead will eventually experience physical death. On the day of their death, their eternal destiny will have been decided. The Apostle John describes their eternal destiny in this way: "But the cowardly, the unbelieving, the vile, the murderers, the sexually immoral, those who practice magic arts, the idolaters, and all liars—their places will be in the fiery lake of burning sulfur. This is the second death" (Revelation 21:8).

The list of sins in this passage reveals the sins of people who have not been washed clean by the water of the Holy Spirit. They heard the gospel message directly or indirectly, but they rejected it. John describes such people as "the unbelieving." They should have repented and turned to God, but they rejected repentance. They refused to be washed with the blood of Jesus Christ that had been shed on the cross.

Some people have prophesied in Jesus name, saying "Lord, Lord" (Matthew 7:22). Others have waited for Jesus' return, like the ten virgins who went out to meet the bridegroom (Matthew 25:1-13). These prophets and five of the ten virgins share one deficiency in common: they did not have, at the end, the Holy Spirit living within. (As we know, oil symbolizes the Holy Spirit.) The five virgins prepared for everything except seeing to it they did not run out of oil. They were well dressed, trimmed the lamps, and waited all night for the bridegroom, but they let the oil of Spirit run out. They later heard the following word from Jesus: "I don't know you" (Matthew 25:12). Those who had prophesied heard the words, "I never knew you." The people who are not born of the Spirit do not know Jesus Christ and do not have a visa to God's kingdom.

5. A Taste of Heaven

Only people who are born of water and the Spirit can enter the kingdom of God. They participate in the celebration of "tasting" heaven while remaining here on earth, enjoying "righteousness, peace, and joy in the Holy Spirit" in this world. At the same time, they are assured entrance into the heavenly kingdom of God. The only way to be sure of heaven is to be born of water and the Spirit here on earth.

Lyle Dorsette, a professor of education at the University of Denver, tasted both hell and heaven as a young adult. Even though he was a professor at a university, he was addicted to alcohol. In spite of his relentless determination to quit alcohol, he was unable to stop drinking. He tried almost every way he could to quit his drinking habit—all the time hating his wife's continuous nagging about it, and hating himself.

At one point, he was alcohol-free for a period of six months. After the six months, he ended up drinking alcohol all night at a bar, celebrating his six month abstention. He ran out of his home, furious that he had failed! His determination to quit had amounted to nothing. Then he went to a bar and drank all night. After that, he drove his car somewhere, and consumed two more six-packs of beer. He drank until he got blind drunk and fainted. When he woke up in the bright sunshine and with the sound of birds singing, he found himself in a grave yard. Since he was thirsty, he picked up a beer can and guzzled it. It was then he suddenly realized that if he kept drinking he would lose his wife, probably his job, and have to live on the street for the rest of his life. In addition to all that, he would go to hell after his death.

At that time, words of his wife came to mind: "Although you cannot quit drinking on your own, Jesus can help you quit your drinking." He cried out, "God, help me. Help me quit drinking!" After a two-day struggle, he knelt down before Jesus and accepted Jesus as his Savior. He never drank alcohol again! A couple of decades have passed since that time. He now teaches education and evangelism at Wheaton College. He has a ministry of evangelism and making disciples.

He is born of water and the Spirit and enjoys the kingdom of God. He has become a very clean and influential figure, hoping to enter the kingdom of God one day. Although he had found himself in a graveyard, nearly crossing the threshold of death, he is now born of the Spirit and has become a citizen of the kingdom of God. Are you born of water and the Holy Spirit? Are you a citizen of heaven, not on your own merits, but on Christ's?

Chapter 19

The Necessity of New Birth

"Flesh gives birth to flesh, but the Spirit gives birth to spirit. You should not be surprised at my saying, 'You must be born again'" (John 3:6-7).

1. Repeated Urging

Nicodemus acknowledged that Jesus was a teacher who had come from God. Nicodemus seemed to praise Jesus Christ's accomplishments, but at the same time bragging about his own. He called Jesus, "Rabbi," considering Jesus to be of the same class or status as his. Jesus called him, in return, Israel's teacher (John 3:10). Nicodemus showed off his broad-mindedness by admitting that Jesus had performed many miraculous signs. He added that many of his fellow rabbis also support his high opinion of Jesus by saying "we know."

However, Jesus, seemingly not impressed, saw, instead, the deep spiritual need of Nicodemus and told him, "you must be born again." Jesus pressed the issue again by saying that everyone must be born again. He explained the reason why Nicodemus and all others must be born again. The main reason was reality— the reality of both life in the flesh and life in the spirit. Although Nicodemus was highly respected for his noble religious and social life, he was a man limited to the reality of life in the flesh. For this reason, wanting an everlasting life in relationship with Nicodemus, Jesus urged Nicodemus, as he does all others, to be born again.

2. The Meaning of Flesh

What is the meaning of the word "flesh" in relation to being born again? First, flesh is used in reference to the human body. Flesh itself cannot commit sin. Although the flesh (body) is the medium for committing sins, human beings themselves control their bodies and use them in acting out their sins.

Often the word flesh refers to the human personality. In other words, human flesh includes intelligence, emotion, and will. Human beings can think, express feelings, and make decisions. The human spirit, or personality, disregards the Holy Spirit. Humans think, feel, and make decisions from a self perspective, experiencing every kind of joy, anger, sorrow, and pleasure there is. Within the flesh are housed the desires that all men have.

A third use of the word flesh has nothing to do with God. Since flesh is only controlled by the principles of this world, it cannot have knowledge of God. Humans can talk about God, but that talking is not the same as knowing God. Knowing God is only possible through Jesus Christ because only Jesus can introduce people personally to God (John 14:6-10).

The Bible clearly declares that "there is no one who understands, no one who seeks God" (Romans 3:11). Since God is spirit (John 4:24), man, in the flesh, cannot know God. The world of flesh and the world of spirit are totally different! For this reason, "The man without the Spirit does not accept the things that come from the Spirit of God, for they are foolishness to him, and he cannot understand them, because they are spiritually (not fleshly) discerned" (1 Corinthians 2:14).

A fourth use of the word flesh is related to the reality of humans who antagonize God. As mentioned before, flesh cannot know God. Therefore, flesh is either indifferent to God because of its separation from God or hostile to God. In other words, flesh has a desire to go against God's will, rather than to obey and follow it. Flesh is driven by evil desires.

This fourth use reveals several positions regarding man's relationship with God. Some people declare that God does not exist, and they are called atheists. Others are not sure whether God exists or not, and they are called agnostics. Many believe in the existence of God, but they think that God has nothing to do with them, and they are called deists. Still others believe that all things in the universe are eventually gods, and they are called pantheists. Regardless of their opinion on God, these are the voices that come only from the flesh.

3. The Characteristics of Flesh

Then, what are the characteristics of "a man of the flesh" who does not know God? First, this man is created by God. He has knowledge and power, but he, inevitably, also has limitations. Only God the Creator can transcend these limits. Second, the man of flesh seeks earthly things (Colossians 3:2). He seeks to eat, drink, sleep, play, study, and fulfill sexual desires. Of course, these things are nothing wrong in themselves. However, when people consider these things as the only things they should pursue, their lives become unbalanced! Spiritual life as well as earthly life is important.

Jesus emphasizes the necessity for a spiritual rebirth in the experience of man by saying that "Flesh gives birth to flesh, but the Spirit gives birth to spirit. You should not be surprised at my saying, 'You must be born again.'" Jesus does not say that flesh is sin. Jesus emphasizes the balance between earthly things and spiritual things when he says that "you should not be surprised." Spiritual things must be added to earthly things.

People who are born of flesh live earthly lives, but they cannot find the meaning or purpose of life through their earthly lives. They lose the balance. If people who are born of flesh only live earthly lives with eating, sleeping, getting married, having babies, and dying, their lives look similar to that of animals.

Thirdly, people born of the flesh will eventually die. If they believe that the earthly lives they pursue are everything in their lives, they make a big mistake because their lives will be evaluated someday and found lacking. All human beings are responsible for their own lives and will be judged by God. For this reason, new birth, spiritual birth, is necessary.

People who are born again are both challenged and enabled to live balanced lives, and they will be led into the heavenly kingdom by God after they pass through the final barrier, death. After all, being born-again is a significant event that controls both present and future lives. From this perspective, nothing is more important than being born-again. We can see the reason why Jesus repeatedly urges Nicodemus to be born-again.

4. Characteristics of the People Who Are Born-Again

People born of the flesh can transcend the limits of the flesh if they seek the meaning of life with questions like "why do we live?" or "what is life?" They can meet Jesus Christ and be born of water and the Spirit. They can live balanced lives at last. In addition, they can live in the tremendous hope that they will someday be led to the place where God dwells.

The first characteristic of people who are born-again is that they still live in their earthly lives. However, these lives are well balanced. Although they make great efforts in their lives, spending time eating, sleeping, studying, working, and enjoying family life, they pursue spiritual life at the same time. They live with a new purpose, a direction, and a new way of life.

The second characteristic of people who are born-again is that they see Jesus Christ in a different way. Before they were born again, they devalued Jesus or considered him merely as one of the great teachers of the world. But now they accept him as Savior. Jesus not only died for man, rescuing them from sin, but also was resurrected for man, making it possible for them to be reconciled to God! People come to love Jesus and receive him as the resurrected Savior. People who are not born again cannot see Jesus in this way because only the Holy Spirit enables them to see Jesus as the Savior and Subject of Love. People who are born-again see Jesus in a different way because of the illumination of the Holy Spirit (John 16:14). One of the works of the Holy Spirit is to illumine Jesus Christ enabling people to see and love him.

The third characteristic of people who are born again is that they lay emphasis on spiritual needs. After they are born again, earthly needs remain stronger than spiritual needs, but the reversal comes as time goes by. In other words, as faith becomes mature, earthly needs decrease, and spiritual needs increase. Such a shift in needs produces more and more joy and peace in their lives. This is evidence of their progress in faith and maturity of personality. They spend more time reading, meditating, and memorizing the Word. In addition, the contents of their prayers go broader and deeper. Such transformation deepens fellowship with other Christians, and gives meaning to the worship services. One step further, they want to share their changed lives with other people because they enjoy the transformed lives that they never knew before.

5. The Earthly and Spiritual Life

Jesus wanted to share this balanced life with Nicodemus, so he repeatedly mentioned the importance of being born-again. Gi-Pung Lee lived a sharply contrasted life in Korea. He was a notorious gangster in Pyung-Yang, Korea. His life consisted of eating, drinking, and enjoying every day. He indulged in an earthly life by all means and at all costs. Since he felt that this was not enough for him, he began to persecute Christians, beginning with missionaries from America and their newly- planted churches. He attempted to kill a missionary, Horace G. Underwood, by striking him with a stone. Even though Underwood was injured, he did not die. Lee was so angry that he burned the church that the missionary had planted. While he was running from the fire, he fell into a ditch and passed out from the fall. When he regained consciousness, he found that he had been nursed by the very missionary he had attacked. He was surprised and shocked, touched by the love of Christians who really cared for such a villain like him.

One day when he was fast asleep, he had a dream in which he saw a man in strange attire. He wore a crown of thorns and was shedding blood from his head, hands, and feet. He approached Lee and said, "I love you." At that moment, he woke up and knelt down before Jesus Christ. He met Jesus Christ as his Savior that day. With his sins forgiven and the Holy spirit in his heart his life was dramatically transformed. He began to pursue heavenly things, and turned away from his former life. Later, he became a pastor and shared the testimony of his transformed life throughout all Korea. Many people were touched by his preaching and his testimony. They too became transformed!

Chapter 20

Flesh and Spirit

"Flesh gives birth to flesh, but the Spirit gives birth to spirit" (John 3:6).

1. Only the Holy Spirit

There is a divine principle about being born again. The principle is that God never uses anything within man to bring about their new birth. Of course, God "convicts the world of guilt in regard to sin" and rebukes it through the Holy Spirit (John 16:8). In addition, God lets them know the necessity for having a personal Savior and draws them to Jesus Christ through the Holy Spirit. Even though God uses human understanding and resolution, people cannot be born again out of their own resources. They can be born again only when God cleanses them of their sins. Furthermore, they can be born again only when God enters into their hearts through the Holy Spirit. This purification and the indwelling of the Holy Spirit are not possible because of something good within human beings. The process is totally the work of God.

For this reason, the life of being born-again is revealed as "entirely made new, the beginning of a truly spiritual life." This spiritual life will later be characterized not only by this newly-born life, but also by a new resurrected body, which will be given to all those who have accepted Christ one day. Therefore the people who are spiritually born again literally become new creatures (2 Corinthians 5:17). Becoming a new creature is, indeed, the work of God.

2. The True Identity of Flesh

Jesus' saying that "Flesh gives birth to flesh, but the Spirit gives birth to spirit" presupposes that there are two kinds of life in human beings. The first kind is physical, given to man through natural birth. The second kind is spiritual, given to man through a supernatural birth of a new heart. Jesus Christ teaches about these two kinds of life in his conversation with Nicodemus. "Flesh" indicates the life of natural human beings, and "the Spirit" means the life of being born again.

What is the meaning of the word "flesh"? When God created a man, man became a living being (Genesis 2:7). The meaning of flesh here is man alive—with body, soul, and spirit. Flesh that is created by God means perfect human beings made in God's image.

The second meaning of flesh speaks of human beings who have fallen into depravity. After the first Adam sinned, the Holy Spirit, who resided in Adam, left him. Therefore, he became a man who had nothing to do with the Spirit. He became a natural man who was spiritually dead. Such a natural person is called flesh. Adam still had intelligence, emotion, and will, but the depraved nature ruled his life because the Holy Spirit left him.

The first humans, Adam and Eve, could communicate with God because of the Spirit of God (Genesis 2:7). However, after they sinned, they no longer could have a conversation or fellowship with God. They were separated from God. For this reason, flesh in the true sense of the word, cannot know God. On the contrary, the flesh strongly desires to turn against God and go in the opposite direction, away from Him.

The flesh is deeply attached to this world and commits and enjoys sinning against God's will. However, that is not the end!

Revelation 20:12-14 tells us that people who have held on to sins of the flesh and not sought God's forgiveness will be eternally punished. Jesus' teaching is right when he says that "Flesh gives birth to flesh." People who live in sin will eventually die in sin.

3. The Effort of Flesh

All people born after Adam are people of flesh who do not have the nature of the Holy Spirit. Such people follow their own sinful natures. They think of sins in their heads, hold sins in their hearts, spew out their sins from their mouths, and commit sins with their hands and feet. People spend much time and money trying to make themselves look more beautiful. Many have plastic surgery to improve their appearance, and spend much time and money on clothes. They may receive praise from other people because of their appearance, but we know that the real problem of people does not lie in their outward appearance, but inward, in their hearts and minds.

Many people also attempt to "decorate" themselves with morality. They may gain recognition from other people because of their morally clean lives. Many try to beautify themselves with good religious thought and action. The lives and ways of thinking of these people may be nobler than other people; however, all these efforts remain nothing more than the adornment of the outward appearance.

Jesus says: Flesh gives birth to flesh. Jesus words summarize that all this adornment comes out of the flesh. The lives of these people are analogous to onions. Removing the outer layer of an onion leads to another coat of an onion. Finally nothing is left to the onion. Like onions, people have coats of home education, school education, morally clean lives, religion, and other things. On the surface, they seem to be beautiful and good, but they are just of the flesh.

Wuest describes this effort of the flesh in the following way:

> The teaching here is that man in a totally depraved condition cannot be improved. Reformation will not change him into a fit subject for the kingdom of God. The flesh is incurably wicked,

and cannot by any process be changed so as to produce a righteous life. What that person needs, Jesus says, is a new nature, a spiritual nature which will produce a life pleasing to God, and which will be a life fit for the kingdom of God. That is, the new birth is a permanent thing, producing a permanent change in the life of the individual, and making him a fit subject for the kingdom of God.

Life before we are born again is nothing more than filth: "All of us have become like one which is unclean and all our righteous acts are like filthy rags—like the wind our sins sweep us away" (Isaiah 64:6). Therefore, we must be born again.

4. The Changed Life

Human beings are not meant to live only earthly lives. Since earthly lives are driven by the flesh, they cannot experience deep satisfaction and peace so they begin to wander. When they see the need to change their ways and turn to Jesus Christ, they are born of water and the Spirit, and are born-again. God's hand of love reaches out to them. With the Holy Spirit working in their lives, new characteristics become prominent.

The first of these characteristics in their lives is that spiritual life begins to spring up. Says that "the Spirit gives birth to Spirit!". The Holy Spirit becomes a reality— becomes apparent to them—in their lives. Although they were driven by the desires of the flesh in their former lives, they no longer need to live that way because the Holy Spirit's power now dwells in them. Instead, they begin to purse the kind of lives that please God through the help of the Holy Spirit.

The second characteristic of people who are born again is their changed relationship with Jesus Christ. They have met Jesus, who died for their sins on the cross and was resurrected, as their Savior and Life-Giver. Since their perspective on Jesus has changed, they begin to obey His commands. Jesus Christ, totally ignored before, now is their Savior and begins to control their lives through the work of the Holy Spirit.

The third characteristic of people who are born again is that they become a part of the community of faith. They begin to worship with fellow Christians and enjoy fellowship with them.

They accept other people's happiness and sadness as their own. They begin to sacrifice themselves for the benefit of others who belong to the same community. This is the work of the Holy Spirit.

Fourth, people who are born again begin to pursue lives that place obedience to God's will over their own desires of the flesh. Of course they might not yet be totally committed to obeying God's will from the very beginning of their newly born lives. However, as they experience meaningful worship of God and deep horizontal relationships with other Christians, their desires change in obedience to God's will. The pursuing of their own desires decreases, and pursuing obedience to God's will or desires increases.

Last of all is the characteristic of love. The will of God is expressed in many ways. The will of God is to love. The born-again person has love for other Christians. Love for other Christians goes deeper and is expressed in more concrete ways, as time progresses. Another way God's love is expressed by those who are born-again is by their showing sincere concern for people who are outside of Jesus Christ. People who are born again really want the uncharted to experience God love through Jesus Christ. When their sincere concerns are expressed in positive ways, we call it evangelism. That is the work of the Holy Spirit.

5. True Beauty

Every human being is born of the flesh. Although the life of flesh contains some noble aims such as morality and artistic expression, in the end, flesh is still flesh. All must be cleansed by water and born of the Spirit. We must not just nod our assent to the phrase "flesh gives birth to flesh," but step forward into the reality of the second phrase "the Holy Spirit gives birth to spirit."

A student was attending Seoul Theological University. She was a beautiful girl both in appearance and personality. She was extremely devoted to her church life and wanted to learn more about God's Word and theology. She was fascinated with literature and everyone noticed her high marks in that area of study. She came to me one day and talked about her faith. It was evident through our conversation that she was not born-again. All her efforts were merely human decoration. Jesus' word, "flesh gives birth to flesh," was applicable to her life. She planned to go back to her home town when the winter break began. I made two suggestions to her. First, I suggested she read the gospel of John to find the truth about the real Jesus Christ. My second suggestion was that she attends the winter retreat of the Joy Club.

After a hard struggle, she finally attended the winter retreat. During that time, she met Jesus Christ: His body torn and his bloodshed on the cross, and his life resurrected from the dead. She experienced being born of water and the Spirit. The guilty feelings that had harassed her for many years disappeared because she was born of water. She began to live a new life and to influence other people, because she was born of the Spirit. The Holy Spirit still "walks with her" and she demonstrates her beautiful life to people all around her. She has become a real beautiful woman who has found true beauty in Jesus Christ.

Chapter 21

Flesh and Spirit (2)

"*Flesh* gives birth to flesh, but the *Spirit* gives birth to spirit"(John 3: 6).

1. Flesh and Spirit

In the moment human beings become born again by water and the Spirit, an amazing experience takes place. It is not an outward experience but one which is internal! The Holy Spirit enters the heart, bringing in "everything (man) needs to live a godly life"—divine power! Peter describes the essence of this experience in this manner: "His divine power has given us everything we need for life and godliness...he has given us his very great and precious promises, so that through them you may participate in the divine nature" (2 Peter 1: 3-4).

Here is something one should think about: Even though he/she has been born again and has experienced the indwelling of the Holy Spirit, they still live in the body. A born-again person, therefore, has two natures within them—the flesh-nature and the new spirit-nature.

Yes, indeed! A born-again person having two natures: flesh and spirit! Wouldn't it be wonderful if a person's flesh nature was totally gone the moment he was born again? No longer would we have to deal with inner conflict. Living a happy and godly life would be so much easier. However, this is not the case. All born-again Christians have flesh and spirit competing with one another—conflict between the two natures comes naturally.

2. The Contrast of Flesh and Spirit

There are several contrasts between flesh and spirit. The first contrast is that which is related to birth. The Apostle John said that everyone is born through natural descent, by way of human decision—therefore, man possesses a flesh nature. Then John speaks of being born of God through the Holy Spirit's transforming work. Born of man and born of God—two natures. From the moment of spiritual birth, born-again people have all the character of both the natural and the spiritual person (John 1:13). Two completely different kinds of birth; one is physical and outward, the other spiritual and inward. Both are necessary, for a life here on earth and a life in the kingdom of God.

The second is a contrast in manner of life. It is evident that it is inevitable for the flesh to have its limits and weaknesses. There is little power here. However, a person born of the Spirit is different. Within a person born again is one whose power is demonstrated in heaven. Life has unlimited possibilities as the work of the Holy Spirit is experienced. Life is enjoyed as one walks with God and receives His peace and joy.

The third flesh-spirit contrast is seen in man's destination. A person born of the flesh comes to earth with sin ready-and-waiting at the door of his heart. It is inevitable. Man falls prey to sin. "Every man has sinned and fallen short of the glory of God" (Romans 3:23). Since "the wages of sin is death" (Romans 6: 23), his last stop is death. The greeter? Satan. The person born of the flesh is made from the dust of the ground (Genesis 2: 7), and he returns to the ground in the end. However, the person born of the Spirit is different. His last earthly stop is death, but then the excitement begins! Because of Christ, "the perishable clothes itself with the imperishable" (1 Corinthians

15: 53)! Eternal life...in the Kingdom! What a contrast in destination!

That's right! Contrasts can be found in terms of time and in terms of eternity. A person born of the flesh belongs to the world, but a person born of the Spirit belongs to God's kingdom. People born once in this world, live with all kinds of limitations, but people born-twice, the last one from above, have the power to transcend all these. Their births determine their future. Blessed is the one who experiences both births!

3. Confrontation of Flesh and Spirit

Being born-again does not guarantee a life void of problems. Eventually, people who are born-again struggle in life and are often pulled in two different directions. One pulls man in the direction of gratifying the desires of the flesh. It is self-centered and world-oriented. The opposite pulls man in the direction of gratifying the desires of the Spirit. This direction is other-oriented and God-centered. Born-again people do not enjoy this confrontation but when conflicts do arise, they need to recognize the potential for spiritual growth, for they have asked an active Holy Spirit to reside in them.

Therefore, truly born-again people always have to choose which direction to go in. But as they chose the way of the Spirit more and more, they find the pull in the other direction less and less. Therefore, what direction a person chooses becomes the most important element in determining his or her spiritual life. "Since you have been raised with Christ....Set your minds on things above, not on earthly things....Put to death, therefore, whatever belongs to your earthly nature...."(Colossians 3:1-5).

This spiritual fight is vividly expressed by the Apostle Paul. He describes the desperate conflict within people who believe in Jesus Christ as their Savior and are born again: "So I say, walk by the Spirit, and you will not gratify the desires of the flesh. For the flesh desires what is contrary to the Spirit, and the Spirit what is contrary to the flesh. They are in conflict with each other, so that you are not to do whatever you want (Ga-latians 5: 16-17). Put no confidence in the flesh. Put all the confidence in the world in the Spirit! For it is God who works in you (Philippians 2:13)!

Paul presents a list (15+) of the fruit (results) that comes from gratifying the flesh in Galatians 5:19. He has these sins listed under one of four categories 1)sexual sin, 2) worship, 3) wrong personal relationships, and 4) self-control problems (Galatians 5: 19-21). However, when a born-again person chooses what the Spirit desires, the situation is totally different. Rather than indulging in the acts of the flesh, he bears the fruit of the Spirit. The Apostle Paul lists the fruit (results) that come from gratifying the Spirit, classifying them in the following way: 1) The relationship with God (love, joy, peace), 2) relationship with others (forbearance, kindness, goodness), 3) relationship within oneself (faithfulness, gentleness and self-control) (Galatians 5:22-23). The results of this inner conflict between the Spirit and the flesh are truly contrasting.

4. Who Is the Winner?

So who determines the direction one should take? Who determines "which dog" to feed—the flesh or the Spirit (Indian legend)? Every born-again believer does! They make life-decisions. They have the freedom to choose what the flesh would choose and they have the freedom to choose what the Spirit would choose. They determine the winner.

The Apostle Paul clearly describes the importance of choice and seriousness of result. Born-again people always live between the two options (Flesh? Spirit?): "Don't you know that when you offer yourselves to someone as obedient slaves, you are slaves of the one you obey— whether you are slaves to sin, which leads to death, or to obedience, which leads to righteousness?" (Romans 6: 16).

According to the Apostle Paul, Christians offer themselves to be either slaves of sin or slaves of righteousness. The choice the Christian makes determines his master (And we know that we can only have one Master!). Here Paul uses the word obedience. Why? Because he wishes to highlight obedience as the Christian's correct response to God's command. God's Spirit within him helps him to make right choices through obedience to His will.

According to Paul, a Christian can choose sin or righteousness. If he foolishly chooses sin, he will walk toward death as a slave of sin. If he wisely chooses God and refuses to sin, he will walk toward righteousness as a slave to obedience. But why does Paul use the word obedience for the choice? Because obedience is the Christian's willing response to God's love. In other words, the Christian obeys God because of His love.

One step further: Paul recognizes that the choice of obedience is the shortcut to spiritual victory. You used to offer yourselves as slaves to impurity and to ever-increasing wickedness, so now offer yourselves as slaves to righteousness leading to holiness (Romans 6: 19). Please pay attention to used to be and now. Used to indicate a period of time before Christians were born again. They used to be in sin, but now have been transformed by water and the Spirit.

However, after the born-again experience, they do not need to live in sin anymore. In fact their sins have been forgiven. The Spirit has come! Obeying God by an act of their will, aided by the Holy Spirit, they can live victorious lives. Paul compares this kind of victorious life to "holiness! That's right! Born-again Christians become victors by their own free will by their responses to the promptings of the Spirit residing within them.

5. A Victor's Story

Yes, indeed! Choosing to be born-again decides who the winner ultimately is. If you choose sin, then flesh is the winner. If you choose righteousness, ah, the Spirit is the winner! Choices! When born-again, you need to continue to choose righteousness. The Holy Spirit will help you, from within, to overcome the pull of the flesh and lead you into holiness. Let's emphasize it again this way: obedient to the Holy Spirit, you can do anything! You can become anything...that He wants you to be! He holds sovereignty over the power of the flesh and over the power of Satan!

In my case, even after I was born again, I used to hate certain Christians. My situation was similar to what Paul mentions in Galatians 5: 20, I was filled with "idolatry and witchcraft; hatred, discord, jealousy, fits of rage, selfish ambition, dissensions, and factions." All prayed for my heart to be changed so that I could love these people, my hatred increased. I prayed eagerly, but nothing changed. Later, I realized that it was not a matter of prayer, but a matter of obedience. I should have been praying, "I will obey! I will love! Help me!"

Later, I did become born-again, but I remained a slave to sin. I lived a life of failure. Peace and joy was gone. I struggled for several months. One day when I was groaning in anguish, a Bible verse came to my mind: For though a righteous man falls seven times, he rises again...h (Proverbs 24: 16). I stood up all of a sudden, and ran into the place where a winter retreat was being held.

On the last day of the retreat, when we were crying out to the Lord in expectation, the Holy Spirit totally filled us. We cried with many tears. From that day forward, the Holy Spirit began to gain control of me. Every morning, quiet time was an important opportunity to encounter the Lord. The Word of God tasted like honey to my lips. Furthermore, this experience was not just a one-time personal blessing. Many precious souls, as I have shared my testimony, have come to the Lord, repenting of their sins. The Holy Spirit brought forth victorious living.

Chapter 22

Man Born of the Spirit

"The wind blows wherever it pleases. You hear its sound, but you cannot tell where it comes from or where it is going. So it is with everyone born of the Spirit" (John 3:8).

1. The Experience of the Spirit

Both the work of God and man's response to it are required for the rebirth experience. First of all, God calls people, even before people call out to Him. Even when people attempt to run away from God, are indifferent to God's calling or try to stand against God, God may still call them. How could human beings ever be born again if there was no such gracious calling!

People respond to God's call in two ways: by repentance and by faith (Acts 20:21). People need to admit their sin, turn away from it, and turn to God in their response to God's call. Responding, people need to fix their eyes on Jesus Christ who died on the cross and shed his blood for them. When they come to Jesus with their eyes fixed on the cross, God responds with grace.

This graceful response of God is expressed as being born of the Spirit. God forgives all sins through Jesus Christ's death on the cross and His resurrection (Romans 4:25). At that very moment of response, the Holy Spirit comes into people's lives and hearts. This is the experience referred to as "born of the Spirit!" They become children of God through the work of the Holy Spirit (Galatians 4:5-6). When people respond to God's call with repentance and faith, He makes the threefold divine-work possible—the forgiveness of sins, spiritual rebirth, and adoption into the family of God.

2. A Certain Experience

Those who respond to God's call become people born of the Spirit, born-again people entering into the kingdom! People hear the sound of the Spirit, but do not know where the Spirit comes from or where it is heading. Likewise, they notice the transformation of people, but they do not know how this transformation happens. Since this experience occurs by the work of the indwelling Spirit, people who are not born-again and look only on the external (human effort and resolve) consider it to be a mystery.

Of course, this internal transformation is inevitably followed by external transformation. For certain people, the external transformation occurs almost immediately, but for most it is a gradual change. Paul is a good example of a person who experienced external as well as internal transformation immediately. As soon as he met Jesus Christ, he experienced vivid transformation in terms of his goal and way of life. He had been persecuting Christians but stopped suddenly and became a witness for Christ after his experience with Christ on the Damascus Road.

The experience of the twelve disciples was quite the opposite of that of Paul. They had not experienced immediate transformation of life even after Jesus called them. Their spiritual lives went-up-and-down for the three years they spent under Jesus' ministry. They began to undergo vivid transformation after their experiencing the resurrected Christ. They soon experienced the fullness of the Holy Spirit taking complete charge of their lives as they submitted to Him. The most remarkable transformation they experienced was to become bold and powerful witnesses of Jesus Christ, as Paul was (Acts 1-2).

After all, the experience of being born-again happens through the indwelling of the Holy Spirit. Paul clearly explains the process of being born of the Spirit, when he says: ⁇And you also were included in Christ when you heard the word of truth, the gospel of your salvation. Having believed, you were marked in him with a seal, the promised Holy Spirit (Ephesians 1:13). To be "included in Christ", the first process is to hear "the word of truth." Here Paul especially refers to "the gospel of salvation." The gospel of salvation, needless to say, is Jesus' death and resurrection. In other words, no one can enter the kingdom of God unless he is born of water and the Spirit. However, if people end up with only hearing the gospel of salvation, they cannot be born of the Spirit. They need to take the second step described as having believed - a positive response to the Gospel.

The third step, the last one, is a very important aspect of being born again. The third process is to be "marked in him with a seal, the promised Holy Spirit." What is the meaning of this? The Holy Spirit comes into their lives, as promised. The Holy Spirit not only comes into their lives, but also marks them with a seal, confirming the fact that they have become the children of God. Since they have become the children of God, God will protect them and offer to be in charge of their lives.

3. Personal Godliness

As mentioned before, people who are born of the Spirit still live in the flesh. Therefore, born-again people experience fierce struggles between the Spirit and the flesh because the Holy Spirit comes into fleshly nature that has existed from the very beginning of their lives. For this reason, people who are truly born again have two natures: the nature of the Holy Spirit and that of the flesh. These two natures compete with each other to control the lives of born-again people.

When the nature of the Holy Spirit wins, people enjoy abundant joy and peace. However, when the nature of the flesh seems to win, people begin to struggle and this inner joy and peace diminishes. God provides several ways for people to regain this lost joy. First, He asks people to reflect on what it was that allowed the nature of the flesh to win over the nature of the Holy Spirit. Then, they need to be frankly honest before God and confess the sin or wrong-doing. John, the Apostle of Love, expresses the importance of confession and receiving assurance of forgiveness: "If we confess our sins, he is faithful and just and will forgive us our sins and purify us from all unrighteousness." "Confessing" means agreeing with God that the sin He has revealed has, indeed, been committed. God promises that if people frankly confess their sins, no longer try to conceal them, God will surely forgive their sins" (I John 1:8-9). If they forsake their wrongdoings, they will experience abundant joy (Proverbs 28:13).

A second way to regain what was lost is to read the Word of God regularly because the Word of God is food for the soul. In many cases, the chief reason why many born-again people are defeated is not sin. Their soul is under-nourished! As people need to eat nutritional food for their bodies, they are required to have the proper food for their spiritual health—on a daily basis. It is no exaggeration to consider that people who do not read the Bible regularly are almost giving up on having a strong Christian life. Healthy people have meals regularly, but people who are ill do not eat well. Likewise, people who do not have the Word of God regularly must be either spiritually ill—or spiritually dead. On the contrary, people who read the Word of God regularly experience joy and grow up to be healthy normal Christians (2 Peter 2:2). They will live vibrant lives!

Third, they need to pray. They need to commune with God to regain joy. As the Word of God is the love-letter God gives to us, so prayer is our love-letter given to Him. If people freely bring confession to God, have a word from God on their lips, and prayer in their heart every day, their souls will enjoy abundant joy and peace. At the same time, they will be better able to encourage many other people, as people born of the Spirit ought to do, to do the same.

4. The Joy of Fellowship

People who enjoy personal fellowship with God inevitably enjoy fellowship with other Christians. They share their time and hearts. They try to meet each other's need. They praise each other's strength and cover each other's weaknesses. They love and encourage each other when they get together, and pray for each other when they are apart. They often enjoy a fellowship that is closer than that which they have with their own biological brothers and sisters.

God already set the stage for this fellowship even before the creation of the world (Ephesians 1:4). God "chose us in him before the creation of the world." Here "us" means the Church. As the existence of Jesus, the head of the Church is true prior to the creation of the world, so the pre-existence of the Church— in the mind of God— before the creation of the world is true. People who form the body of Jesus Christ are born-again Christians. Christians enjoy the fellowship of the Church, which God saw before the creation of the world.

Needless to say, fellowship in the Church has two dimensions: fellowship with God and fellowship with fellow Christians. For this reason, born-again people must worship God, as well as be involved in a local church. Through worship, people deeply experience God and, at the same time, share love and fellowship with fellow Christians. This two-fold fellowship is a beautiful characteristic to see in an obedient and growing local church!

After the first local church was born in Jerusalem, this two-folded fellowship was a sight to see! Fellowship activities of the people there are concisely summarized in the Book of Acts: They devoted themselves to the apostles teaching and to the fellowship, to the breaking of bread and to prayer (Acts 2:42).

One more thing is accomplished through the fellowship of Christians: spiritual discipline! Born-again people should mature. For spiritual growth, people need to experience spiritual discipline. They spiritually grow when they worship together, share their lives together, laugh and cry together, and learn together. They learn beliefs and life styles from their mentors. In addition, they pass on their learning and experience to new believers. And, more importantly, God is pleased!

People who are born of the Holy Spirit are not alone. They are surrounded by a great cloud of witnesses (Hebrew 12:1). People born of the Spirit can join this line of witnesses through their spiritual growth and their triumph over the temptations of the world. The Church is described as the body of Christ, and born-again people as parts of His body. Therefore, born-again people must be involved in a local church (1 Corinthians 12:12).

5. The Fragrance of People Born of the Spirit

According to John 3:8, people who are born of the Spirit are like the wind. They quietly approach unchurched people and softly and gently spread their fragrant spirit of life and share the story of God's extravagant love. The warm wind of the Spirit in born-again man falls upon people who shiver in the cold; a peaceful wind of the Spirit in born-again man falls gently over people who have toiled endlessly and gives them rest; and a moisture-filled wind of the Spirit in born-again man comes to quench a spiritually dry and thirsty people.

Even though they do not know where the wind comes from and how it comes to them, they know people stirring up the wind. The wind comes from the Holy Spirit. People who are born again are filled with the wind of the Holy Spirit. Wherever they go, they spread it. We can find numerous stories that show the wind of the Spirit spreading along with the fragrance of born-again people. One of these testimonies comes from Kim-Cheon, South Korea.

An elder heard a groan from under a bridge and decided to go down to investigate. He found a leper family. The time was soon after the Korean War. There were many leper families in Korea. The elder took the leper family to his home and began to take care of them. Other lepers who heard that good news gathered at his house one by one. Finally, a rehabilitation facility for lepers was established.

As their living conditions improved and they got proper treatment, they became healthy. They raised chickens, and their chickens produced eggs in abundance. In addition, they were able to save enough money to buy land to farm. They always had a good harvest of rice every year. Many lepers came to believe in Jesus Christ and were born again, following the footsteps of the elder. Their lives, along with that of the elder, were filled with the fragrance of Christ's Spirit.

They built a church building on their own and invited a good pastor to their church. In addition, they shared God's love with other poor people, taking the example of the elder. They planted several daughter churches and provided living expenses of their pastors. Nobody knows how far their fragrance was spread by the wind. Their praise, fellowship, love, and fragrance are still spreading under the guidance and power of the Holy Spirit.

Chapter 23

Man Born of the Spirit (2)

"The wind blows wherever it pleases. *You hear its sound, but you cannot tell* where it comes from or where it is going. So it is with everyone born of the Spirit" (John 3:8).

1. The Indwelling of the Holy Spirit

People, born of the Holy Spirit experience a great spiritual mystery. No one knows the origin and destination of the wind despite knowing that the wind is indeed blowing. But the time comes when the Wind of God gives opportunity to man to respond to God's invitation to receive Christ. Those who respond positively are born-again. They experience new life. They now have the Holy Spirit guiding them. They sense their lives going in a new direction. Their inward nature is changing—they can sense that change occurring. Their lives take on new purpose, and there is a new joy in living! All about them they are experiencing re-birth! Such changes may often be seen and felt immediately. Others take more time—the Spirit's time—to develop. It certainly is a great mystery as to how this all comes about, but it does happen. It is hard to explain, yes; but it is experienced.

Why can only the people who have experienced such a change understand the work of the Holy Spirit? The reason is very simple! The indwelling Holy Spirit cannot be seen or touched by human hands. The presence of an active and creative Holy Spirit within man is the best gift God could ever give to human beings. Earthly gifts can only provide temporary relief to the people who receive them. This gift can change people's lives forever.

The indwelling presence of the Holy Spirit not only gives joy and peace to people who receive him, but it totally transforms their lives. A person's goals, purpose, and way of life change. These changes cannot happen through human effort. Only the Holy Spirit coming into people's hearts makes them possible. People in their attempt to explain the mystery of the Holy Spirit's indwelling and working in man have used other terms to help explain this mystery. The indwelling of the Holy Spirit is often referred to as: being "in Christ," having "the seal of the Holy Spirit," and, given "the gifts of the Holy Spirit." These terms are all important elements of this experience, but the full mystery remains.

2. "In Christ"

People, who experience the indwelling of the Holy Spirit, are often referred to as people who are "in Christ." The Apostle Paul uses the term "in Christ" about one hundred times in his New Testament letters. First, when people are born of the Holy Spirit, they have come "out of Adam" and have gone "into Christ." Even though human beings are born under the sin that has been passed down from Adam, they become new creatures in Jesus Christ when they are born of the Spirit (2 Corinthians 5:17) given at the time of Jesus' departure to heaven. Because of the disobedience of Adam, all human beings are spiritually dead from the moment of their birth (Ephesians 2:1). Such a spiritual death cannot be overcome by human efforts, but human beings can escape from Adam into Christ through the grace of God. This born-again experience can be described as being "in Christ." Paul describes the process of this change: "For as in Adam all die, so in Christ all will be made alive" (1 Corinthians 15:22).

Second, in Christ he emphasizes that people are united with Christ as soon as they are born of the Spirit. From the beginning, Christ is in God and God is in Christ (John 14:10), meaning that God and Jesus Christ are forever one. When people are born of the Spirit, they are in Christ and Christ is in them (John 14:20), which also signifies that people who are born of the Spirit are one in Jesus Christ. "If anyone is in Christ, he is a new creation; the old has gone, the new has come" (2 Corinthians 5:17)! That Christ and born-again people are one refers to their becoming children of God, as Christ is the Son of God. Furthermore, they participate in Jesus' death and resurrection (Romans 6:4-5). One step further, people who are born of the Spirit is seated with him in the heavenly realms in Christ Jesus (Ephesians 2:6). In other words, people who are born of the Spirit are equal to Christ in terms of position, status, and privilege.

Third, "in Christ" emphasizes a moral life. People who are born of the Spirit become new creatures. The old self was spiritually dead because of "transgressions and sins" (Ephesians 2:1), and "followed the ways of this world and of the ruler of the kingdom of the air—gratifying the cravings of our sinful nature" (Ephesians 2:2-3). Ultimately, the old self cannot meet the moral standard of God, nor the social norms, nor a good conscience. But people who are in Christ are different, because the power to live a moral life is given to them through the indwelling of the Holy Spirit. In addition, a heart that desires to imitate the life of Jesus Christ is also given to them.

People who are born of the Spirit are "created in Christ Jesus to do good works, which God prepared in advance for us to do" (Ephesians 2:10). Likewise, they begin to live moral lives because of the work of the triune God.

3. "The Seal of the Holy Spirit"

As quoted above, Paul mentions the "seal of the Holy Spirit" in the following way: "And you also were included in Christ when you heard the word of truth, the gospel of your salvation. Having believed, you were marked in him with a seal, the promised Holy Spirit" (Ephesians 1:13). "Sealed with the Holy Spirit" means that the Holy Spirit comes into the people who are forgiven. People who believe in the redemptive work of Jesus Christ and are justified by God enter into a covenant relationship with God. The mark of the covenant relationship is the seal of the Holy Spirit.

As circumcision became the seal of the covenant with Jews (Genesis 17:10), the indwelling of the Holy Spirit becomes the seal of the covenant to people who are born of the Spirit. As Jews enter into the covenant relationship with God and belong to God through the seal of circumcision, so people who are born of the Spirit belong to God through the seal of the Holy Spirit. Paul claims: "Nevertheless, God's solid foundation stands firm, sealed with this inscription: 'The Lord knows those who are his'" (2 Timothy 2:19).

God knows the born-again people who are sealed with the Holy Spirit. "Knowing" here means "belonging to God." When God judges the whole human race on the last day, God does not want to judge his own people. So God has marked his people with a seal. The seal signifies "ownership" and "protection": "Do not harm the land or the sea or the trees until we put a seal on the foreheads of the servants of our God" (Revelation 7:3).

"Sealed with the Holy Spirit" refers to a guarantee as well as "protection." According to Paul, God "set his seal of ownership on us, and put his Spirit in our hearts as a deposit, guaranteeing what is to come" (2 Corinthians 1:22). The seal of the Holy Spirit assures man of the indwelling of the Holy Spirit. At the same time, the Holy Spirit works as a deposit, which means a guarantee of things to come.

As soon as people confess their faith, God shows them that they are born again by paying a deposit, the seal of the Holy Spirit. However, God will pay the balance on behalf of them at the last Day. In addition, God invites them to enter into the kingdom of God. To put it plainly, people who are born of the Spirit will surely meet God on the last day when Jesus returns to the earth. God seals them with the Holy Spirit as a guarantee.

When people are born of the Spirit, God, through the seal of the Holy Spirit, guarantees that they will be perfectly changed when Jesus returns (2 Corinthians 5:4-5). When Jesus returns, "the perishable has been clothed with the imperishable, and the mortal with immortality" (1 Corinthians 15:52-53). Moreover, guaranteed by the Holy Spirit, they will enjoy their eternal inheritance in the kingdom of God, where God abides (Ephesians 1:14). This guarantee is the seal of the Holy Spirit.

4. The Gifts of the Holy Spirit

People who are born of the Spirit must be a part of the body of Christ, a local church (1 Corinthians 12:13). Furthermore, people who are members of a local church have roles of ministry for the health of the body, just as parts of a body such as eyes, ears, hands, and internal organs play certain roles in the body. When each part of the body plays its unique role, the body is healthy. Likewise, if people who are born of the Spirit fulfill their roles in the body, the body is healthy.

The Spirit dwells in the hearts of people when they are born of the Spirit and he gives definite gifts to them. The Holy Spirit can either give just one gift to a person or several. The gifts they receive are apportioned by the Holy Spirit, the number depending upon the will and concernment of the Giver (Ephesians 4:7-8).

According to the New Testament (I Corinthians 12:4-11), the Holy Spirit gives people three different kinds of gifts. First, there are those gifts which are used through their mouths (teaching, encouraging, and more). Second, there is another group of gifts which are used with their hands (contributing to the needs of people, serving, and more). There is a third group of gifts which are related to the performing of miraculous signs (speaking in a tongue, distinguishing between spirits, and more). What kinds of gifts are given to them is not important, because the Holy Spirit wisely determines the gifts according to his purpose. It is more important that we serve each other using the spiritual gifts we have been given, regardless of the kind of gifts. Having a sense of inferiority or superiority by comparing each other's gifts is unwise. More emphasis should be put on "actual usage" of the gift for the glory of God and His church. For example, people who have the gift of teaching need to teach, and people who have the gift of contributing to the needs of others need to give generously.

If all people born of the Spirit receive certain kinds of spiritual gifts, how do they discern them? Giving specific examples may help us understand more clearly. One born-again person likes to read and study the Bible, and many people benefit from his or her study and teaching. He or she is encouraged by people positive responses of his or her teaching and goes deeper in studying the Bible. He/she apparently has been given the gift of teaching.

All born-again people should contribute to the development of other people's faith by using their spiritual gifts. For this purpose, they need to find their own spiritual gift. Then they should develop it. For example, people who have the gift of teaching must study diligently and accumulate the resources they need. Lastly, they should use their gift for the health of the church. Using one's gift to serve the church brings about great joy to the church and to oneself.

5. The Witness of the Holy Spirit

One important way to keep the believers healthy and the Kingdom growing is to share the gospel with unchurched people. When Nicodemus began his conversation with Jesus, Jesus directly spoke to him that "no one can see the kingdom of God unless he is born again." Why did he say that? The most important reason for Jesus coming into this world was "to seek and to save what was lost" (Luke 19:10). People are lost...and in need of a Savior!

Jesus' main concern was the salvation of souls. For their salvation, Jesus died on the cross, enduring terrible suffering.

Through Jesus' suffering, he saved precious souls. Those who were saved were born of water and the Spirit, and they became the children of God. In other words, they were born of the Spirit. The people who are born of the Spirit should share the gospel with people who are not.

When people who are born of the Spirit share their testimony with unchurched people, the Holy Spirit helps them in their witness. The Holy Spirit awakens the minds of people to realize their sinfulness and to recognize their need to be rescued from it. In addition, the Holy Spirit shows that all the accomplishments and good deeds of people turn out to be nothing more than filthy beggar-like clothes in the heart and mind of God. The Holy Spirit also reminds them of the fact that they will be judged by God on the last Day (John 16:7-11). So He points them to Jesus Christ as the way out of their earthly dilemma. A dilemma which has taken them farther and farther away from God's kingdom!

These awakenings are the testimony of the Holy Spirit. As born-again Christians share the gospel, the Holy Spirit works together with them. People who are born of the Spirit must witness for Jesus Christ, and then they will experience the witness of the Holy Spirit. They will naturally taste great joy. As a result, their churches will eventually grow. Born-again people have the great privilege of walking with God and to witnessing to others through the wisdom, guidance, and power of the Holy Spirit.

Chapter 24

Man Born of the Spirit (3)

"The wind blows wherever it pleases. You hear its sound, but you cannot tell where it comes from or where it is going. So it is with everyone born of the Spirit" (John 3:8).

1. The Wind and the Holy Spirit

The similarity between wind and the Holy Spirit is remarkable. First, the Holy Spirit and the wind move regardless of human decision and will. They both move mysteriously, whenever and wherever they please. A second similarity is their influence. A powerful wind can change people's lives forever. The work of the Holy Spirit can also change lives forever—transforming people spiritually. A third similarity is seen in the inability to stop them. Neither the determined power of the wind nor of the Holy Spirit can be stopped by human beings. When the wind blows hard, few humans can stop its destruction. So too, the work of the Holy Spirit will break any human prejudice and rebellion that interferes with what He wishes to accomplish!

Fourth, sometimes the wind blows gently; but sometimes it blows very hard. Similarly, sometimes the Holy Spirit deals very gently with man, and sometimes He "divides the waters!" No human being can predict the intensity of either force. Fifth, human beings cannot see the movement of the wind nor the Holy Spirit, but their movements can be felt and events experienced. A sixth, and last, similarity of the wind and the Holy Spirit is their necessity. If the wind does not blow, many plants will die. Likewise, if the Holy Spirit does not move, humans will continue to live in a condition of spiritual death. When the wet, warm winds blow, plants revive. When the Holy Spirit acts, the spiritually dead are stirred!

2. The Proof of God's Word

People born of the Spirit were once living among the spiritually dead, "following the desires and thoughts" of their sinful natures. But they had been "made alive" by the work of the Holy Spirit Who they had asked to come into their lives (Ephesians 2:1). People who have experienced this spiritual change show several proofs of this happening, just as many proofs of birth follow when a new babe is born. A newly-born babe cries, breathes, sucks the breast, and relieves itself— growing healthy and strong as time passes by.

Several proofs of spiritual birth are seen. The first one comes from the Word of God. The fundamental proof that born-again people have renewed spiritual life can be found in the Scriptures. This proof is extremely important because even born-again people have feelings and emotions that may fluctuate. Sometimes, they may feel doubts about their having had this second birth. Whenever they feel this way, they need to go back to the Word of God for reassurance. Had they taken the steps God said were necessary to change their lives?

Peter emphasizes the fact that people are born again by the Word of God; "For you have been born again, not of perishable seed, but of imperishable, through the living and enduring word of God" (1 Peter 1:23). The Word of God testifies that born-again people have eternal life. The Apostle John claims, "I write these things to you who believe in the name of the Son of

God so that you may know that you have eternal life" (1 John 5:13).

The Word of God indicates that people who are born of the Spirit have eternal life (John 5:24). At the same time, the Word confirms that people born of the Spirit become the children of God. God's Word claims that they call God Father because they become children of God through the work of the Holy Spirit; "Because you are sons, God sent the Spirit of his Son into our hearts, the Spirit who calls out, Abba, Father (Galatians 4:6; also see Romans 8:15).

The Word of God not only testifies that born-again people are children of God, but it also explains the reason for this. How do people have this life and how do they become the children of God? This happens because God forgives their sins. Sin prevents human beings from coming close to God. A major gulf exists between man and God and man cannot cross over it by himself. Isaiah spoke of it in Isaiah 59:1-2, "the arm of the Lord is not too short to save....But your iniquities (sin) have separated you from your God."

However, God sacrificed His Son to tear down this gulf. In other words, God forgives the sins of people through His Son, Jesus Christ. God's Word strongly testifies to the forgiveness of sins: "For he has rescued us from the dominion of darkness and brought us into the kingdom of the Son he loves, in whom we have redemption, the forgiveness of sins" (Colossians 1:13-14). When the problem of sin is solved, the gulf is demolished, and we are privileged to become God's children, and to have eternal life in the Holy Spirit (John 1:12). God's Word testifies to these facts. He has made the way straight for man. The gulf has been filled in by the death and resurrection of Jesus Christ. The child of God has walked across!

3. The Proof of the Holy Spirit

The second proof is related to the witness of the Holy Spirit. If people who are born of the Spirit did not have the witness of the Holy Spirit, this would be a strange thing. Of what does the Holy Spirit testify? The Holy Spirit testifies that they are children of God. The following word confirms it: "The Spirit himself testifies with our spirit that we are God's children" (Romans 8:16). The Holy Spirit testifies through the new actions and spirit of born-again people.

Our spirit that is now reborn, reveals that we have met God, responded to Him, and are now living new lives. The Holy Spirit indirectly testifies that we are children of God through our new spirit. What does it mean to become a child of God? It means that we have entered into a new relationship with God—like what children have with their earthly father— turning away from an antagonistic relationship with Him and turning to Him.

The witness of the Holy Spirit that people have been born of the Spirit and are now children of God signifies that a tremendous positional change has occurred. They once belonged to this world and lived under the influence of Satan (John 8:44; Ephesians 2:2-3), but they have come out of that and have entered into the kingdom of God. They have become members of the family of God (Ephesians 2:19) and enjoy their many privileges as God's sons and daughters.

One of their privileges as children is that they become co-heirs with Jesus Christ. The inheritance that will be given to Jesus as the firstborn Son will be tremendous and honorable. However, people born of the Spirit share the same glorious right of inheritance as Jesus Christ does. Paul expresses this in the following way: "Now if we are children of God, then we are heirs▫\heirs of God and co-heirs with Christ, if indeed we share in his sufferings in order that we may also share in his glory" (Romans 8:17).

God's children not only have the privilege of inheritance but also share in Jesus' suffering. This reasoning is quite evident. People born of the Spirit no longer conform to the pattern of this world. In other words, they are different from other people. The people who are not tolerant of this difference not only do not accept people born of the Spirit, but also persecute them (1 Peter 4:4).

What do people born of the Spirit inherit? They will inherit an eternal inheritance. Peter states that God has given us "new birth...into an inheritance that can never perish, spoil or fade—kept in heaven for you" (1 Peter 1:4). The inheritance is called "a kingdom" (Hebrew 12:28), "a better country" (Hebrew 11:16), "the crown of life" (James 1:12), "the crown of righteousness" (2 Timothy 4:8), and "an eternal glory that far outweighs them all" (2 Corinthians 4:17).

4. The Proof of Experience

The third proof that one is born of the Spirit comes from experience. If the Holy Spirit comes into and seals people's heart, the impact and impression of that experience is indelible. They begin to enjoy peace with God (Romans 5:1), the product of a restored relationship with God. In addition, they taste unspeakable joy, and they will long to share that joy with other Christians.

Their goals in life also change. In previous times, they only dreamed of success for themselves, but now they begin to live for the glory of God. Before they used any means necessary to achieve their goals, but now they try to live honest and transparent lives. Their previous destiny was death and eternal punishment, but now they will enter into kingdom of God. Thinking of the glory of God makes joy overflow from their hearts (Romans 5:2).

How can people born of the Spirit live for the glory of God? To begin with, they need to live according to God's will. For this, they need to find God's will in the Bible. Therefore, people born of the Spirit read and meditate on God's Word day and night (Psalm 1:2). In other words, the standard which Christians live by is found in the Bible.

People born of the Spirit have strong and holy desires to live up to God's Word. But sometimes their actual lives do not meet His standard. For example, God commands us to Love your enemies, do good to those who hate you, bless those who curse you, pray for those who mistreat you (Luke 6:27-28). However, sometimes people born of the Spirit may experience difficulty in obeying this teaching of Jesus. These commands seem hard to do at times!

After all, people born of the Spirit experience this obedience-gap between God's Word and their actual lives. Struggling with this is the experience of many people born of the Spirit. If people do not struggle with this gap, they have probably not experienced the new birth. The reason for this struggle comes from the fact that human nature still remains in spite of the indwelling of the Holy Spirit.

The good news is that people born of the Spirit can end this internal struggle. They can overcome this struggle through the infilling of the Holy Spirit, an experience of holiness. In fact, this painful gap between God's Word and day-to-day experience could be a necessary trial because it leads to more dependence on Jesus than before going through the struggle. While they go through the struggle, they finally learn to give up their own efforts and ways and begin to depend exclusively on Jesus, leading to experiencing the fullness of the Holy Spirit (Ephesians 5:18).

5. The Proof of Evangelism

People born of the Spirit recognize that an inner struggle is going on in their heart and mind. A struggle between their obeying God's Word and their submitting to their own wills—God's way or their way. It is assuring to note that this can be a noble one. People in this world do not have a high standard of life and, therefore, do not experienced any noble struggle. If they do have any inner struggle, it is usually a struggle with their own desires. On the other hand, people born of the Spirit can enjoy peace and joy, even while they undergo this noble struggle. Their lives will only become richer as they increasingly learn to allow the Holy Spirit to do his work.

People born of the Spirit naturally want to share with unchurched people the special lives they enjoy. The strong desire for evangelism is another proof of born-again people. This desire to share the gospel is given by the Holy Spirit, who prompts us to tell the good news that God wants to transform lives and has revealed that desire of His personally. People who are moved from darkness to light naturally look back on their lives and want to help those who still remain in the darkness enter the light.

People who are born of the Spirit provide noticeable testimonies that demonstrate the truth of their having had the second birth—they testify to God's Word supporting what has taken place, they testify of the Holy Spirit leading their lives, and they testify of their own experience of changes in their lives. When these proofs are combined, they will naturally produce strong motivation for evangelis

Chapter 25

Man Born of the Spirit (4)

"The wind blows wherever it pleases. You hear its sound, but you cannot tell where it comes from or where it is going. So it is with everyone born of the Spirit" (John 3:8).

1. A Remarkable Characteristic

People go through three experiences on earth: birth, life, and then death. Each person sets out on his life-journey accumulating personal goals and ambitions, thoughts and accomplishments, good and bad experiences. Death seems too far away to be concerned about. However, each person, at one time or another will be confronted by God with a choice: to turn around and go 180 degrees in the opposite direction with God or to continue on in life, leading, ultimately, to nowhere without God! To make that "turn-around" will take much more than academic or economic achievement. In fact, it will be an amazing and mysterious experience, one that will not be accomplished through any kind of human effort, but by God's.

How can God accomplish this experience? Well, it's God's own plan. He will, and can, do it. Secondly, the plan will be executed by His Son, Jesus Christ. Jesus' death on the cross and His resurrection from the dead will be the means by which God's plan will be successful. Lastly, the Holy Spirit will provide the power to enable man to travel down this new life-journey. How? By the Holy Spirit entering receptive hearts and man experiencing that "second birth!"

After all, the most remarkable characteristic of people born of the Spirit is the indwelling of the Holy Spirit. The teaching that the Holy Spirit enters into people hearts and lives is an unprecedented one. The indwelling of the Holy Spirit is not something that happens in other religions nor can it be accomplished by human efforts. It is the most mystical and practical experience that human beings can have. It is no longer a faint hope that is often hidden in other religions but a living reality.

Jesus claims the wind blows wherever it pleases. You hear its sound, but you cannot tell where it comes from or where it is going. So it is with everyone born of the Spirit. In other words, people born of the Spirit not only can hear the sound of the wind, but also know the direction.

2. The Inspiration of the Holy Spirit

To follow the direction of the Holy Spirit is analogous to following the will of God. How do people born of the Spirit discern and follow the will of God? Most of all, we find God's will in the Bible, not the will of God in a general sense, but God' will in a practical sense applicable to everyday lives. Of course, the Holy Spirit helps us discern this will of God.

The Word of God was written under the inspiration of the Holy Spirit. 2 Timothy confirms this, "the Holy Scriptures—are able to make you wise for salvation through faith in Christ Jesus. All Scripture is God-breathed and is useful for teaching, rebuking, correcting and training in righteousness, so that the man of God may be thoroughly equipped for every good work" (2 Timothy 3:15-17). Here, Paul emphasizes that all Scripture is God-breathed. This means that God breathed His Spirit into the writers of the Bible and they were inspired by the Holy Spirit to write as God willed.

The Apostle Peter puts it this way: For prophecy never had its origin in the will of man, but men spoke from God as they were carried along by the Holy Spirit (2 Peter 1:21). After all, the original author of the Bible is God, though God allowed all the writers of the Bible to write using their own culture and personality. Some 40 different authors, within a period of 1500 years, ensure tremendous consistency in writing the history of what God willed for man.

What is God's will for man according to this God-breathed Bible? As mentioned earlier, we find two very clear desires of God. First, the Bible was written to tell of God's love for man, and His plan to save them. "For God so loved the world that He gave his one and only Son, that whoever believes in him shall not perish but have everlasting life" (John 3:16). The second desire of God's is to then enable them, by the indwelling Holy Spirit, to live the holy lives He has planned for them (2 Timothy 3:16). This is done by His people searching His Word and obeying what they soon discover to be the will of God. The Holy Spirit will be their guide, and the power behind their obedience.

3. The Illumination of the Holy Spirit

Man without the Holy Spirit has a problem. Because the Word of God was written under the inspiration of the Holy Spirit, and the Author is not yet in man, they may regard the Bible as the Word of God, but they do not easily understand it. Although the Bible is on the best-sellers list of books, regrettably, not many people live the holy lives prescribed in it.

What is the reason for this inability to live a holy life? One of the reasons is that many people treat the Bible as they do a literary masterpiece. Many masterpieces have been produced and give substantial lessons for life. They can be inspirational, but no masterpiece can produce born-again Christians who live holy lives except the Bible. They may be masterpieces, but they are all of fallible human origin.

As mentioned before, the Bible has man's handwriting, but it is God's word for man. For this reason, the Bible cannot be totally understood through various methods of analysis and criticism, as people do with other masterpieces. We need the help of the Holy Spirit to understand God's Word and to find God's will in it, and to do what it says.

Jesus Christ focused upon this problem by saying quite clearly, "but the Counselor, the Holy Spirit, whom the Father will send in my name, will teach you all things and will remind you of everything I have said to you (John 14:26). This work of the Holy Spirit related to man's understanding of God's Word is called the illumination of the Holy Spirit. When the Holy Spirit is present and illuminates the Word of God, then people open their eyes to the Bible and are seized by it. The will of God found in this way captivates them and true holy life begins.

In addition, they begin to positively influence other people around them. We can find many good examples of people, insignificant in the eyes of the world, changing history because he or she was captivated by the Holy Spirit and the Word of God.

4. The Work of the Holy Spirit

Dwight L. Moody is a good example. He did not even graduate from high school. Many people mocked his sermons because of his incorrect grammar. However, after about 20 minutes, people who had been mocking his sermon would begin to cry. Many cried out for salvation and were born of the Holy Spirit. People estimate that more than one million people experienced spiritual change through the ministry of Moody. But his influence did not end with the number of converts. Moody started Moody Press and the Moody Bible Institute in Chicago, both of which became possible by the leading of the Holy Spirit.

Do people born of God automatically find the will of God through the illumination of the Holy Spirit? Do they automatically apply the will of God to their everyday lives? Of course not! Born-again people must have an attitude of obedience. They must be ready to obey the will of God when the Holy Spirit reveals it in their lives. God works through the Holy Spirit given to people of obedience (Acts 5:32).

God says to us through Samuel, "Does the Lord delight in burnt offerings and sacrifices as much as in obeying the voice of the Lord? To obey is better than sacrifice, and to heed is better than the fat of rams." (1 Samuel 15:22). If we relate this word to a worship service today, sacrifice may be analogous to the worship service and the fat of the ram may be analogous to offerings or service. These things are important to born-again people, but obedience is far more important.

If people born of the Spirit read the Bible with the intention of total obedience to it, God will surely reveal His will through the illumination of Holy Spirit. For this reason, people born of the Spirit need to read the Bible on a daily basis, along with memorizing and meditating on it. The illumination of the Holy Spirit always resonates with investing the time and effort into Bible-reading that is characterized by full obedience to it.

Furthermore, people born of the Spirit must treat the Word of God as they would treat God Himself. Additionally, they need to open the Bible with the earnest prayer to seek the will of God in it. God who does not show favoritism reveals His will to the people who come to God with a prayer and an attitude of obedience.

5. Man of the Holy Spirit

Another person who demonstrated this illuminating power of the Holy Spirit was John Song, an Asian. John Song was born the son of a Chinese pastor. He went to America to study, holding an ambitious dream in his heart—he desired to be a Christian theologian. There, he graduated from university and graduate school with honors and earned a doctoral degree in chemistry.

While in America, John entered a seminary to fulfill his vow to God but the seminary was very liberal where people no longer considered the Bible as the Word of God. He was influenced by liberal theology. He was rapidly becoming a liberal and humanistic theologian. However, one day, he attended a revival meeting out of curiosity. There a strong presence of the Holy Spirit left an indelible impression upon his heart. He repented of his liberal theology and his original belief was restored.

Then problems began to arise. Conflicts of opinions arose between him and his humanistic professors in the classroom. They could not understand the transformation that had taken place in John. They concluded that he was insane, and forcibly put him in a mental hospital.

He stayed there for nine months, devoting himself to the study of God's Word. The Holy Spirit was with him, illuminating the meaning of the Bible. John Song began to understand the Bible, written under the inspiration of the Holy Spirit, through the illumination of the Holy Spirit. Before long he became a man of the Holy Spirit. He became a man of God, now captivated by the Words of God.

Finally, Song returned to China, and the Holy Spirit used him for the work of God. He traveled all around China and many places of Southeast Asia, preaching the Word of God. Numerous people became born of the Spirit through his preaching and people who were born again began to live more holy lives. Even though John Song has gone to Heaven, the seeds he sowed through the work of the Holy Spirit have born fruit all over the world to this day.

Chapter 26

Man Born of the Spirit (5)

"The wind blows wherever it pleases. You hear its sound, but you cannot tell where it comes from or where it is going. So it is with everyone born of the Spirit" (John 3:8).

1. A Transformed Life

People who are not born of the Spirit do not know about the moving of the Holy Spirit within man, just as people do not know where the wind is heading and from where the wind comes. On the contrary, people born of the Spirit know the work of the Spirit because the Holy Spirit dwells in their hearts. Because of the indwelling of the Holy Spirit, born-again people can live transformed lives.

What does it mean to live a transformed life? Does it mean breaking totally away from one's past life? Of course not! The transformed life has several implications. First, the transformed life is concerned with the change of direction in their thinking patterns. Before the second birth, people are indifferent or hostile to God. Afterward, however, their thinking begins to revolve around God.

These changed attitudes and behaviors naturally follow God-centered thinking patterns. The transformation of born-again people begins within their hearts. Out of this internal transformation, they begin to experience external change. Human beings cannot create this transformation themselves. Only the presence and indwelling of the Holy Spirit make it possible. In other words, only born-again people can enjoy this transformation.

People born of the Spirit demonstrate several evidences that they walk with the Holy Spirit. This chapter enumerates the following three evidences: the faith of victory, the life of obedience, and the strength of victory over sin. Each of these three evidences reveals the demonstrative power of the Holy Spirit needed to bring them about.

2. The Faith of Victory

The first evidence that one walks with God is the faith of victory that accompanies a life of obedience. People are born again when they repent and receive Jesus Christ by faith. Faith refers to a personal resolution involving intelligence, emotions, and the will. Intellectually, the fact that Jesus died and was resurrected must be affirmed personally. Emotionally, a grateful heart needs to be given to Jesus Christ who sacrificed himself for us. Volitionally, our lives need to be entrusted to Jesus Christ for our salvation.

The faith of victory differs from the faith of salvation. When we are saved by faith, that faith is for a brief moment of time, but the faith of victory is a persistent one that endures for the rest of life. Furthermore, the persistent faith continuously grows. Without continuous growth, that faith is not the faith of victory. How can faith grow continuously? The revelation of God mediates the growth of faith.

The revelation of God that makes faith grow has two prongs. The first one is the revelation of the Word, and the second, the revelation of experience. The moment people born of the Spirit find revelations of God that they had never known before, faith increases on the basis of the newly revealed word of God. One step further, when the word of God is obeyed and experienced, faith grows. So, faith grows when the Word and a God-given experience intersect.

For example, when the Israelites had their experience of crossing the Red Sea, their faith in God grew. When God's people today are confronted with some difficult situation and they begin to cry out to God, God leads them into an experience that will enable them to have the faith to overcome that difficulty. In that moment, their faith increases again. Therefore, their faith grows when the revelation of the Word and the experience intersect. They continue to enjoy the faith of victory.

How great it would be if perfect faith were given to us from the very beginning of our salvation! However, that is not the way of God. The reason why God does not allow us perfect faith from the beginning is that we must learn to live life relying deeply on God. When we deeply depend on God, God makes us great people! This is quite true! The great people of God are those who greatly depend on God. Truly great people of faith are those who kneel down before God.

When born-again people depend on God, their faith grows. When they do not depend on God, their faith does not grow. Through repeated stumbling and restoration, God turns their weak faith into victorious faith. Therefore, they can overcome predicaments and temptations using their tempered faith. For this reason, people born of the Spirit must live life by the faith that reflects the verse, "Let us fix our eyes on Jesus, the author and perfecter of our faith" (Hebrew 12:2). Through this faith, we overcome the world (1 John 5:4).

3. The Life of Obedience

As faith is concerned with the promise of God, so is obedience concerned with the command of God. For this reason, faith and obedience are significant signs of people born of the Spirit. Faith that does not accompany obedience is not true faith, even though the faith may look to be beautiful. James explains the relationship between faith and obedience as follows: "As the body without the spirit is dead, so faith without deeds is dead" (James 2:26).

Since God loves people born of the Spirit, He gives them both promises and commands. As mentioned before, God's promises should be received by faith, and God's commands, by obedience. The faith and obedience of born-again people are responses to God's love. Through their positive responses, blessings and power are given to them. This is quite true! When people respond to God's promise by faith, God's blessings flow out to them. When people receive God's command by obedience, God's power is poured down upon them (Acts 5:32).

There are so many commands of God in the Bible. In the Pentateuch alone are written as many as 613 commands. How many additional commands of God can be found in the whole Bible? There are so many! People born of the Spirit are only in the process of knowing these commands, let alone obeying them. Here is the secret of God's wonderful love: God gives commands according to the depth of their faith. For example, a mother does not give her daughter the task of washing and drying dishes when she is three years old because she cannot possibly do it. However, the mother will give her daughter that same task when she is fifteen years old because by that time she can handle it. This is like God's dealing with us. God calls us to do according to the measure of faith we have been given.

God reveals a command/shares his will with each born-again Christian at a time that he knows will be of benefit to that believer's spiritual development. To one person, God may give a command to love his or her enemy. Another person may be asked to tithe faithfully. Still another person may be commanded to regularly attend the worship service. A command may be given to honor his or her parents. Some people may be encouraged to have daily devotions or to engage in evangelism.

God's specific order given to a specific person is called a commandment. Jesus mentions the importance of obeying these commands in the following way: "Whoever has my commands and obeys them, he is the one who loves me. He who loves me will be loved by my Father, and I too will love him and show myself to him" (John 14:21). In other words, when people obey commands given to them in a specific moment, they demonstrate that they love God. Furthermore, being faithful in that one thing may be rewarded with more of God love and more of Jesus' revealed will. On the contrary, if someone does not obey God's command, he or she will not rise to an advanced level but will stay at the same level or even regress.

4. The Victory over Sin

The third evidence is victory over sin. People born of the Spirit overcome sins with the help of the Holy Spirit. This does not mean that they never commit sin. They too can commit sin. As mentioned previously, the desire of the flesh still remains in them. Although struggles between the desire of flesh and the desire of the Holy Spirit exist, those born of the Spirit overcome sin. I John 5:3-4 reads, "This is love for God: to obey his commands, his commands are not burdensome, for everyone born of God overcomes the world."

When these Christians are tempted and commit sin, an inner conflict occurs because of the Holy Spirit who dwells in them and the longing of a jealous God (James 4:5). If a person does not experience this inner conflict or struggle, he or she is probably not born of the Spirit. If inner conflict is resolved by His holy love, peace, and joy, he or she is born of the Spirit. The conflict and struggle is resolved, and he or she continues to enjoy victory over sin.

Of course, people born of the Spirit must fight against and seek conquest over sin. Their attitude is very important when they are being tempted or have committed sins. If they attempt to excuse their sins, to shift the blame onto the shoulders of others, or to play the silly game of denial, they will degenerate into lethargic Christians. However, if they admit and confess their sins, they can overcome them.

When people born of the Spirit commit sin, fellowship with God--not the relationship with God--is severed. For this reason, they will lose love, peace, and joy. Therefore, they must confess their sins: If we confess our sins, he is faithful and just and will forgive us our sins and purify us from all unrighteousness (1 John 1:9). According to this verse, fellowship with God is immediately restored when they confess their sin and accept God's forgiveness by faith.

Unfortunately, even people born of the Spirit can commit sin even after they are forgiven. They must confess their sins and be forgiven. Whenever they confess their sins for forgiveness, they must come forward to the Cross because only the cross resolves the problem of sin. They who commit sins begin to hate themselves in front of the cross, seek forgiveness, and again thank Jesus for the forgiveness given.

People born of the Spirit can discover the reality of self at the Cross. They can realize that part of the true self which repeatedly commits the same sin and ask God to take it away. In addition, they discover the love of Jesus who forgives any sin. Furthermore, they realize at the Cross that they have been crucified with Jesus. Victory comes as it did to the Apostle Paul, "I have been crucified with Christ and I no longer live, but Christ lives in me. The life I live in the body, I live by faith in the Son of God, who loved me and gave himself for me" (Galatians 2:20). Victory over sin comes to the one born again by the Spirit!

5. Mysterious Leading

People born of the Spirit are led by the Holy Spirit. This leading of the Holy Spirit is a privilege of all Christians. If these people obey God's command, then God leads them to the next level. For example, if born-again people begin to read the Bible on a regular basis, then the Holy Spirit leads them to pray. If they pray to God regularly, then the Holy Spirit leads them to love other people. When they begin to love other people, their hearts are broadened and they share the gospel. Jesus is pleased with this sharing and leads them to be filled with the Holy Spirit.

After all, born-again Christians are people who are led by the Holy Spirit. Therefore, they must wait and pray to God in order to be led by the Holy Spirit before important decisions are made. If they are not led by God prior to making an important decision, they must repent and again learn obedience. If born-again people wait for the guidance of the Holy Spirit, the Holy Spirit leads them with a gentle whisper, through the Word of God; revelation that comes from his creation (Romans 1:19-20); the fellow believers; and the amazing inner peace which comes from the Holy Spirit..

Born-again people need to make important decisions on many things throughout their lives, such as marriage, job, and children. For these times of decision-making, they must kneel and pray to God in order to be led by Him. Many Christians do not enjoy the privilege of being led by the Holy Spirit during difficult times because they do not practice this in normal times. Let us enjoy the privilege of being led by the Holy Spirit from this time forward.

Chapter 27

Man Born of the Spirit (6)

"The wind blows wherever it pleases. You hear its sound, but you cannot tell where it comes from or where it is going. So it is with everyone born of the Spirit" (John 3:8).

1. Wonderful Blessings

Although we can hear the sound of the wind and feel the movement of it, we do not know where the wind is heading and from where it comes. Likewise, people born of the Spirit know each other and know they are born of the Spirit because they have wonderful blessings from this relationship. However, unchurched people around them do not know the indwelling and work of the Holy Spirit. Paul explains the reasoning as follows:

We have not received the spirit of the world but the Spirit who is from God, that we may understand what God has freely given us. This is what we speak, not in words taught us by human wisdom but in words taught by the Spirit, expressing spiritual truths in spiritual words. The man without the Spirit does not accept the things that come from the Spirit of God, for they are foolishness to him, and he cannot understand them, because they are spiritually discerned" (1 Corinthians 2:12-14).

This is true! People born of the Spirit can be compared to the movement of the wind. In addition, they need to come to the Holy Spirit if they want to know the movement of the Holy Spirit. Otherwise, discerning it is almost impossible. People born of the Spirit know where it is heading and from where it comes. In other words, people born of the Spirit know both the starting point and destination point on their spiritual journey. Furthermore, they enjoy the "road signs" that discern the direction to take while on this journey.

2. Holy Love

The most remarkable blessing for these people to receive is God's holy love. Holy love best describes this blessing because the character of God, the object of worship and obedience, is best described as holiness and love. Most of all, God is holy. God Himself declares, "I am holy" (Leviticus 11:44-45, 19:2; 1 Peter 1:15), and angels confess the same (Isaiah 6:3).

The Holy God is called the God of love at the same time. The Bible claims that "God is love" (1 John 4:8). If this is so, and it is, how did God demonstrate His love for us? The love of God was best demonstrated in gift of His Son, Jesus Christ for us. John 3:16 wonderfully expresses it as follows: "God so loved the world that he gave his one and only Son...."

Why did God give His Son as an expression of His love? The reason is that God is holy. There must be a relationship between God's love and holiness. Of course! Since God is so holy, he cannot ignore injustice and sin. God cannot help but judge injustice and the sins of people. If He didn't judge, He would no longer be holy.

The God of judgment is simultaneously the God of love, so He wants to forgive sinners. How does He solve the dilemma of judgment and forgiveness? The only way to resolve it is through the sacrifice of Jesus. Jesus died on the cross because he took the judgment of sinners on his own Self. Since God punished His Son instead of sinners, God character of holiness was also satisfied. The character of the love of God was satisfied too, by forgiving sinners through the death of Jesus.

People who experience such a love are the people born of the Spirit. The Word of God expresses it in this way: "And so we know and rely on the love God has for us. God is love. Whoever lives in love lives in God, and God in him"(1 John 4:16). People who have experienced the love of God through Jesus Christ cannot help but express the character of God, because they abide in God.

Of course, this loving, holy God abides in us through the Holy Spirit, which the Bible explains in this way: "...God has poured out his love into our hearts by the Holy Spirit, whom he has given us" (Romans 5:5). Since people born of the Spirit abide in God and God abides in their hearts, they can express the character of God--holiness and love. Thus, people born of the Spirit have, and express, holy love.

3. Spiritual Peace

The second blessing for those born of the Spirit is spiritual peace. Here, spiritual peace does not mean the peace that depends on circumstance and situation. How can we have the peace that transcends our circumstances and situation? For people born of the Spirit, having that kind of peace is not difficult because they have already experienced it. When they were born of the Spirit, they experienced the love of God, and that love drove out fear. God clearly declares through His Word, "There is no fear in love. But perfect love drives out fear, because fear has to do with punishment. The one who fears is not made perfect in love" (1 John 4:18). Instead of fear, they enjoy the peace provided by God. They enjoy peace with God (Romans 5:1), with other born-again people, and with nonbelievers as well.

The peace that people born of the Spirit enjoy does not depend on circumstances and conditions. This is a privilege that only born-again people enjoy. Of course, even people born of the Spirit can lose spiritual peace momentarily, because they live in a world that is hostile to them and, almost endlessly, tempts them. The twelve disciples of Jesus illustrated this vulnerability.

The disciples were overwhelmed by fear when Jesus Christ died on the cross. They sensed that the same kind of death could happen to them. When they withdrew themselves in fear, the resurrected Jesus came and said to them, Peace be with you (John 20:19). The word of Jesus was a word of restoration to the disciples who had violently lost their peace. In fact, Jesus had already spoken to them of this peace and the fear of losing it in John 14:27, "My peace I give you. I do not give to you as the world gives. Do not let your hearts be troubled and do not be afraid." In fact, a more victorious statement of hope had been given to the disciples later on in John 16:33, right after he had told his disciples of the need for the Holy Spirit to come: "I have told you these things, so that in me you may have peace. In this world you will have trouble. But take heart! I have overcome the world."

Later, Jesus repeated the same expression, "Peace be with you" to the disciples in John 20:21a. This time "Peace be with you" is spoken in the context of sending his disciples out into a post-resurrection world; "As the Father has sent me, I am sending you" (John 20:21b). Jesus promised a peace that would go far beyond the circumstances and situation that he and his disciples had just gone through. He would soon be sending his disciples out into a world that would attack them with clenched fists and gnashing teeth. He will be sending them out to their deaths! Peace...for them and a very troubled, evil, and unbelieving world!

4. Miraculous Joy

The third blessing for people born of the Spirit is the spirit of joy. This joy takes a miracle! It is expressed both internally (a feeling of joy in your spirit) and externally (a deep sense of peace escapes from your spirit). The joy that born-again people possess is different from the joy of the world. Many kinds of joy in the world are pure and good: the joy of reuniting with close friends, the joy of having things we have longed for so long, the joy in visiting a place where we really have wanted to go— but this joy takes no miracle from God!

The joy that people born of the Spirit enjoy is different. This kind of joy is not temporary and this-worldly. This joy does not come from an external factor, but from the Holy Spirit, extending far beyond circumstances and situations. If people who are born of the Spirit do not have this joy, their relationship with God may have been altered in some way. They may have lost their internal joy because they have disobeyed or compromised God's commands, or they may have committed a sin, and guilt has crept in.

People born of the Spirit enjoy and express the miraculous joy that goes beyond the limitations of time and place. Paul strongly claims that this joy is a Kingdom-gift when he says "For the kingdom of God is not a matter of eating and drinking, but of righteousness, peace, and joy in the Holy Spirit" (Romans 14:17). In Hebrews 12:2, it was said that Jesus, "for the joy set before him, endured the cross, scorning the shame...sat down at the right hand of God." Is joy only theoretical? No! Real joy...miraculous joy from the Holy Spirit!

Paul had ministered on several mission trips. He aimed to go to Asia, but the Holy Spirit turned his direction elsewhere. Through the clear guidance of the Holy Spirit, he went to Macedonia. Contrary to his expectation, he was put in prison. He might have asked, Lord, why do I need to be in a prison, since I moved to Philippi under your direction? Was I misled? Paul could become resentful, or he could have joy. He obeyed the words of Jesus, "Blessed are you when people insult you, persecute you and falsely say all kinds of evil against you because of me. Rejoice and be glad (have joy!)" (Matthew 5:11-12). Paul rejoiced and expressed it by praying and singing hymns to God, while the other prisoners were listening to them (Acts 16:25).

Paul's joy not only glorifies God, but also deeply touches people's hearts. God opened the gate of the prison, as He remembered His promise to Paul, for Paul was not yet in Jerusalem! In addition, many people who had heard the singing of joy came to believe in Jesus and were saved (Acts 16:34). This miraculous joy produced a church in Philippi. Joy, as God's miracle, is a powerful instrument for the work of the Holy Spirit.

5. Continuous Testimony

As mentioned before, people who are born of the Spirit enjoy holy love, spiritual peace, and miraculous joy. These blessings are so valuable that it is impossible for them to exist at any low level of spiritual attainment—in a life that puts the things of the world above all else. The Apostle John strongly urges us, "Do not love the world or anything in the world....For everything in the world—the cravings of sinful man, the lust of his eyes and the boasting of what he has and does...."(1 John 2:15).

What is the meaning of not loving this world? Does it mean that people born of the Spirit should leave this world to live holy lives? Does it mean that they should hate the world, or transcend all the things that belong to this world? Of course not! Loving this world refers to a life that follows the principles of this fallen world. The principles of this world signify a system that hinders and even goes against the life of people born of the Spirit. In other words, the principles of this world stand against the principles of God. For example, the principles of this world say that people should hate and take revenge on enemies, but people born of the Spirit live under the principles of loving and praying for their enemies (Matthew 5:44).

After all, people who are born of the Spirit are holy beings who speak, act, and think according to the principles of God as written in the Word of God. Their style of life is not one that fallen people in this world can understand and imitate. Their lifestyle is only possible because of the power and help of the Holy Spirit. This lifestyle differs from that of non-believers. Often it becomes a significant witness that draws them to pursue the holy life, the spiritual peace, and the miraculous joy that born-again people experience. Let us glorify God who blesses people born of the Spirit to live according to the principles of God.

Chapter 28

The One Who Came from Heaven

'How can this be?' Nicodemus asked. 'You are Israel's teacher.' said Jesus, 'and do you not understand these things? I tell you the truth, we speak of what we know, and we testify to what we have seen, but still you people do not accept our testimony. I have spoken to you of earthly things and you do not believe; how then will you believe if I speak of heavenly things? No one has ever gone into heaven except the one who came from heaven—the Son of Man' (John 3:9-13).

The Third Question

Nicodemus asked three questions when he had his conversation with Jesus. The first question can be found in verse 2. Although it appears hidden in the form of a statement, the actual content implied a question. The question? Perhaps something like, "Who are you, miracle-worker, really?" The second question occurred in verse 4 when Nicodemus asks "how can a man be born when he is old? Surely he cannot enter a second time

194   Born of the Spirit

into his mother's womb to be born!" Then, the third question followed soon afterwards in John 3:9: "how can this be?"

Jesus never disregards or ignores Nicodemus. This Pharisee asks frank questions followed by Jesus' providing serious answers to them (3:3, 5-8 and 10-21). A closer look at Jesus' answers reveals that his answers go deeper and deeper each time. It is important to note that Jesus uses the expression, "I tell you the truth," (3, 5, 11) three times to introduce his replies to Nicodemus. Jesus' frequent use of this expression is to emphasize that whatever he says, he speaks truth—for He is the Truth! In this case, a positive response from Nicodemus to the content of Jesus' answers is vital. No entrance into God's Kingdom will take place without it!

2. Nicodemus' Response

Nicodemus' third question came right on the heels of his second question! He had asked Jesus, "How can a man be born when he is old?" He received an answer, the essence being, "By being born of water and the Spirit. Flesh gives birth to flesh, but the Spirit gives birth to spirit." Even more confused now, Nicodemus asked a follow-up question, "How can this be?"

Jesus rebukes Nicodemus for his third question "How can this be?" Jesus replied to him, "You are Israel's teacher and (still) you do not understand these things?" Nicodemus was not just any ordinary teacher of Israel; he was their chief teacher, and therefore, held a highly-prestigious social and religious position in Jewish society. Yet he could not understand Jesus' teaching of a great heavenly truth!?

Israel's people attempted to live lives based on the words of the Old Testament. Nicodemus must have been very familiar with such passages as Jeremiah's prophecy of a new covenant God would make with Israel (Jeremiah 31); Ezekiel's teaching of cleansing and a new heart and new spirit being given (Ezekiel 36); and Psalm 143's "No one living is righteous." Along with his OT knowledge, he might well have heard of the message of John the Baptist concerning baptism with water and a coming baptism with the Holy Spirit (Matthew 3). Still, Jesus' words of a new birth seemed too far away for Nicodemus to grasp.

However, Nicodemus heard this message through the prejudicial ears of a Pharisee, so pre-occupied with obedience to the laws of God's kingdom that they did not pay attention to the importance of the transformation of the heart. They missed the more important call to internal change, while stressing the externals. This prejudice was preventing Nicodemus from accepting Jesus' teaching of the necessity of being born again in order to enter God's kingdom!

Nicodemus' ignorance was quite understandable. He had been taught about God (intellectual knowledge) and was trying to be obedient to Him in his own strength. He knew very little about "knowing" Him through a personal relationship (Do you remember the chapter four study of the two verbs *oida* and *ginosko* regarding "knowing"?). Therefore, when Jesus seemingly rebuked Nicodemus by asking, "Do you not understand these things?" he implied that being born of the Spirit required a personal relationship with God, made possible by having a born-again experience. Jesus seems to be just another wonderful religious teacher. Although he acknowledges Jesus' miraculous signs and wonderful teachings, he still cannot get rid of his prejudice. He needed more time. He needed more knowledge about Jesus in order to make a decision. Although he is a serious seeker, he still looks at Jesus through the lens of prejudice.

3. Jesus' Testimony

Jesus never gave up on Nicodemus, this man of prejudice. He continued to speak: "I tell you the truth, we speak of what we know, and we testify to what we have seen, but still you people do not accept our testimony" (John 3:11). Jesus knows that Nicodemus does not understand. Besides, Jesus testifies "we know and have seen" what Nicodemus does not know. Knowing is a part of intellectual activity, but seeing is an experiential one.

Then, why does Jesus say "what *we* and what *we* seen" instead of "what I know and I have seen?" The reason comes from the fact that testifying of knowledge and life's experiences is not only the work of Jesus, but also that of all those who follow him. People who have experienced Jesus have the same kind of testimony. Thus, many people can testify about Jesus with their lives, and are called to do just that.

Jesus uses the legal term witness in describing the act of testifying what people know and have seen. Witnessing means testifying to what people see and hear without making any changes or adjustments. People who testify in a court are called witnesses. Witnesses must tell the truth and are often threatened because of their truthful testimony. Note that the term witness can be translated as martyr. What should Christians witness of at the risk of their lives? Jesus speaks of the content of our witness being related to both earthly and heavenly things (John 3:12). Christians need to give testimony to not only what they have experienced, both externally and internally, here on earth, but what there is for them to experience when they enter heaven itself.

What are these earthly and heavenly experiences? The born-again person has had wonderful experiences here on earth! They have sensed God loving them and the Holy Spirit guiding them. They have had the thrilling experience of surrendering to Christ and receiving His love and forgiveness. They have been baptized and seen their own growth in becoming more Christlike as well as the spiritual growth of others. They have had friends and family come to Christ and have their lives changed. They shared their lives in fellowship with other believers! Experiences in the kingdom of God began on earth, but they do not end there at death. Heavenly experiences begin! Paul suggests such experiences in Philippians 3. He speaks of one day experiencing the resurrection from the dead (v. 11), and then goes on to say that he "presses on toward the goal to win the prize for which God has called (him) heavenward (v.14)! What prize experiences there will be in heaven! There are so many: Christ no longer a Gift but a Presence; maturity as a follower of Christ; receiving the "fruit" monthly from the Tree of Life; no more spiritual hunger nor thirst! The list is long! See the Book of Revelation! Yes, Christians are called to tell others of both the earthly and heavenly experiences that await them ...but they "must be born again"!

4. The Object of Faith

Although Jesus tells Nicodemus earthly things, Nicodemus does not understand Jesus' testimony. However, Jesus does not give up on him, and kindly teaches him about faith and the object of faith; "No one has ever gone into heaven except the one who came from heaven—the Son of Man" (John 3:13). Through this passage, Jesus reveals three things about himself, the Object of faith.

The first revelation is that Jesus is the one who came from heaven. All human beings including Nicodemus are born in the earth. However, Jesus Christ, who came from heaven and has existed from before the creation of the world, became a human being, one who has time and space restraints. In other words, the Creator came into this world "being made in human likeness" (Philippians 2:7). The one who belonged to heaven became one who belonged to the earth, and told Nicodemus who belonged to the earth about earthly things.

The second revelation is that Jesus is the Son of Man. Originally the title, the Son of Man was used in Daniel (Daniel 7:13-14), but it becomes Jesus' favorite expression to describe himself. This title has two meanings indicating both Jesus Christ of the earth and of heaven after his glorification. Therefore, Jesus Christ, the Son of Man, has both a fragile human nature and a glorious divine nature.

According to Daniel, the Son of Man was given "authority, glory, and sovereign power" and his rule was to never end" (Daniel 7:14). This description is also found in the Lord's Prayer, "For thine is the kingdom, and the power, and the glory, forever. Amen" (Matthew 6:13, KJV). As a human being, Jesus Christ suffered many hardships, but at the same time, he demonstrated divine power equal to God's. Without divine power, he could not have cast out demons, could not have healed people unable to walk, nor healed the deaf and blind.

The third revelation is that Jesus is the one who ascended into heaven. The title Son of Man describes the earthly life of the one who came from heaven and the one who has gone into heaven. It connects Jesus' incarnation (the one who came from heaven) and Jesus' ascension (the one who has gone into heaven). As Son of Man is the title that links human nature to the divine nature of Jesus, the above connection is naturally expected.

Only the one who came from heaven can go into heaven. We can take the example of Satan. Even though Satan did not come from heaven the same way as Jesus did, he attempted to ascend into heaven where God is seated. The result is well known. Instead, he descended into hell (Isaiah 14:12-13). Only the One who came from heaven to earth through supernatural birth can go into heaven again. For this reason, all human beings, including Nicodemus, who are born of the earth must "hold on to" Jesus Christ in order to go into heaven with him. The only way to hold on to him is to believe in him, receive him as Savior, and live with the indwelling Holy Spirit.

5. From Earth to Heaven

Jesus Christ still gives clear answers to the questions of people who have religious prejudice. Although Nicodemus asked the question, "How can this be?" a long time ago, many people, especially those who have religious prejudice, also ask the same question. As Nicodemus asked honest questions and sought answers earnestly, we need to ask frank questions and pursue answers seriously.

Robert Coleman is a man who did just that. Though he was born in a Christian home, he spiritually wandered because he had no assurance of salvation until he attended the university. One night his long spiritual pursuit ended when he personally experienced Jesus Christ. They praised the name of Jesus Christ all night. The day after he was touched by Jesus Christ, he and his friends shared their testimonies about Jesus Christ and their experiences that night.

Overwhelmed by the joy of salvation, he attended a seminary and became a doctor of theology. While teaching evangelism at seminaries, he traveled all over the world, sharing his overwhelming joy with people. His initial joy remains today! He is now over eighty years old, but he still preaches, both in America and in many other places of the world, about Jesus Christ, the One who came from heaven

Chapter 29

The One Who Has Gone into Heaven

"No one has ever gone into heaven *except the one who came from heaven—the Son of Man*" (John 3:13).

1. Jesus, the Unique Object

The previous chapter dealt with Jesus explaining earthly matters and heavenly matters. In addition, he explained the Object of faith. He had a clear purpose in doing this. The Object of faith in Christianity is different from that of objects of faith in other religions. The objects of faith (leaders such as Mohammed and Buddha), of other religions have all died. Their followers are left to achieve eternal life through obedience to the thoughts written by these founders or their disciples.

Of course, Christianity has its own scriptures, the Old and New Testaments, written by men. Christians put a high premium on them. They live the Christian life by being obedient to the will of God contained in them. Then how is Christianity different from other religions? Christians do not attempt to achieve eternal life by observing all of the commandments and laws written in the Bible, because they know that in their own power they cannot fully do so, however hard they may try.

Eternal life can only be attained through Jesus Christ. Jesus Christ is the Alpha and Omega, the Beginning and the End, of the Christian faith (Revelation 1:8)! He is the Object of the Christian faith. Eternal life comes when people meet Him personally, for He is alive! Yes, he died upon a cross and was buried in a tomb...but he rose again! There is no other religion that can make the claim of a founder's resurrection from the dead. You can meet Him. You must meet Him! Your life can be, and must be, changed—by Him.

2. The One Who Came from Heaven

Why did Jesus call himself the one who came from heaven, and why did people have such a difficult time believing so? "I have spoken to you of earthly things and you do not believe; how then will you believe if I speak of heavenly things?" (John 3:12). No human being can know or understand heavenly things. No human has ever seen nor had a physical conversation with God. Human beings, with their limited earthly wisdom and power, cannot come to know God.

Jesus Christ who has been with God from the beginning is different. However, not only that He has been with God from the beginning but also participated in creating the heavens and the earth with God, and also shares the very will of God. Christ has come to reveal the will of God (Jeremiah 1:15-16). Morover, intimate fellowship with God to people who are living in spiritual darkness is absolutely needed. Christ came down from heaven for this very purpose.

In other words, he came to earth as a man, abandoning all the glory he had in heaven, to make it possible for men to know God and be able to have a personal relationship with Him. He came down to earth—entered into history as the Incarnate One."Though he was God, he gave up his divine privileges; he took the humble position of a slave and was born as a human being" (Philippians 2:6-7). He spent his whole life, a lowly life, in the midst of "enemy territory." He was "made in every respect" like man.

His life was brief, and he suffered the humiliation of being slain on a cross (Revelation 5:9). Jesus Christ who came down from heaven to deliver God's will to human beings end his earthly life on a cross. Then, was he successful in delivering God's will to human beings? Yes! He spoke of God's will to the multitudes. They saw evidence of God's will through the miraculous signs he performed.

However, more wonderful than all of his teachings and miraculous signs was his personal demonstration of God's will. Jesus displayed God's will through his death on the cross, the most degrading form of punishment. It is no wonder that he desperately prayed "Father, if you are willing, take this cup from me; yet not my will, but yours be done" before he took up the cross (Luke 22:42). He lowered himself to the point of extreme humiliation in order to demonstrate God's will to human beings.

3. The Son of Man

In the last chapter we learned of the double-meaning of the title Son of Man. It refers to the Jesus who was "given a position lower than the angels"—his humiliation in becoming a man—and to the Jesus who was to be "crowned with glory and honor"---his later ascension and glorification as Son of God. We see Jesus being truly man, as he was truly God.

Why did Jesus make frequent use of this title? First, Jesus wanted to emphasize that he was not the Messiah the Israelites were expecting. They were waiting for a political messiah, but Jesus was a spiritual messiah, contrary to their expectation. Secondly, he wanted to hide his true identity from the people who do not sincerely seek him. Third, on the other hand, he wanted to reveal himself to people who seriously seek him.

According to the gospel of John, Jesus intensively used this title on three occasions. First, the title was used in reference to his death. For example, Jesus said, "Just as Moses lifted up the snake in the desert, so the Son of Man must be lifted up" (John

3:14). Needless to say, the meaning of "lifting up" indicates Jesus' death on the cross (John 8:28). On the second occasion, Jesus used this title when he taught, again, about his death, saying that---"I tell you the truth, unless you eat the flesh of the Son of Man and drink his blood, you have no life in you" (John 6:53). On the last occasion, Son of Man referred to the eschatological power of Jesus, when Jesus said, "And he (God) has given him (me) authority to judge because he is (I am) the Son of Man" (John 5:27).

Jesus was calling people to seek religious faith. Son of Man, in using this title, people will come to know God, through personally accepting Jesus as their personal Saviour. By being obedient to death on the cross, Jesus will be eternal. Jesus gives solemn warning to Nicodemus to find God or else get punished.

4. "The One Who Has Gone into Heaven"

According to God's Word, only a couple of people have gone into heaven without experiencing death: Enoch (Genesis 5:24) and Elijah (2 Kings 2:11). In addition to these two, when Jesus returns to earth, saints who are still alive will be transformed and meet Jesus in the air (1 Thessalonians 4:17). Who else has come down from heaven? No one! Only Jesus has ever come down from heaven and later gone back to heaven!

Only Jesus knew the will of God, and he came down from heaven to reveal God's will to man. Jesus revealed God's will with words and deeds. His final deed— crucifixion on a cross, an act of obedience to the Father, was for all people without reservation. God elevated Jesus by raising him from the grave three days later. The apostle Peter notes both Jesus' humiliation and elevation in Acts 2:27, "because you will not abandon me to the grave, nor will you let your Holy One see decay." Peter said very clearly, "(Jesus) suffered physical death, but he was raised to life in the Spirit" (I Peter 3:18). Jesus could not be made powerless by death. Since he obeyed God to his death, God raised him again. From that moment, God's will for the salvation of sinners began; "He was delivered over death for our sins and was raised to life for our justification" (Romans 4:25).

When Jesus finally finished his ministry on the earth, he returned to his Father. He no longer needed to live within the limitations of man. He no longer had to go through human hardship. He is now at the right side of God, carrying out his heavenly ministry. What kind of ministry is he carrying out? His ministry of intercessory prayer for Christians who remain on earth!

The title of Son of Man covered the whole ministry of Jesus for the salvation of human beings. He is the atonement for Nicodemus and for all human beings who sincerely desire to pursue the truth (Mark 10:45). He urges Nicodemus to kneel down before him and to receive him as his redeeming Savior. "At the name of Jesus every knee (must) bow...every tongue confesses---that Jesus is Lord to the glory of God the Father" (Philippians 2:5-11)!

5. Humiliation and Exaltation

Why was Jesus humiliated and exalted? Because of Jesus' humiliation and exaltation, the salvation and exaltation of human beings who suffer from limitation and deficiencies was made possible. Many people have suffered humiliation because of his guilt feelings and corruption but have been exalted through Jesus' death on the cross and his resurrection. The former took away sin; the latter, gave them the power to become children of God!

The author knows well a young man who grew up in several orphanages and had an unhappy adolescence. Eventually he was put into an orphanage where he met an American missionary. He attended a Christian school and a local Christian church. He was very interested in learning conversational English. He became involved in the Joy Mission where he learned English and deepened his faith, but he still suffered from a deep inferiority complex because of his orphan background.

One day he attended a Joy Mission Conference for leaders and experienced an amazing transformation. When he listened to another member share the Word of God in an early morning prayer meeting, he felt the Holy Spirit speaking to him and he received the assurance of salvation. He realized that all of his past sins and shame had been taken away by the blood of Jesus Christ. His perspective on life was transformed. His faith matured as he read about the will of God for him in the Bible and he became a leader in the Joy Mission.

This young man began to influence many other young people. Eventually, he became a preacher, proclaiming the gospel message. He was involved in co-ministry with Rev. Daniel Lee, one of the finest preachers in South Korea. His preaching's effectiveness demonstrated that he was deeply touched by Jesus. Through his message, many people have been transformed.

Led by the Lord, he planted a church in the state of New Jersey in the United States, and this church has become a growing and healthy church. He has a good reputation as a faithful minister there. He is a very competent minister in terms of preaching, teaching, and training people. How was all of this possible? This transformation took place because he had been personally touched and humbled by Jesus, the One who had come to earth to die for him, and who was alive, with the Father, actively involved in enabling him to live...forever!

Chapter 30

The One Who Is Lifted Up

"Just as Moses lifted up the snake in the desert, so the Son of Man must be lifted up, that everyone who believes in him may have eternal life" (John 3:14-15).

1. The One Who Has Gone into Heaven

Jesus introduced himself in the following way: "No one has ever gone into heaven except the one who came from heaven—the Son of Man" (John 3:13). This passage provides the "bookends" ("from heaven" and "into heaven") that express the essence of the gospel. There are several ways of expressing the gospel found in this passage. Some people explain the gospel as the "good news" of Jesus' death and resurrection (1 Corinthians 15:3-4). He came down to die, so that others might live. He was raised to life again, and ascended to the Father, that man might be raised to new life on earth and, later, in heaven. According to others, the "good news" is that the Kingdom of God has come into the world, initiated by Jesus, the Son of God. The Kingdom is to continue on in heaven. Others, limiting the impact of God's entrance into the world, believe that the gospel is the "good news" that he has come down from heaven to offer us inward peace. Jesus was a wonderful religious teacher, but that—teaching that one can have inner peace— is as far as the "good news" can go!

Jesus' introduction of himself as "the only one who came down from heaven and has ever gone (back) to heaven" implied that he had come to earth as God-Incarnate on a mission to transform man. The expression "the one who has gone into heaven" meant that he would finish the ministry for which he was sent and return to the place where God resides.

What was the mission given to Jesus? To teach deep spiritual truths never taught before? To perform many wonderful and miraculous signs that no one in human history has ever done before? Is it to live a good consistent and moral life before men to show them how to live from beginning to end? No, as good as those things are, Jesus was sent on a much more valuable mission.

2. Background

In order to explain His ministry, Jesus introduced a well-known Old Testament incident. He knew a story from the Old Testament that would make Nicodemus, still full of religious prejudice, more attentive to his teaching. Jesus spoke of the time in the desert, soon after Moses had led them out of Egypt, when the people of Israel rebelled against following God (Numbers 21:4-9). He told them: "And as Moses lifted up the bronze snake on a pole in the wilderness, so the Son of Man (Jesus himself) must be lifted up, so that everyone who believes in him will have eternal life" (John 3:14-15). Jesus' OT story might reach the heart of Nicodemus because its familiar truth would give him a connection to what Jesus was trying to get across to him regarding being born-again and entering into the Kingdom of God. Perhaps Nicodemus might still reach out to Jesus! He needed only to "look up, trust, and do so expectantly!" He, Jesus, was the answer to man's problems. Only God had the power, and the plan, to make all things possible. Believe in grace, the work of God; believe not in works, the work of man— to get you to that Promised Land! Be born-again...purely by a "heavenly action" (John 3:12).

3. Judgment

The people of Israel had been disgruntled and disobedient all along the wilderness route. They opposed Moses' leadership. They wanted to return to Egypt. From a human perspective, their complaints were understandable. They grieved over the loss of both Aaron and Miriam whom they had loved and trusted so much (Numbers 20:1, 28). Moses, their leader, would not be allowed to lead the Israelites into the Land of Promise as a result of God's judgment on his failure to honor God before the people (Numbers 20:12).

On the top of that, they endured deep physical sufferings as time in the wilderness progressed. Because of all the pain and difficulty they had endured, they weakened in their trust of both God and Moses. Their current physical and psychological pains and difficulties overshadowed all the glory of the past miracles they had experienced. The mercy and power that God showed to them along the wilderness trek failed to stop their complaints. God's generous provisions of their everyday needs did not satisfy them.

The Israelites, of course, blamed Moses, the leader God had exalted. They spoke out against God as well. Finally, from Mount Hor along the route to the Red Sea, things came to a boiling point! In Numbers 21:4-5, we read, "The people grew impatient...spoke against God and Moses saying, 'Why have you brought us up out of Egypt to die in the desert? No bread...no water...and we detest this miserable food!'" As God had poured out His wrath on the Egyptians who had rejected God, so God's wrath was poured out upon Israel. He sent venomous snakes among them. Many died. They came before Moses and cried out that they had sinned and asked him to pray to God to take the snakes away! Again, the people of Israel experienced God's mercy. They faced judgment they received, again, mercy!

4. Repentance

God's discipline and punishment always have a clear purpose. God does not discipline because he enjoys doing so, neither does he punish because he enjoys punishing. He desires that all men come unto Him. Of course, the Last Judgment time "runs out." Man has run out of opportunities to repent and be born-again. For this reason, God disciplines and punishes people, patiently giving man more time to come to Him.

The Israelites were no exception. Although God's judgment upon them by sending venomous snakes into their lives was harsh, it also implied that God had not totally given up on them. God desired a restored relationship with them. This could come only through repentance. A harsh judgment might lead to a deeper repentance, which might produce a surer way of restoration. Paradoxically, a harsher judgment of God may mean a deeper love of God. Eventually, the Israelites did repent. Finally they said to Moses, "We sinned when we spoke against the Lord and against you" (Numbers 21:7a).

Their repentance was a confession of sin and an acknowledgment that they were unable to overcome sin themselves. The Israelites had been bitten by venomous snakes. Since they acknowledged that this judgment had come from God, they confessed that only God could take the judgment away. They waited for God's mercy and grace.

This attitude signifies true repentance. Repentance involves the confession of sinfulness, an acknowledgement of the inability to deal with it yourself, and a humbled heart that waits for God's abundant mercy and grace. God never abandons people who come to God seeking His mercy. God not only provides a way out (1 Corinthians 10:13), but also provides an opportunity to take a new leap of faith. God not only listened to the Israelites' prayer of repentance, but made it possible for them to continue to live and enter into a deeper relationship with Him.

5. The Bronze Snake

"The Lord said to Moses, 'Make a snake and put it up on a pole; anyone who is bitten can look at it and live'"(Numbers 21:8).

As a solution to the problem of venomous snakes, God gave two commands and one promise. First, God instructed Moses to make a snake and put it up on a pole. Second, God instructed the people who are bitten by snakes to look up at the snake on the pole. Both actions were steps of faith requiring acceptance of God's Word and obedience to it. The Israelites did not ask for a detailed explanation in terms of science on how the snake on the pole can save their lives. The people totally trusted God's word that totally doing so would bring to them life. Look and live! The Israelites repented first, and then stepped out in faith. As a result, they not only saved their lives, but also rose to a new level of trust in God.

An interesting thing is that God instructed Moses to make a snake, but Moses made a bronze snake. Venomous snakes were the tools of God's judgment sent to the Israelites. In order to remove the tools of God's judgment, God's justice needed to be satisfied. Since Moses understood God's intention, he made a bronze snake— bronze signifying God's judgment in the Old Testament.

Jesus explains our salvation using this incident with which Nicodemus is very familiar. As the snake on the pole means the snake under God's judgment, so Jesus is hung on the pole, signifying Jesus under God's judgment. Just as whoever is bitten by venomous snakes can be healed when they look up at the bronze snake on the pole, so whoever looks up at Jesus Christ on the cross in repentance and faith will have eternal life. Won't you look up at Jesus on the cross in faith and repent of your own sins?

Chapter 31

The One Who Is Lifted Up (2)

"Just as Moses lifted up the snake in the desert, so the Son of Man must be lifted up, that everyone who believes in him may have eternal life" (John 3:14-15). (2)

1. The Meaning of Being Lifted Up

Jesus Christ said that the Son of Man must be lifted up. What is the practical meaning of being lifted up? John 12:32-33 reveals the meaning: "'But I, when I am lifted up from the earth, will draw all men to myself.' He said this to show the kind of death he was going to die."

Needless to say, "Jesus being lifted up" signified his death on the cross. After the Israelites had committed sin before God, they hovered between life and death. They struggled to free themselves from the threat of the snakes of judgment, but they realized that they could not get free on their own. Therefore, they concluded that the only way they could gain freedom would be to repent and receive God's mercy.

As soon as they turned to God, He extended a hand of mercy to them. They had only to look up, and believe their "salvation" would come. Jesus was that "snake" put up on the pole. The snake symbolized salvation. Jesus was going to be put on a cross, and people of all nations seeking salvation would have to look up to Him and believe. Nicodemus needed to realize that his pursuit of God by depending upon his own deeds would be futile (Romans 9:31-32).

2. The Being Lifted Up of Justice

The story of Moses lifting up a snake in the desert to save them was very well known to the Israelites. However, they soon forgot that it was not the bronze snake which saved them. It was God. Later, they foolishly worshipped the bronze snake that Moses had made and burned incense to it (2 Kings 18:4). The bronze snake was actually nothing but a piece of bronze—created by God.

Nicodemus clearly knew that when the Israelites committed sins, God punished them. And when they repented, he forgave their sins. The bronze snake demonstrated God's holiness and love. When they repented of their sins, God expressed his holiness by judging the snake instead of their sins. As soon as they looked to the snake, He displayed His love through His forgiveness.

The case of the bronze snake is also applicable to Jesus in terms of revealing God's holiness and love. Why was Jesus lifted up like the bronze snake? Was Nicodemus blaming God for all the trouble in his life, like the Israelites had done? No, Nicodemus did not directly blame God as they did. It appears that he felt he had none. He lived an exemplary life, compared to others, in terms of education, social position, morality, and religion.

Would his good life make it possible for Nicodemus be born again? Of course not! He cannot even begin to understand the meaning of being born-again. The reason is very simple! He does not understand the holiness of God, one of the most basic foundations of Christianity. According to God's holiness, Nicodemus is just an unrighteous man who cannot escape God's judgment. His righteousness is nothing but the self-righteousness he has accumulated throughout his life (Romans 3:10).

Presumably, Nicodemus' internal sin could be more serious than the external sins of the Israelites' complaints. Although Nicodemus was a religious leader who influenced the Israelites, he does not know the basic truth of the new birth. As a teacher who would mislead his people if spiritual truth did not come from his teachings "From everyone who has been given much, much will be demanded; and from the one who has been entrusted with much, much more will be asked (Luke 12:48), it was even more important than ever that Nicodemus understand Jesus' word. More than just his earthly life depended upon it.

Jesus lets Nicodemus know about the holiness and judgment of God, through his own life "being lifted up." God will punish Jesus Christ instead of Nicodemus. As Moses put the bronze snake up on the pole in place of the Israelites, God likewise put Jesus Christ up on the cross in place of Nicodemus. As the Israelites are required to look up at the snake on the pole, so Nicodemus must look at Jesus Christ on the cross and believe. So must all men!

3. The Lifting of Love

If God offered Nicodemus only His holiness and justice, Nicodemus still would have no hope. He would continue to live a boastful life, depending on his prestigious social position and high morality—as well as holding on to his religion and beliefs—to get him into the Kingdom of God. When his life on earth came to an end, entrance into the kingdom would be certain. However, God knew that when he died he would stand before the God of justice, and He knew that Nicodemus was not ready for that!

God is the God of love as well as the God of holiness. Because God loved him, Nicodemus was offered the opportunity to be born of water and the Spirit. To be born-again! If he is spiritually born again, he would not need to die twice. He would live eternally! If he was not born-again, he would be thrown out of the presence of God forever. This is the second death (Revelation 21:8).

As mentioned before, God had a purpose in judging the Israelites. His judgment was designed to warn them and urge them to repent. When they finally accepted God's warning, and repented, He demonstrated His love by healing them and letting them live. Though God judged the Israelites with His justice, at the same time He offered, and gave, forgiveness.

The lifting of the bronze snake onto the pole was God's offer of forgiveness to Israel. In the case of Nicodemus it was the same only it would be Jesus who would be lifted up. Nicodemus' sins could not be seen by man, but God knew of them, as He does every man's. They are the object of God's judgment. Nicodemus was relying on his own righteousness for forgiveness. He, like every man, cannot escape God's eyes. God's love is expressed via the cross of Jesus Christ. Jesus had told him, Nicodemus, ⸢Just as Moses lifted up the snake in the desert, so the Son of Man must be lifted up (John 3:14). Nicodemus does not know it yet but Jesus is to be hung on (a pole) in place of him! As a willing Substitute!

So we see that Jesus Christ taught Nicodemus the meaning of "being lifted up." In order to avoid any more misunderstanding, he had taken an incident from the Pentateuch to further explain! The lifting up of the snake is an expression of God's holiness and love. Since Jesus Christ loves Nicodemus, he had this serious conversation with him hoping it would help change his heart.

4. The Power of Being Lifted Up

The snake Moses lifted up in the desert was the solution to the problem of the Israelites. People who were dying because they had been bitten by snakes (sin) could be healed if they looked up at the bronze snake on the pole. The bronze snake—that had no poison—healed the people who were poisoned. Poisonless, it was put up on the pole in place of poisoned people. The bronze snake, judged by God, defeated the power of the venomous snakes. The divine power that turns death into life was displayed there.

Jesus Christ who died on the cross has the same power. Even though he was sinless, he died for sinners. Who are the sinners? Everyone born into this world is a sinner. Jesus died on the cross for all the people who are bitten by the poison of sin and are dying. Therefore, every sinner can be saved by looking to Jesus through the eyes of faith.

This way of salvation seems to be foolish to the mind of people, but it is the wisdom and power of God. God's wisdom and power are beautifully seen in the writing of Paul: "Jews demand miraculous signs and Greeks look for wisdom, but we preach Christ crucified: a stumbling block to Jews and foolishness to Gentiles, but to those whom God has called, both Jews and Greeks, Christ the power of God and the wisdom of God" (1 Corinthians 1:22-24).

Jesus relates his being lifted up on the cross to the power of salvation, saying "But I, when I am lifted up from the earth, will draw all men to myself" (John 12:32). The word, "I am lifted up" is the same as the word of Jesus to Nicodemus; "the Son of Man must be lifted up." The word "I will draw all men to myself" he corresponds to Jesus the word to Nicodemus, everyone who believes in him may have eternal life" (John 3:15).

God intends that if Jesus, who has no sin, is lifted up on the cross, He will give eternal life to all those dying of sin who will look up to Him for salvation. When Jesus says "I will draw all men to myself" he is saying that he will remove the problem of sin and its impact upon people, in order for them to come to Him in this world for entrance into the next. Therefore, Jesus, being "lifted up" is so powerful that it can remove the problem of sin and its results.

As soon as sin is removed, they will become clean. How clean? They will become clean like Jesus. They will become the righteousness of God. They will have the righteousness of Jesus instead of their own self-righteousness (II Corinthians 5:21). This is the power of "being lifted up."

5. Justice and Love

God is holy and God is love. These two moral characters of God are clearly demonstrated at the cross. God displays not only His holiness, but also His love. Because of His holiness, he must judge sin. The result of God's judgment is eternal punishment. Although sinners know about this, they cannot themselves remove the inevitability of death and God's judgment. The only thing they can do is to wait for death and judgment—unless they seek God!

However, since God is love, He has provided a solution to the problem sinners' had—His Son. "For God so loved the world he sent his son that whosoever believeth in him should not (have to) perish, but (could) have everlasting life. For God did not send his Son into the world to condemn the world, but to save the world through Him"(John 3:16-17). In other words, He resolves the problem of sin and death by judging Jesus on the cross. Although human beings are sinners, if they come forward to Jesus who died on the cross on their behalf, God forgives and accepts them. Jesus' cross is at the intersection of God's holiness and love and man's sin.

An ancient man who tried to explain this intersection of holiness and love was Hammurabi, a king of the Babylonian Empire during the time of Abraham. He is known for enacting the Code of Hammurabi. He ruled over the empire with strict justice and love. The story is told that he had a lovely son who would inherit his throne. The Code of Hammurabi is famous for its strictness and detailed instruction on specific sins and their corresponding penalty. One day, his son committed a sin, the penalty for which one's eyes were to be plucked out. Although the vassals cried out for forgiveness, Hammurabi refused to forgive his son because he believed that ruling his country with justice outweighed saving his son's eyes. Finally, the king ordered to have his son's eyes plucked out.

The executor hesitated to follow the king's order, but he had no choice but to pluck out one of the son's eyes in front of the vassals. The pain the prince experienced was beyond description, even apart from the shame he received. At the moment when the executor attempted to pluck out the prince's other eye, Hammurabi ordered him to pluck out one of his own eyes in place of his son's. Thus, Hammurabi kept the law and showed his love for his son.

God, the eternal judge, cannot but judge all people with justice. At the same time, He wants to save them. His justice and love are intermingled on the cross. He sacrificed His one and only Son in man's place. If people look to Jesus by faith, he will save them, just as the Israelites were saved by looking up at the bronze snake on the pole.

Chapter 32

The One Who Is Lifted Up (3)

"Just as Moses lifted up the snake in the desert, so *the Son of Man must be lifted up*, that everyone who believes in him may have eternal life" (John 3:14-15).

1. The Double Meaning of Being Lifted Up

All the Jews, including Nicodemus, were waiting for the Messiah. They believed that though they were ruled by the Romans and enduring all kinds of oppression, such conditions would come to an end at the appearance of the One called Messiah. The political and religious situation of Israel would be reversed, and the Jews would rule not only the Roman Empire, but also the whole world. Their hope? The emergence of this Messiah! They were waiting for the Messiah who would be "lifted up" as a king.

A prophecy that gave hope to the Israelites is found in Zechariah: "Rejoice greatly, O Daughter of Zion! Shout, Daughter of Jerusalem! See, your king comes to you, righteous and having salvation, gentle and riding on a donkey, on a colt, the foal of a donkey. I will take away the chariots from Ephraim and the war-horses from Jerusalem, and the battle bow will be broken. He will proclaim peace to the nations. His rule will extend from sea to sea and from the River to the ends of the earth" (Zechariah 9:9-10).

According to this passage, their Messiah would come to conquer and rule the whole world. However, the Jews overlooked the fact that the king would come as one humbled in status. He is "gentle and riding on a donkey." Isaiah further described the lowliness of the Messiah: "despised and rejected of men....led like a lamb to the slaughter....poured out his life unto death" (53:3,7,12). These descriptions indicate that before the Messiah is "lifted up" as a ruler, he must be "lifted up" a cross.

2. The Cursed Snake

God instructed Moses to put up a bronze snake on a pole to save the Israelites who were being bitten by snakes. What did God's instruction mean? First, people themselves cannot solve the problem of the death. Second, the bronze snake is put up on the pole in place of the snakes that bite the Israelites. Third, the bronze snake is cursed on behalf of the people who are bitten by snakes.

If we accept the above meanings, the reason why Jesus compared the bronze snake of Moses to himself is more easily understood. First, all human beings are sinners. The problem of sin cannot be resolved by their own means (Romans 6:23). That is why they need to be born-again.

Second, Jesus Christ must be lifted up on the cross to solve the problem of human sin and ultimate death. As the snake had done, Jesus would be the Substitute for man's sin. He would take the punishment for sin, not man. Jesus Christ the son of David, the son of Abraham— Son of God, the One sent from God—had to die.

Third, Jesus' crucifixion on the cross indicated that he was one cursed of God. As Nicodemus knew, "...anyone who is hung on a tree is under God's curse" (Deuteronomy 21:23). Jesus was to be cursed on behalf of the people.

Bronze symbolized God's curse and judgment in the Old Testament. The offerings slaughtered in place of sinners were put on the altar made of bronze (Exodus 27:1-2). The offerings must be burnt on the bronze altar under God's judgment (Leviticus 4:25-26).

What brought about such harsh judgment to the Jews? According to Deuteronomy 28, they were judged by God when they disobeyed God's Word. A Bible verse describes God's judgment in the following way: "The sky over your head will be bronze, the ground beneath you iron" (Deuteronomy 28:23). The expression the sky will be bronze denotes God's judgment is inevitable. Bronze is also used when the Bible introduces Jesus as the judge; "His feet were like bronze glowing in a furnace" (Revelation 1:15).

As the bronze snake is cursed and judged on the pole, so Jesus is cursed on the tree in place of sinners who have the curse of death because of sin. Paul clearly explains that fact as follows: "Christ redeemed us from the curse of the law by becoming a curse for us, for it is written: 'Cursed is everyone who is hung on a tree'" (Galatians 3:13). Here "everyone" means us, and "redeeming" means paying the price for sin. Jesus hung on the cross, like the bronze snake on the pole, for the sake of redeeming sinners.

3. My Thoughts

God's order for people who were bitten by a snake was very simple. First, whoever was bitten had to look up at the bronze snake that hung on the pole. Yes, they probably thought that that was too easy. Let's try medication! There is no medication that can get rid of sin. Since the bite from venomous snakes symbolized the judgment of God against Israel's sin, only God can cure the people.

Second, they were not to depend on other people, even their leaders Moses and Aaron. As mentioned before, only God can remove God's judgment. Depending on other people is analogous to clutching at a straw. As a straw cannot save sinking people, other ways apart from God's cannot save people's lives.

Third, the people who are bitten by snakes were not told to fight against the snakes. People already bitten were dying and it appeared that this attack by snakes would continue on. A fight would be useless because they were fighting against God and his judgment upon them. Sinners cannot win the battle against sin. God had His way.

Fourth, people who are bitten by snakes should not give offerings to the bronze snake. The bronze snake had been made by Moses. It could not accept any offerings. It was only a man-made object cursed and judged by God in place of the people. Even if they brought a lot of offerings to the bronze snake, their problems would not be solved. The offerings would just lie unconsumed by the inanimate object. There are church-going people who attempt to solve their sin problem through ministry and offerings rather than look up to Jesus for forgiveness.

Fifth, people who are bitten by a snake were not asked to pray to the bronze snake. Praying can be a desperate means, especially to people who are dying, just like many religious people today seriously attempt to solve the problem of their sins through prayer. However, God does not order the Israelites to pray to the bronze snake. Their earnest efforts and exhibition of deep religiosity are admirable, but they are refusing God's way presumptuously.

Sixth, people bitten by snakes should not look at their wounds. Looking at their wounds only makes them feel worse, like many church people today become more miserable when they dwell on their own sins. Such people may indulge in self-pity and self-torment, which only make things worse, instead of becoming a means to the solution of the problem. They should lift up their eyes to see the snake, not lowering their eyes to see their wounds, concentrating on themselves.

4. Active Commands

What kind of commands did God give to the Israelites? Let's look again at the bronze snake passage in the Book of Numbers. The Lord said to Moses, "Make a snake and put it up on a pole; anyone who is bitten can look at it and live" (Numbers

21:8). According to this passage, God instructed Moses to do three things: to make a snake; to put it up on a pole; and for those bitten, to look at the snake for deliverance.

What was the practical meaning of the first instruction? The Israelites were sinning against God and He judged them for it. But Moses interceded on their behalf. God would be the only One who could remove His own judgment on man. God's way of salvation may seem foolish from the perspective of human wisdom, but God had said "Do this." And Moses did. The problem of being bitten by snakes could not be resolved any other way than intercession and obedience.

What was the meaning of the second instruction "put it up on a pole"? Numerous people had been bitten by snakes. In order to remove their problem, God's way of salvation must be applied to all of them. For this reason, God ordered the bronze snake to be put up on a pole. It was publicly hung on the pole. Everyone would see it, and those who sought God's healing, could look up at it—and live!

What was the meaning of the third instruction? People are required to give up all other means they have invented to save themselves including scientific, medical, and their own religious means. Instead, they are told to look at the bronze snake on the pole. Their lives would revive only when they followed God's way again. Anyone who is bitten by a snake must make an individual decision to follow God's command. No matter how much pain is involved in being bitten by the snakes, no matter how much dread in the approaching death, and no matter how much people wish to be healed, each individual had to look at the bronze snake on the pole. No one was forced to do so, but they were free to do so!

For God's plan to work, each willing person had to take two steps. First, they had to confess their sins. They must admit that this judgment comes from their complaints against God and Moses. Admitting one's sins corresponds to repentance. Secondly, faith was required. Although this seemed to be foolish from a human perspective, people had to look at it with belief in God's word and promise. Then whoever looked at it would live.

5. The Same Command

God's way of salvation is beyond our understanding. The Israelites needed to look at the bronze snake. In turn, we should look at Jesus Christ on the cross who was cursed by God like the bronze snake on the pole. Jesus Christ is the way of salvation which God has predetermined. Only God's way of salvation can save us. Jesus was hung on the cross like the snake that was lifted up on the pole. Jesus was cursed on the tree in place of all sinners. He was hung high on the cross so all sinners could look at him. He was publicly executed for all the people. However, by being judged on the cross on behalf of the people, Jesus offered life to all who fear death.

The third instruction regarding the bronze snake is given to all sinners. It let them know that every individual has to make a decision. The sinner must admit that he indeed is a sinner and must turn to the cross. Furthermore, he must look up in faith at Jesus, the One who has taken upon himself the curse of sin, dying on the cross in place of him. Only in this way can sinners be saved.

God's word is clear: "Let us fix our eyes on Jesus, the author and perfecting of our faith" (Hebrew 12:2). In other words, Jesus Christ is the object of faith and the fulfiller of our faith. Fix your eyes on Jesus and accept the invitation of salvation: "Turn to (that is, look at, come to) me and be saved, all you end of the earth; for I am God, and there is no other." (Isaiah 45:22). Look at Jesus Christ, who was lifted up on the cross!

Chapter 33

The One Who Is Lifted Up (4)

"Just as Moses lifted up the snake in the desert, so *the Son of Man must be lifted up,* that everyone who believes in him may have eternal life" (John 3:14-15).

1. Glorious Lifting Up

Let's look at some of Jesus' words spoken shortly after his triumphal entry into Jerusalem: "Now it is the time for judgment on this world; now the prince of this world will be driven out. But I, when I am lifted up from the earth, will draw all men to myself.' He said this to show the kind of death he was going to die" (John 12:31-33).

These verses reveal two important truths. First, the prince of this world will be driven out. The prince of this world means the evil power that rules over this world. How will Jesus being lifted up end this evil power? The answer is seen in the second truth; Jesus will draw all the people to himself by dying on a cross. In other words, many people will be born again through his death.

On the surface, Jesus "being lifted up" seems to be a defeat, since he died on the cross. However, further examination shows that "lifting up" includes both death on the cross and exaltation. What came after death? Jesus Christ was not one whose life stopped at death, but he was resurrected from the dead. After his resurrection, he ascended into heaven and sat down at the right hand of God (Hebrew 1:3). Sitting at the right hand of God, he drove out the evil power. He is there now!

Jesus being lifted up is the wonderful way of salvation from self-righteousness and every kind of unrighteousness. One step further, his lifting is the way of driving out the evil power that rules over the world.

This truth becomes a source of power to Christians who live the life of victory. Such a life of victory is not only applicable to Christians today, but was also applicable to the Israelites back centuries ago.

2. The Complaints of the Israelites

The ultimate purpose of God's deliverance from Egypt was to bring them into the promised land of Canaan where they would prosper under His rule (Deuteronomy 6:23). If the escape from Egypt was the first half of their deliverance, bringing them into the land of Canaan would be the second half. Before entering into Canaan the Israelites had to pass through the wilderness. This journey in the desert would be long and hard— indeed a testing ground for them.

Although the Israelites had experienced wonderful deliverance from Egypt, many obstacles began to block their way in the wilderness. They again began to blame their leaders and resent God. They tested God ten times (Numbers 14:22). The first three testing occurred on the way to Mount Sinai, but God showed mercy to them (Exodus 15:24, 16:2, 17:3).

However, after the Israelites had experienced God's special presence and had been given His instructions on how to live at Mount Sinai, the situation changed. Before they learned God's words at Mount Sinai, they were like children of growing faith and God bore patiently with them. Now, however, after the experience at Mount Sinai, they ought no longer to have considered themselves children. They had been taught many lessons by God in the exodus from Egypt, and had been given many words of instruction for their future, including the Ten Commandments and other laws.

The Israelites should speak and act in accordance with their maturity. From now on, whenever they grumbled against God, He would discipline them. This was God's treatment for matured people. The Israelites disobeyed God seven times on the way to Canaan, and seven times they were severely disciplined! God disciplined them with fire (Numbers 11:1), a severe plague (Numbers 11:33), leprosy (Numbers 12:10), and death (Numbers 14:29, 16:31-32).

The Israelites had left Egypt, crossed the Red Sea, and began their journey to the land God had promised them, experiencing the actions of a powerful and loving God. They experienced God's salvation and became His redeemed people. Nevertheless, they soon forgot God's love and power, continuously blaming God for their troubles along the way. They knew they would be disciplined by God whenever they disobeyed Him—they had learned that. Why did they fail to keep their relationship with Him? Was God unable to change their ways? Was their God powerless to do anymore?

On the contrary, God could, and would, continue to do more. He would again give mercy to an Israel continuing to be disobedient. It was at the "bronze serpent pole," on the route along the Red Sea, that the conflict between God and his people again came to a head! They "grew impatient on the way; and spoke against God and against Moses"(Numbers 21:4-5). They wondered why they had ever left Egypt! God's people were to eventually enter the land of Canaan. God had plans for them there. But they needed to be obedient people! The Lord sent venomous snakes which might have killed them all, but God, again, offered them an opportunity for deliverance.

3. From Defeat to Victory

The Israelites never really came to a point on their wilderness journey when their complaining and disobedience stopped for any length of time. They seemed to ride a spiritual rollercoaster. Their disobedience and God's discipline that followed seemed to go on almost endlessly. Far from being humbled and drawing closer to God, their complaints, especially of what they thought to be a lack of fleshly provisions, seemed to become stronger and stronger as time progressed. Their focus continued to be on themselves and their needs rather than on the needs of others and a personal relationship with God. God's desire to give them "a new heart and a new spirit" within them (Ezekiel 36:26) was yet to be!

The coming of venomous snakes—the judgment of God, and the lifting up of the bronze snake—the salvation of God, marked a turning point in the heart and mind of the Israelites (And for all mankind later on!). Now, through this event, the Israelites realized one thing, that their own ways and wisdom could not overcome the sin problem. The pole? Another offer of mercy from a holy God, but one that would require faith on the part of each Israelite!

For the first time, they saw their own inability and recognized their own limitations. They had to choose between two options: they could either die being bitten by the snakes or continue to blame God, or they could live by kneeling before God and receive His mercy. They chose the second option. For the first time since the Exodus they humbled themselves and repented of their complaints. They emptied themselves of guilt and entrusted their lives to God.

God immediately responded to their repentance, having had patiently waited for it, because He loved them— even back in Egypt, God had called Israel His "firstborn son" (Exodus 4:22). God offered a way of salvation to "His son" through the lifting up of the bronze snake. When they accepted God's offer and, staring death in the face, obeyed God's word by looking up at His offer, healing came to them. Life was theirs again!

New life for the Israelites did not stop at that pole! Their disobedience did not either. But the God of love finally brought them to enter into the land he had promised them.

4. The True Identity of the Snake

Two events in the Bible tell of a snake being involved in "turning points" in man's history. A snake appeared for the first time in the lives of Adam and Eve. The snake approached Adam and Eve and tempted them to disobey God— the snake was Satan; "The great dragon was hurled down—that ancient serpent called the devil, or Satan, who led the whole world astray. He was hurled to the earth, and his angels with him" (Revelation 12:9).

Adam and Eve did not overcome temptation by the snake. The snake tempted them to doubt God's word to them and disobey Him. The snake that tempted Adam and Eve to disobey God's command was judged by God. And so was man. Since that time, sin entered into all human beings. In spite of experiencing God's love and mercy, their sinful nature/freewill led them into disobedience—more sin. Men have continued to blame others or God for their troubles rather than themselves ever since.

When did a snake(s) appear to mark another "turning point" in the history of the Israelites? We have been talking, in this and previous chapters, about the time another snake appeared—this time a bronze snake. Although they had experienced God's miraculous deliverance when they left Egypt, they had repeatedly blamed God for their troubles and had committed sin because of their own sinful nature. They were attacked by snakes, venomous—deadly, just like sin! Their very lives were threatened. Death came. Again, God would have to judge sin. And He did—through a bronze snake, one made by man, but used by God to judge and curse the venom of sin! This snake was lifted high upon a pole, this time to "heal" all those threatened with death. Their sins had been judged the moment they looked at the bronze snake. Their lives had been spared!

Sad to say, this did not end Israel's sinning. The Israelites continued to look away from the bronze snake. The only thing left should have been further victories over the "enemies" and their entrance into the Promised Land. They finally entered but sin entered in with them and on into Jesus' day!

5. The Snake and Jesus

Jesus used this episode in Israel's history when he talked with Nicodemus about his need, and the need of all men, to be born-again. Why did Jesus compare himself to a hideous bronze snake? The reason is very simple: As the bronze snake "attracted" the Israelite to look up at it in the belief that God would save him---give him life again—so Jesus would "attract" all those to look up at him upon a cross (of curse and judgment), and by having faith in God's power and love, to take away sin—be born-again.

Jesus told Nicodemus that he (the Son of Man) would die on "a pole" like the bronze snake in the wilderness. He would be the one who would take all the sin away that Nicodemus had committed. However, his being lifted up would not be just for the sins people committed. Jesus will be lifted up on a cross for the believer's sinful nature too. In other words, Jesus would die on the cross to solve the problem of the sinful nature of all Christians including Nicodemus.

Nicodemus could be hung on a cross because of his personal sins. Furthermore, he could be lifted up on a cross because of his sinful nature. However, Jesus is to die on a cross in his place. If we see this triangle of Nicodemus, snake, and Jesus with spiritual eyes, we can realize that the three are one. Nicodemus is supposed to die on the cross. No, the snake is supposed to die. However, Jesus dies on the cross.

As soon as an Israelite looked at the bronze snake lifted up on the pole, they became one with the snake. They became the snake and the snake became them. Their sinful nature is overcome through the experience of losing one's identity in each other. Nicodemus should look at Jesus who is lifted up on the pole like the snake, for his sins to be forgiven and be born again—with new life and new nature! Although this experience is important, it is just a beginning.

We, like Nicodemus, must come to the cross before we can be born again. We must experience a new birth, dying to self (to our will), looking to Jesus, the One whom God, not Moses the man, has sent to judge sin on the cross. At that moment, we become one with Jesus Christ. At that moment, we experience that we are crucified like the snake and Jesus, and then move on to a life of spiritual victory.

I once secluded myself in a room and prayed seriously, "God, what can I do? What should I do?" There seemed to be no way out of the spiritual situation I was in! I continued to pray in anguish. I prayed on my knees. I prayed on my feet. I prayed with my face on the floor. I prayed with my eyes to the ceiling. I do not remember how long I was struggling in prayer. All of a sudden, a scripture verse flashed before me: "I have been crucified with Christ! It is no longer I." It was a new revelation!

At that moment I realized that I have been crucified with Christ. What a glorious moment! "I have been crucified with Christ!" As a lay person, I had to speak at JOY Mission that evening. I shared with them this wonderful fact—crucified with Christ! The Holy Spirit met us there in a very powerful way, and many precious souls received Jesus Christ as their Savior and were graciously saved. It was not I, but Christ who worked through me.

Chapter 34

God's Love

"*For God so loved* the world that he gave his one and only Son, that whoever believes in him shall not perish but have eternal life" (John 3:16).

1. Unconditional Love

Can you guess what most people's favorite word is? It is "love." Why do you think that is so? Perhaps the reason is that in every person's heart and life is the need to love and to be loved. The love relationship between men and women appears to be almost universal. So, too, is the love between parents and children. Of course, there are additional kinds of love that appear to be universal: the love between friends, love for pets, love for jobs, and love for hobbies.

A much greater kind of love is God's love, which differs from all the others in its intensity. All kinds of love have conditions attached except for God's love. God's love is offered with no strings attached. Why does a man love a woman? The man loves her because she looks good to him and has a personality that he finds attractive. She does things for him. Why do parents love their children? Needless to say, they love their children because they are "their" children. An ownership type of thing! Love between friends, love for pets, love for hobbies develop because people like to have friends and pets around them because they give "something" back. Hobbies keep one's mind occupied and body alert and strong.

However, as we have said, God's love is unconditional. God does not love people because they catch His fancy or because they are lovable. Imagine a man giving a beggar ten dollars. He does not give it because the beggar is lovable or catches his fancy. He gives it out of his own compassion and generosity. That is unconditional love. He loves because he is love.

2. The Object of Love

Love always has an object. There are objects of love between men and women, and the love between parents and their children. All kinds of love have their objects. Then who is the object of God's love? John 3:16 says, "God so loved *the world.*" The object of God's love is the world. The world in this verse refers to all people who live in this world: People of all nations—Koreans, Americans, French, Latinos, Chinese, and many, many others.

What kind of people does God love? His love is for all different kinds of people— rich and poor, educated and uneducated, men and women, the old and the young...God's "whoever"—the "good, the bad and the ugly" levels of human natures! He loves them all! Everyone has a sinful nature, and God has a solution for every one—His love. No one is worthy of this love. Those who believe they are righteous. Those who know they are not. God's love extends to all!

Many people do not know why they live: they eat, they sleep, they go to work, they rear their children, and they die. These activities are often done with little thought as to their having any purpose in life or that they have any definite direction to go in life. The way they live and the decisions they make in this world are seen as having little to do with determining their eternal destiny. In fact, they spend little time thinking of judgment from God or their eternal destiny. For this reason, people are afraid of death. But there is one common characteristic in people as they come closer and closer to the end of life—fear, fear of what the future, if there is one, holds for them! There is another thing all men have in common: a God who loves them. In fact, He has loved them from the very beginning of their lives. And His love is unconditional! God loves people even though their lives are full of sin. For this reason, no greater love can be found than God's love.

3. The Gift of Love

Loving people always want to give. When a man and a woman love each other, they want to give to each other and receive from each other. Parents want to give gifts for their children. People who love their pets give gifts to them as a symbol of their love. People who love sports spend much of their time practicing and playing those sports. God loves mankind. His love was also demonstrated by the giving of a gift. John 3:16 claims that "God so loved the world that he gave his one and only Son...." What did God give to people? Power? Money? Honor? No! Then what did God give? God gave *his one and only Son as* ultimate expression of love.

Why did God give his only Son? The reason was very simple! Material things cannot satisfy the problem of loneliness. Material things cannot bring happiness. They cannot provide meaning in life? They cannot solve the problem of sin. Material things cannot resolve the problem of death. They cannot come to the rescue of man. It has to be a man. But not just any man!

God knew that the sin problem would eventually destroy man. He wanted them to be in a love relationship with Him. But they refused to let go of sin. They tried to deal with sin in their own way. And they were powerless to do so!

For this reason, God sent his only Son to earth as His love-gift to all humanity. God knew only too well that people would ultimately die for their sin and would be punished with death. God's action? He gave his only Son and sent Him to die instead.

In other words, Jesus Christ would take upon himself the sin of mankind and experience death for every man! God's gift of love is Jesus Christ who would be man's substitute.

4. The Purpose of Love

When a man and a woman exchange gifts, each has purpose in their action. They want to express and confirm their love for each other. When parents give gifts to their children, they, too, are expressing and confirming their love. God had a clear purpose in giving His only Son as a gift of love for the sinful world. His purpose: "God so loved the world that he gave his one and only Son, that whoever believes in him shall not perish but have eternal life." This is true! God did not let his only Son die on the cross without a purpose. God's purpose is to save people from death and eternal punishment—to keep them from "perishing." And to give them a new and different life!

"Whoever believes in him *shall not perish*." What does it mean to perish? First, it means death; they shall surely die. All people— including the poor and the wealthy, the weak and the strong—will die. Everybody faces death some day. The second meaning involves judgment to come after death. Everyone who does not know God will die and be judged. Punished eternally in hell! However, people who accept God's gift of love "shall not perish!"

What about the words that appear after this word "perish"—"but have eternal life?" Eternal life literally refers to man living forever. How can people live forever, and more importantly, live eternally with God? They can live forever when they actively receive God's gift of love. In other words, they must believe, put their trust in Jesus Christ. Then, they will receive the eternal relationship God has always wanted them to have with Him! They will then be able to enjoy peace both in this world and in heaven.

Jesus Christ died on the cross to take away sin...to release man from its bondage. But, so vital—he was resurrected three days after his death! New life came to Him! Why was he resurrected? God wanted to confirm that people who believed in Jesus Christ would also come to life after their own death. Death could be conquered! The Conqueror was Jesus! People who believe in the One who died on the cross and was resurrected from the grave will enjoy eternal life!

5. The Condition of Love

When a man and a woman truly love each other, they give gifts. Each enjoys the other's gift. When a person accepts a gift, the gift belongs to him/her to enjoy. When children accept gifts from their parents, they receive them with joy. When friends give gifts of love to their friends, their friends receive them with joy. God's gifts are the same. Gifts are useless if people do not accept and enjoy them.

John 3:16 claims, "For God so loved the world that he gave his one and only Son, that *whoever believes* in him shall not perish but have eternal life." Even though God loved people so much that he gave his only Son to die for them, the gift is useless, unless they "believe" and accept him into their lives. They must accept Him and what He has done for them with open hands and grateful hearts. Without accepting God's Gift in this way, they do not have Him to enjoy—forever!

The act of accepting the gift is expressed in this verse as "believing." Believing means accepting Jesus Christ as God's gift to man. How can they do this? They accept Jesus when they admit that they are sinners, that Jesus died on the cross for their sins, and that He was resurrected on the third day to show that he had the power to give them new life.

Who can believe? "*Whoever!*" Whoever accepts God's Gift and is willing to open it!

6. The Fruit of Love

On October 19, 1963, a terrible murder case was reported. An entire family of six was murdered in a rural area in South Korea. When the case came out in the national newspapers, South Koreans trembled as they read about the cruel murder. To make matters worse, nobody knew why the family of Lieutenant Major Deok-Ju Lee was murdered. When the murderer, Jae-

Bong Ko, was arrested 25 days later, he refused to reveal any motivation for the murders.

A deacon in a local church, a Mr. Ahn, heard the report and knelt down to pray for Jae-Bong Ko, wondering how a man could axe to death six innocent people without reason. His mind went to the Bible's account of the robber who had been crucified alongside Jesus Christ but was saved at that time. Mr. Ahn believed that God would reach out to the man who now was imprisoned.

While he prayed for the murderer every day, one day he heard the clear voice of the Holy Spirit: "Deacon Ahn, you must go to him and share the gospel with him." Deacon Ahn heard this voice several different times. Three months later, he heard that several pastors had visited Jae-Bong Ko to share the gospel with him, but all of them had failed. Deacon Ahn thought, "How can I share the gospel with him, and do what the pastors were not able to do? How can I open such a closed heart? What kinds of words could open his heart?"

He was heavily oppressed with these thoughts, but he heard the voice of the Holy Spirit again, "Open his heart not by your words but by the Word of God." Finally, Deacon Ahn decided to visit the murderer and share with him John 3:16. When he came to visit Jae-Bong Ko, he imagined meeting a very violent, horrifying person with a ferocious face. Although thoughts of fear coursed through his mind, he prayed, "Lord, you commanded me to be your witness to the ends of the earth and I consider murderer Ko to be the end of the earth."

Praying continuously, Ahn entered into the visitors' room of the prison. As soon as he saw Jae-Bong Ko come into visitors' room, he was surprised to see that Ko was a small young man and looked very vulnerable. Judging him by his looks, people would wonder how this small young man could murder six innocent people with an axe.

Deacon Ahn read the Bible verses from John 3:16-20 and told him who God was, who Jesus was, and what God could do for him. Then, a miracle happened. Ko changed his mind, and decided to reveal his motivation for the murder. His heart had been opened through Ahn's prayer during those three months and his sharing of the gospel during those fifteen minutes in prison. The power of the Holy Spirit, not the power of man, had made this change possible.

Jae-Bong Ko had had a deprived childhood and joined the Army. He ran errands for a Lieutenant Major Park at his house. But because he had stolen things, Lieutenant Major Park turned him over to the military police for rehabilitation. The military police put him in a military prison for seven months. While Ko was in prison, he decided to kill the whole family of Lieutenant Major Park as revenge, and then kill himself. As soon as Ko got out of the prison, he tried to carry out his terrible plan.

But while Ko was in prison, Lieutenant Major Park moved out of his house, and Lieutenant Major Deok-Ju Lee and his family moved in. Ko did not know this and killed the entire innocent family. When Ko realized it, he felt that the world had caved in. The day when Ko read the Bible Ahn had given him and he repented, acknowledging his salvation, he cried out so loudly that the whole prison seemed to shake.

> "You should have let me know about Jesus Christ. If I had known Jesus earlier, I would not have killed six innocent people!" Crying out all night, Ko shouted these words over and over again. After that night, like a wind of the Holy Spirit, the murderer Jae-Bong Ko became a prison evangelist, like a whirlwind of the Holy Spirit. Many of the other prisoners were saved through the witness of Jae-Bong Ko. After several months, Ko shouted out to Ahn, "Deacon Ahn! Leave the evangelism in this place to me. You must go to the tiger's den. Many people are waiting for you there."

The "tiger's den" refers to the red-light district where Deacon Ahn had done evangelism since his sophomore year of college. He spent his whole life in evangelism, in prisons, in red-light districts, and in sanitariums. He is now a pastor of a local church, sharing Christ. He knows now that transformation is not the work of man but of God. Jesus Christ transformed the murderer Jae-Bong Ko, not Deacon Ahn. Only Jesus' power is successful, men are just small errand boys for Jesus Christ.

Chapter 35

God's Love (2)

"For *God* so loved the *world* that he gave his one and *only Son*, that whoever believes in him shall not perish but have eternal life" (John 3:16). (2)

1. The Extract of Love

John 3:16 summarizes the whole Bible and is the essence of the gospel. John Wesley described this verse as follows: "This was the very design of God's love in sending him into the world." Many people have realized the importance of this verse and have meaningfully applied it to their ministry and life. Dwight L. Moody, a man mightily used by God, was one of them. There is a famous story of Moody's where he shares how the verse of John 3:16 helped him realize the depth of God's love.

While Moody was in England, he had met a young pastor named Moorehouse who had mentioned to Moody his intention to visit the United States. Moody half-heartedly promised to give him an opportunity to preach in his church, if he ever came to Chicago. One day, Moody received a telegram from

Moorehouse, saying that he had arrived in Chicago. Although Moody was unenthusiastic about it, he gave Moorehouse an opportunity to preach because of the promise he had made to him. Then Moody left Chicago to lead revival meetings elsewhere.

Later Moody returned to his home and asked his wife about Moorehouse's sermons he had preached. According to his wife, Moorehouse was a greater preacher than Moody and had been successfully leading revival meetings for a week. Moody had thought that the revival meetings were already ended, but he went to his church to listen to Moorehouse's preaching. As on the other days, Moorehouse preached about God's love, based on John 3:16. Moody confessed that he had been deeply awakened to God's love for the first time.

We have briefly surveyed, in the previous chapters, John 3:16 in terms of the object of love, the gift of love, the condition of love, and the purpose of love. In thesechapters we will be looking briefly at some other key words used in this passage. In this chapter we will look at God, the world, the only Son, believe, perish, and eternal life.

2. God

Who is God? Although God is transcendent (beyond the limits of all possible experience and knowledge) over all human beings—the Holy One, at the same time, he is imminent (operates within the domain of reality) in them—the Loving One! The Bible describes God's transcendence and immanence as expressed in God's relationship with human beings as holiness and love. If people cannot understand the relationship and harmony between holiness and love, they may have difficulty in further understanding of the essence of the gospel.

Since God created human beings, He is known as their Creator. Later, people who experienced His redemption called Him "Father." The Apostle Paul in Galatians 4:4-6 explained the latter term: "But when the time had fully come, God sent his Son, born of a woman—that we might receive the full rights of sons. Because you are sons, God sent the Spirit of his Son into our hearts, the Spirit who calls out, 'Abba, Father'." He is relational—because he wants to be! Because he loves to be!

God is the Father of holiness and love. The holy God is the Father of justice, so he cannot overlook the sins human beings have committed. If God the Father ignored human sins, He would no longer be God. As Judge he cannot overlook human sins, but as God the Father he can deal with them. How does he deal with them? As the holy Judge, He must deal with sin, for sin does harm to man. But before he pours out His wrath, He, the loving Father, offers an opportunity to repent of their sins (Romans 2:4-5). When people admit and repent of their sins, God the Father forgives them. He not only forgives them, but also adopts them into His family (Romans 8:15; John 1:12; Galatians 3:26). Needless to say, we see, then, that God is the Father of love. Therefore, God the Father is both a holy and loving God, both attributes of God introduced in John 3:16.

This verse describes God as the Father who has deep interests in caring for His children. However, if people really want to realize and experience the Father's love, they must realize that God is also a holy God. They must come to the realization that they are sinners responsible for their sins and will be judged one day. They will "perish." However, when people come face-to-face with the fact that they are sinners before a holy God, they have the opportunity to know the love of God the Father who will forgive them unconditionally and accept them when they believe in Jesus. For this reason, the love of God the Father is described as *holy love*. The declaration of "God is love" presupposes God's declaration of "I am holy."

3. The World

The second key word we want to look at is the word "world." We need to go back to the beginning...to the first chapter of Genesis. The "world" speaks of man, "man created in (God's) image!" Since man (Adam) was created by God, the "world" was good. God was delighted, in fact, with all He had created: "God saw all that he had made, and it was very good. And there was evening, and there was morning—the sixth day" (Genesis

1:31). The Psalmist (Psalm 8:4-6) cried out, "What is man....You made him a little lower than the heavenly beings and crowned him with glory and honor....You put everything under his feet!"

The most striking teaching of the New Testament on this word "world" refers to man quickly falling from his position of "glory and honor." After the disobedience of the man Adam, people in this world became estranged from God. They claimed to be wise but became fools. "The wrath of God (was) revealed from heaven against all the godlessness and wickedness who suppressed the truth by their wickedness" (Romans 1:18,22).

Sin went even further! This world (that is, the people in the world) hated and persecuted those who tried to live Godly lives. Sin abounded! This hatred came from Satan and the influences behind him. People in this world followed "the ways of this world and of the ruler of the kingdom of the air" and were directly or indirectly controlled by them (Ephesians 2:2). Paul described the sin-battle in the following way: "For our struggle is not against flesh and blood, but against the rulers, against the authorities, against the powers of this dark world and against the spiritual forces of evil in the heavenly realms" (Ephesians 6:12).

God loved this "world" so much that "he gave his one and only Son, that whoever believed in him should not perish but have everlasting life....no condemnation!" God's love is unconditional love for all. John 3:16!

4. The Only Son

How do people know that God so loved the world? God demonstrated His love by giving his one and only Son. Although the expression of giving his one and only Son is simple, its meaning is deep. We can find at least three implications in this expression. First, God sent His only Son, Jesus Christ, into the world as a human being. This act of God is called the Incarnation. The fact that God sent His Son to be born of the Virgin Mary reflected God's grace and supernatural gift. God wanted to provide man with an opportunity to return to Him. The virgin birth of Jesus symbolizes God's sovereignty that transcends nature and creation. Jesus was born in such a way—possessing the nature of man and the nature of God—that he served as a bridge between God and sinful human beings. Through this supernatural birth of Jesus, human beings are given an opportunity to live with God.

God's "giving his one and the only Son" involved the death of Jesus Christ, God's Son. The writer of the Book of Hebrews speaks of Jesus as "one who had been tempted in every way, just as (every man is)—yet was without sin" (Hebrew 4:15). Nevertheless, he was crucified, the cruelest punishment at that time, not because of his sins, but because of man's. According to God's justice, people who have committed sin against both God and man must be punished. However, because of God's unconditional love, He sent his Son Jesus to die in place of sinful people, instead of punishing them. Since God's justice has been satisfied by Jesus' death on the cross, their sins are forgiven and they, through faith in Him, become children of God. Yes, it is true! God sent His only Son to die a redemptive death. So that man could be born-again.

Second, "giving his one and only Son" implies Jesus' resurrection on the third day. Even though God allowed His only Son to die on the cross, this would not be the end. After Jesus' death, God resurrected His only Son (Hebrew 13:20). By doing so, God solved the problem of death, which had been inevitable because of man's sin (Romans 6:23). Death could no longer keep "whoever believeth in Him" away from living with God.

One step further, solving the problem of death meant that the problem of sin had been solved. Jesus' resurrection is an affirmation of God's forgiveness. Paul proclaims God's forgiveness through Jesus' resurrection: "He was delivered over to death for our sins and was raised to life for our justification" (Romans 4:25). The word justification refers to the forgiveness of sins. God resurrected his only Son in order to bring life out of death and to proclaim forgiveness of sins.

5. The Throne of Glory

The most amazing event in the history of mankind is found in God "giving his only Son." How can it be that the Son of God became man? Is this a mythical story—like Greek mythology? No, this is an historical event. Jesus Christ became a man, taught wonderful things and performed the most amazing miracles. But that was not the end of the story. Although he lived a righteous life, he was put on trial by his enemies who accused him of blasphemy. He was condemned to death. His flesh torn and his blood shed—on a cross. He died willingly. For man! He was resurrected from the grave. He ascended into heaven. The Bible states that "Jesus, the author and perfecter of our faith, who for the joy set before him endured the cross, scorning its shame, and sat down at the right hand of the throne of God" (Hebrew 12:2).

The expression "sitting down at the right hand of the throne of God" describes a most glorious scene in heaven. This scene signified that Jesus had finished all his redemptive work for the salvation of man (the world). Man would have to do nothing to have a relationship with God—but just receive the Gift! Furthermore, He is at the side of His Father, praying—interceding for all those who have been saved by faith in him (Romans 8:34). He will one day return to earth as the glorified Lord!

Chapter 36

God's Love (3)

"For God so loved the world that he gave his one and only Son, that whoever believes in him shall not perish but have eternal life" (John 3:16). (3)

1. Other Terms

God so loved this world and gave the only Son. To whom was the only Son given? As mentioned before, God gave his only Son to the world and this world refers to all the people who live, and have lived, in it. The Apostle John claims that Jesus Christ was given to all the people in this world, saying that "He is the atoning sacrifice for our sins, and not only for ours but also for the sins of the whole world" (1 John 2:2).

Does this mean that the people who commit all kinds of sins are unconditionally saved because of the gift of God's only Son? If there are conditions, what are they? What happens if the conditions are not satisfied? Is God's unconditional love enough to make up for those conditions man is powerless to attain? Or is there still a price to be paid? John 3:16 provides an answer for these questions.

We are not yet finished with searching out the wonderful message of John 3:16. Let's look at three words: faith/believe, perish, and eternal life. We have looked at them before, but, perhaps, we can search a little more deeply into them. With each one we will be focusing on the depth of God's love.

2. Faith/Believe

God did everything necessary for the salvation of sinners. This can be summarized in the death and resurrection of Jesus Christ. God delights to see people in this world respond positively to His actions. This positive response is called "faith". The verse highlights faith by saying "whoever believes in him---." Why does God require human faith in Jesus? The reason is very simple! God requires our faith because even the best gift needs to be accepted. To be "forced" to receive a gift renders the gift useless because it will not truly be opened by man's heart.

The act of receiving God's gift, Jesus Christ, is called faith. Faith requires one who has stood against God to do an about-face and reach out to Him, the One who offers the gift, if he wants to receive it. Turning around is a pre-requisite for receiving the gift. This turning is called repentance. Thus, repentance and faith are complements of one another. The words "believe in Him" involves believing in Christ, repenting of sin, and stepping out in faith, "They must turn to God in repentance and have faith in our Lord Jesus"(Acts 20:21).

True faith must have the following three ingredients: knowledge, emotions, and will. To begin with, knowledge is the intellectual ingredient of faith. People should know about the Jesus Christ whom the Bible introduces: his birth from a virgin; his righteous life; his miracles and teachings; and his redemptive death and resurrection on behalf of all the people in this world.

However, intellectual knowledge about Jesus alone does not guarantee eternal life. People must personally accept Jesus Christ as the Truth and as their Savior, based on their knowledge about Jesus. They must also believe and receive Jesus with a grateful heart (John 1:12). The emotional factor refers to this grateful reception of Jesus.

Trust is required for complete faith. Born-again people know very well that they cannot be saved by other ways and means. They must trust and depend only on Jesus Christ for their salvation (Acts 4:12). In other words, they must totally surrender themselves to Jesus Christ. Thus, trust and surrender make up the third ingredient necessary to have faith: the human will.

This is true! Personal saving faith includes knowledge, the emotions, and the will. Combining these three ingredients together, the Heidelberg Catechism defines true faith as follows: "True faith is not only a certain knowledge, whereby I hold for truth all that God has revealed to us in his word, but also an assured confidence, which the Holy Ghost works by the gospel in my heart. God requires us to have faith and gives us faith as a gift."

3. Perish

The verse of John 3:16 declares—"whoever believes in him should not perish." God intends that no one perishes. The heart of God is love and the practical expression of His love is to give His only Son as a gift. No human being has ever been able to express this sacrificial love or receive this kind of love from any other human. This sacrificial love can only be found in God.

What happens if people reject such a sacrificial love? God knows that every human being is heading toward eternal destruction, and God blocks their way, telling them that the road leads to eternal destruction. How does God block the road? God puts the cross on it, hanging His only Son on it, and exclaims "turn around and believe in my Son who died in your place." This warning means that if they do not receive Jesus Christ, God's only way for their salvation, they will perish.

Practically, what does it mean to perish? First of all, it means present destruction. There is a destructive factor that destroys people's present lives when they reject God's sole means of redemption, Jesus Christ. Their footsteps always leave the trace of sin. Because of this, they often struggle against God. Also, they do not experience the amazing life of fellowship with God. This is a natural result of being separated from God.

Furthermore, without the faith which transforms, they take advantage of other people, hurting them, and ending up in isolation from other people. In addition, since they hurt each other, they struggle with all kinds of wounds and injury. People experience all kinds of pain: the pain between husband and wife, pain between parents and children, the pain of disease, pain of a bad economy, the pain of saying farewell, the pain of war, the pain of disaster, and finally, the pain of death. When people reject Christ, they are choosing the road to destruction, leading to all kinds of pain.

Perishing does not end with present destruction. Beyond death eternal destruction is waiting for people who choose not to believe in Jesus. Their existence does not end with physical death; they remain separated from God, and suffer forever. The Bible teaches that the place where they will live is hell. As heaven is a clear teaching of the Bible, so is hell. They will fall down into hell and cry out in eternal pain.

The Bible describes hell as darkness where people leave the presence of God, the Light and life (Matthew 8:12; Jude 12). Moreover, hell is described as fire (Matthew 25:41; Revelation 19:20), the Abyss (Revelation 9:1, 2), and torment (Romans 2:9; Revelation 14:10). Hell is the place where people who reject God's gift, Jesus Christ, will suffer forever under the wrath of God. Since God does not want people to go to such a place, He sacrificed His only Son.

4. Eternal Life

Jesus uses the term eternal life twice in his conversation with Nicodemus (John 3:15, 16). The term "eternal life" can be substituted for the terms "born-again" or "salvation." In the former conversation, eternal life is substituted for being born-again (John 3:3, 5) and for salvation (3:17) in the later conversation. Do these words have the same meaning? Although each term highlights a different emphasis, they are deeply related to each other.

Being born-again highlights instantaneousness, salvation emphasizes process, and eternal life accentuates transcendence. The indwelling of the Holy Spirit at the time when people are washed by water stresses the instantaneous work of God. However, salvation emphasizes the whole process of salvation, including the spiritual salvation of the past, the life salvation of present, and the body salvation of the future. God's concept eternal life is that which transcends the human concept of time.

The Apostle John uses the term *eternal life* as many as seventeen times in his gospel. What kind of life does *eternal life* indicate? Eternal life does not signify time that simply drags on endlessly. At its base, the term *eternity* indicates the character of God. God's eternity is expressed in the Bible as "I am Alpha and the Omega, who is, and who was, and who is to come" (Revelation 1:8).

Eternal life is God's life which Christians inherit. When do Christians inherit eternal life? Does it begin when life as we know it here on earth ends? No! Eternal life begins from the moment the Holy Spirit enters into people's hearts and lives, their being born-again. This is very clear because the Holy Spirit, the eternal God, has entered into their lives.

Life exists in God and life is given to the people who believe in Jesus (John 1:4). For this reason, the Apostle John expresses his conviction in the following way: "Dear friends, now we are children of God, and what we will be has not yet been made known. But we know that when he appears, we shall be like him, for we shall see him as he is" (1 John 3:2).

Eternal life emphasizes not only life in the future, but also life in the present age. Christians will fully enjoy the character of God, such as His holiness and love, in eternity. But they also have the privilege of partially enjoying God's holiness and love in the present. Therefore, Christians enjoy eternal life in their hearts even in this limited world. Paul states, in I Corinthians 13:12, "Now we see but a poor reflection as in a mirror; then we shall see face-to-face. Now I know in part; then I shall know fully, even as I am fully known."

5. From Perishing to Eternal Life

All sinners are destined to perish, but they have been given the opportunity to turn the direction of their life around by accepting the sacrificial love of God. All they must do is to light the embers of faith, which is the grace of all graces. Through the stepping stone of faith, any sinner can change his or her destiny from eternal death to eternal life. Here is an actual story of a man whose hope was restored through the stepping stone of love in the midst of pain and despair.

> I was on the way home after work and crossing the crosswalk in front of my house when I see the car coming toward me, it was too late, I was seriously injured. I was rushed to the emergency room; they said it was a miracle that I survived. But I was deeply depressed as soon as I gain consciousness because I had lost my sight. I could no longer see nor do anything. I was being transferred from the intensive care unit to the general ward when I met a seven-year old girl.
>
> "Hey, mister, why did you come here?"
> "Little girl, do not bother me. Go somewhere else."
> "Mister, why do you have a bandage around your eyes? You look like a mummy."
> "Little girl, go away and play with your friends."
> She was a patient who shared the same room.
> "Mister, do not be angry at me. You are not the only one who is sick. Many people in this room are sick. Come on, why don't you be my friend?"
> "Little girl, could you leave me alone?"
> "Yes, I am Jeong-Hye. Jeong-Hye Oh. This is a very boring place. Did you say that I bothered you?"
> Then she went out.
> On the next day, she said, "Mister, why do you sigh so deeply?"
> "Did you say you are Jeong-Hye? Imagine that the world became dark overnight. That is a scary thing. I sighed deeply because I am scared."
> "My mother told me that a disease can be cured by positive thinking. If I think that I am a patient, then I am a patient. If you do not think you are a patient, you are not a patient. A few days ago, a girl who used your bed went to heaven. My mother told me that she would become a star because she was a good

child. She will shine on people in the dark night when they are scared."
"Okay, what brought you to the hospital?"
"That is a secret, but the doctor told me that I will get better soon and after a month will not need to come to the hospital."
"Is that true? That's a good thing."
"Mister, since you cannot see after a month, even though you want to see me, why don't you just play with me? Please stop sighing."
I unconsciously smiled at her. Her words were very encouraging, like a bright sun shining in the shade. After that time, Jeong-Hye and I became best friends.
"Jeong-Hye, it is time to get a shot."
"I do not like geting a shot. Is it possible to get my shot after thirty more minutes?"
"Then you cannot marry me. If you want to grow fast and marry me, you need to get your shot!"
The idea of marrying him persuaded her to get her shot. She and I became the most famous couple in the hospital. She became my eyes and we took a walk every evening. She described people and the landscape around us with wonderful images, considering her young age.
"Mister, do you know what Mr. Kim looks like? His nose is red and his mouth looks like that of a hippo. Also, his eyes are similar to those of a weasel! On the first day I came to this hospital, I cried as soon as I saw him and asked to return to home."
"It's very funny because his voice is wonderful like actors or voices on TV programs."
"Well, what is your dream, Jeong-Hye?"
"My dream is to marry you."
"Why do you like me so much? Am I a handsome guy?"
"You are so ugly, like a monster in Pokémon."
My parting from her came earlier than I had expected. After two weeks, I was discharged from the hospital. My friend was crying and asked, "Mister, you must come back to the hospital when I leave." Even though I was not able to see her, I promised her I would come back to the hospital.
Two weeks later, my phone rang.
"Hello?"

"Are you Ho-Seop Choi?"
"Yes, I am."
"Congratulations! A donor gave you his eyes."
"Really? Please thank him for me!"
I was so happy that I felt that I was soaring up to the sky. After a week, I received an eye transplant and three days after the operation I began to see again. I was so thankful that I wrote a letter to the hospital. Further, I asked them if I could meet the donor. I fainted at the news that the donor had been Jeong-Hye. Later I found out that a week after my discharge, she was supposed to have an operation, She had been diagnosed in the last stage of leukemia. Since I had never seen her previously, I had assumed she was healthy. I was so sad that I decided to meet her parents.
"My child liked you very much."
"Yes."
"She really wanted to see you on the day of her operation."
Jeong-Hye's mother could not continue her words.
"Jeong-Hye wanted to give her eyes to you in case she went to heaven. She asked me to give you this letter." The letter was filled with the neat writing of a seven-year old girl and she told me her story: Hello, Mister! I am Jeong-Hy. It is time for me to enter the operation room.

Several weeks ago, a girl from the bed beside me went to heaven in the operation room. I am not sure what will happen to me, so I want to tell you this before I go into the room. If I go to heaven, my eyes will become yours, so that I can live with you. But if I come out of the operation room alive, I will marry you. I want to marry you and live a happy life.

Streaks of tears ran down my cheeks.

Chapter 37

God's Love (4)

"For God so *loved* the world that he *gave* his one and only Son, that whoever believes in him shall not perish but *have* eternal life" (John 3:16). (4)

1. Three Verbs

The Apostle John is the one who summarized God's love in a very short verse but one with very deep implications. John is known as the Beloved Disciple. The gospel of John describes his special relationship with Jesus at the Last Supper: "One of them, the disciple whom Jesus loved, was reclining next to him" (John 13:24). Since he had experienced Jesus' love deeply, we would be wise to continue to take an in-depth look at his summary of God's deep love in John 3:16.

John 3:16 introduces several interesting and heart-opening verbs. We have already studied two important verbs "believe" and "perish" in previous chapters. This chapter deals with three others verbs found in the verse: "love," "give," and "have." God's greatest motivation for giving His only Son was love. Because of God's "love" for the world, He "gave" His only Son to die for the world. We "have" eternal life because of His love and His action! God's love always wants more than itself! These three verbs together are a bridge to a relationship. A relationship between God and His creation, man! Sinners can now be born-again. The "image of God" restored to them, God's nature becoming theirs!

2. "Love"

One of the most important characteristics of God is love. Of course, God's love is different from all other kinds of love. His love is different from parents' love because their love is conditional, limited mostly to their own children. God's love is different from the love between friends, because the latter is contingent on conditions of friendship.

In contrast, God's love is unconditional! But actually, there *is* one condition a person must meet if he wants to receive God's love. What is that condition? Contrary to people's general assumption, the condition is not hard to decipher. The condition they should meet is that they must be undeserving of love. God's love is an unconditional love that God pours out on undeserving people.

First of all, God's love transcends geography. God is not a local God who only loves people in particular area. For a long time, Jews believed that God especially loved them and treated other people as unworthy of His love. For awhile, white people believed that they were God's favorites and did not hesitate to ravage the world, establishing colonies throughout the earth and ruling over those they considered to be inferior.

However, God is not a God who favors people from a certain area or specific people groups. God loves equally all peoplegroups. Paul describes God's love in this way: "Now he commands all people everywhere to repent" (Acts 17:30). God's love is for both Jews and Gentiles (Romans 1:16, 2:10). Paul also says, "From one man he made every nation of men, that they should inhabit the whole earth" (Acts 17:26).

Second, God's love transcends the individual. It does not exhibit favoritism based on a person's ability, appearance, sex, age, health, wealth, or education. If anyone comes to God with hands outstretched, God will accept him or her with love. Paul proclaims: "There is neither Jew nor Greek, slave nor free, male nor female, for you are all one in Christ Jesus" (Galatians 3:28).

Third, God's love transcends time. There is no one He cannot touch because of when they lived. God loved Abraham and David. They lived thousands of years ago. God loved Dwight Moody. He lived more than a hundred years ago. God loved John Song in China and Sadhu Sundar Singh in India in more recent days. Such love, which has not changed throughout the course of human history, can be found in no one else's heart but God's!

3. "Give"

God's love that transcends places, people-groups, individuals, and time periods in history is not an abstract love but a practical one. This love is so practical that sinners can feel it and are moved by it. Love is an abstract noun, but the act of giving gives shape to it and makes it a reality. Since God is love, He gives. His giving is different from any expected inheritance given to children. God's giving is purely unilateral. It is not mutual. He cannot be forced into giving it, as good as that "force" might be.

What did God give to the people who became estranged from and even stood against Him? Does He give them food, clothes, or houses? No! He gave them a gift more valuable than any of these things. His gift was not any of this world's material wealth, nor power, nor honor, but God's Son, His only Son. And his gift would die!

If we meditate deeply on the fact that God gave His only Son to this world, we note a number of things. The first is that His Son became a man— the Incarnation of Christ...later to be separated from the Father. Paul describes this in his Letter to the Philippians: "Christ Jesus: Who, being in the very nature God, did not consider equality with God something to be grasped but made himself nothing...made in human likeness....he humbled himself and became obedient (to the Father) to death—even death on a cross" (2:6-8). God and His Son had never before been separated. God sent his only Son to earth to die for sinners. God the Father gave up his intimate inseparable fellowship with Jesus, his Son.

What was the life of Jesus like here on earth? The life of Jesus was one of profound loneliness from the very beginning. Jesus was born in a stable---there had been no room for his parents in an inn! The family had to flee to Egypt out of fear of what Herod might do to him. After they returned to Israel, Jesus grew up in Nazareth, a rural area which nobody paid attention to. Who can understand the loneliness of Jesus? No one really knew the purpose of his coming. At the end of his life he found himself upon a cross? Reflecting his loneliness, Jesus cried out, while dying on the cross, "My God, my God, why have (even) you forsaken me?"

The second thing we see is that giving implies sacrifice. Of course, separation itself is a kind of sacrifice. However, when God gave His only Son to us, God endured much more sacrifice than just separation. What is the sacrifice? Needless to say, it is the death of Jesus Christ—and a horrible death on the cross at that. We can hardly find another example of such a huge sacrifice in human history. Such a noble man became humiliated and died on the cross. He gave himself as a sacrifice!

Third, giving entails a glory that goes beyond sacrifice. Jesus' resurrection is the glory we, too, can realize. There is remarkable glory found in the transformation of sinners. They had lived in sin, and were destined for God's punishment in the future. However, they become God's children. Whoever believes becomes a child of God, because "He was delivered over to death for our sins and was raised to life for our justification" (Romans 4:25). Born-again, man receives forgiveness and a new life in God.

4. "Have"

The third verb, *have*, implies a result. God wanted His agape love to be distributed to all the people. As God desired, many people have received God's love with the outstretched hands of faith, but they have received other gifts as well. The first gift they have is, needless to say, God's only Son. They can have the Son—such a wonderful gift! (Romans 8:32).

When they have the Son as a gift, they also have eternal life. The Apostle John explained the relationship between the Son and eternal life: "He who has the Son has life." (1 John 5:12). "Have" in this passage is the same word as "have" in John 3:16. In short, whoever has the Son as a gift will also have life. Life in 1 John means the same as eternal life in the gospel of John.

What other gifts do people who have eternal life in Jesus Christ possess? They receive a gift of peace. They enjoy peace regardless of situation and circumstances. They enjoy peace even in war, in economic crisis, in poor health, or in separation from family members. This peace is like the calm of the deep sea, even though the waves are high on the surface.

Why can people enjoy this peace? Very simply, they enjoy peace because they begin to experience peace with God. Originally, human beings were God's enemies (Romans 5:10). But when they were reconciled with God through the sacrifice of Jesus Christ, they begin to enjoy peace with God (2 Corinthians 5:18). After people are restored by this peace of God, they begin to see other people from God's viewpoint. They begin to enjoy peace with other people.

God's peace does not end with these new relationships with God and other people. People who receive the gift of eternal life respect life. They begin to have peace with life itself. Furthermore, people who have life begin to have peace with them. Even though they know that they are not perfect, they begin to accept themselves as they are being transformed by God.

5. Giving Love

Have you ever experienced the joy of giving? The story below happened on an airplane.

I put my carry-on in the luggage compartment and sat down in my assigned seat. It was going to be a long flight. "I'm glad I have a good book to read. Perhaps I can also get a short nap," I thought. Just before take-off, a line of soldiers came down the aisle and filled all the vacant seats, totally surrounding me. I decided to start a conversation: "Where are you headed?" I asked the soldier seated nearest to me.

"Great Lakes Air Base. We'll be there for two weeks for special training, and then we're being deployed to Iraq."

After flying for about an hour, an announcement was made that sack lunches were available for five dollars. It would be several hours before we reached Chicago, and I quickly decided a lunch would help pass the time. As I reached for my wallet, I overheard the soldier ask his buddy if he planned to buy lunch. "No, that seems like a lot of money for just a sack lunch. Probably wouldn't be worth it. I'll wait till we get to Chicago."

His friend agreed.

I looked around at the other soldiers. None were buying lunch. I walked to the back of the plane and handed the flight attendant a fifty dollar bill. "Take a lunch to all those soldiers." She grabbed my arms and squeezed tightly. Her eyes wet with tears, she thanked me. "My son was a soldier in Iraq. It's almost like you are doing it for him."

Picking up the lunches, she headed up the aisle to where the soldiers were seated. She stopped at my seat and asked, "Which do you like best: beef or chicken?" I replied, wondering why she asked.

She turned and went to the front plane, returning a minute later with a dinner plate from first class. "This is our thanks."

After we finished eating, I went again to the back of the plane, heading for the restroom. A man stopped me.

"I saw what you did, and I want to be part of it. Here, take this."

He handed me twenty-five dollars. Soon after I returned to my seat, I saw the Flight Captain coming down the aisle, looking at the aisle numbers as he walked. I hoped he was not looking for me, but noticed he was looking at the numbers only on my side of the plane. When he got to my row he stopped, smiled, held out his hand, and said, "I want to shake your hand."

Quickly unfastening my seat belt, I stood and took the Captain's hand. With a booming voice he said, "I was a soldier, a military pilot. Someone once bought me a lunch. That was an act of kindness I never forgot." I was embarrassed when applause was heard from all the passengers.

Later, I walked to the front of the plane so I could stretch my legs. A man who was seated about six rows in front of me reached out his hand, wanting to shake mine. He left another twenty-five dollars in my palm.

When I landed in Chicago, I gathered my belongings and started to deplane. Waiting just inside the airplane door was a man who stopped me, put something in my shirt pocket, turned, and walked away without saying a word. Another twenty-five dollars.

Upon entering the terminal, I saw the soldiers gathering for their trip to the base. I walked over to them and handed them seventy-five dollars. "It will take you some time to reach the base. It will be about time for a sandwich. God Bless You."

Ten young men left that flight feeling the love and respect of their fellow travelers. As I walked briskly to my car, I whispered a prayer for their safe return. These soldiers were giving their all for our country. I could only give them a couple of meals. It seemed so little.

A veteran is someone who, at one point in his life, wrote a blank check payable to "The United States of America" for an amount of "Up to and including my life."

This is honor, and there are way too many people in this country who no longer understand it.

Chapter 38

God's Love (5)

"For God *so* loved the world that he gave his one and only Son, *that whoever* believes in him shall not perish *but* have eternal life" (John 3:16).

1. Auxiliary Words

John Wesley, who transformed England after the moral and religious atmosphere had fallen into decay, frequently described himself as a "burning stick snatched from the fire" (Zechariah 3:2). David Livingston, who loved black Africa, especially loved the last promise of the Great Commission of Matthew: "And surely I am with you always, to the very end of the age" (Matthew 28:20). John Newton, who wrote the famous hymn "Amazing Grace," loved the following passage: "But where sin increased, grace increased all the more" (Romans 5:20). Martin Luther, a great reformer who paved the way for Protestantism took his motto from the Bible: "For in the gospel a righteousness from God is revealed, a righteousness that is by faith from first to last, just as it is written: 'the righteous will live by faith'" (Romans 1:17).

Many Christians may have their own favorite Bible passage, but a passage that every Christian loves is John 3:16. This verse summarizes the message of the whole Bible and is the essence of the gospel. When we look closely at it, we find some auxiliary words that add meaning to the primary words we have studied in the previous chapters. These auxiliary words, at first glance, seem to be insignificant, but they are actually very important. Let's look at some of them.

2. "So"

The first auxiliary word we see in the verse is "so." This little word is translated as *hootos* in the Greek Bible. Since "so" is hidden amongst so many important words such as God, the world, and love, it does not capture people's attention, until they take a closer look. Here we see the word taking on significant importance.

Grammatically, "so" modifies the verb "loves," highlighting the intensity of God's love. How is the intensity of God's love expressed? It is expressed by the universality of God's love offered to all people. The intensity of God's love is revealed through the depth of His sacrificial love. His love is so real, so rich, so deep!

God's love is so inclusive, so universal, that John refers to it as reaching out to "the entire world." It is true! God loves all the people in the world. The Apostle John describes the world as a place of depravity and rebellion against God (1 John 2:15-17). Nevertheless, the object of God's love is this very sinful world. "So" modifies the word love in order to express the vast and inclusive love of God which reaches out far beyond the area of Judea into all the various regions of the world.

Jesus tells his disciples to "go into all the world and preach the good news to all creation" (Mark 16:15) and to "make disciples of all nations" (Matthew 28:19)! "All nations" refers to all the people who live in the world; they must hear the gospel because they are all objects of God's love. Whoever hears the gospel can become disciples of Jesus regardless of their ethnicity.

Moreover, "so" expresses the intensity of God's love by highlighting the intensity of His sacrifice. We paraphrase the John 3:16 verse in the following way: "God loved the world so much that he spared nothing and even gave His only Son." We find a similar scene in the Old Testament—Abraham's willingness to sacrifice his only son on the altar of God; "But the Angel of the Lord said...so now I know that you fear God, since you have not withheld your son, your only son, from Me" (Genesis 22:12).

Did God really have to sacrifice His only Son whom He loved so much, to save a world so deeply contaminated by sin and rebellion against God? Could He have withheld his only Son? Was there no other way to express the full extent of his love for us? It appears not. If this is true—that there was no other way—then God's act of love is the noblest, most intense act ever done in the world because God sacrificed His only Son for the salvation of the world.

3. "Whoever"

The second auxiliary word we need to look at in John 3:16 is the word "whoever." John 3:16 begins with God as the Subject. This is evident, since the salvation of human beings begins with God. God not only planned for salvation, and He, as its Source, acted upon it. And, the object of salvation is the world. Although "world" is a collective expression that refers to all human beings, "whoever" signifies a personal invitation. The object of God's love is the world, but the whole world will not turn to God. Men will reject God's offer of love.

Herein lies the importance of "whoever." God created all human beings in His image (Genesis 1:26-27), but the essence of God's image included freedom of will for each individual. God did not create human beings to be robots. God gave everyman the freedom to make moral choices and eternal decisions.

Although Adam and Eve used their free will to disobey and, therefore, became corrupt, God continued to pour out His love upon all human beings. Therefore, human beings can respond favorably to God's call through free will. We can find God's call in numerous passages in the Bible. "Come to me, all you who are weary and burdened, and I will give you rest" (Matthew 11:10) and "Believe in the Lord Jesus, and you will be saved" (Acts 16:31) are just some examples. God calls for man to take action, to come to Him and receive eternal life.

The object of God's love is the world, but the whole world has not decided to receive the gift of eternal life. Millions have, but millions have not. As soon as people turn away from their sins and fix their eyes on Jesus Christ, believing that he sacrificed himself, for them, by dying on the cross, their sins are forgiven. In other word, they are born of the water and the Spirit and begin to enjoy eternal life. The word "whoever" calls for a personal decision.

God's will is that humans be born again and enjoy eternal life with Him. God's pleasure and will is that man would come to Him. People who hear such marvelous news of God's love must accept that love. God put in place a beautiful offer of salvation that required a human response to it. Human beings must, by faith, receive God's work of grace.

4. "That"

The third auxiliary word in John 3:16 is "that." This word is buried in a long list of primary words, rarely drawing people's attention. However, the Greek Bible illuminates its importance. According to the Greek Bible, the structure of John 3:16 is as follows: "God so loved the world" –cause; "he gave his one and only Son" –result; "*that* whoever believes in him shall not perish but have eternal life" –purpose.

This supportive word signifies that the "cause" and "result" seen in this passage clearly show God's "purpose": "that whoever believes in him shall not perish but have eternal life." This is really true! Two different kinds of eternities await all human beings. Every individual must decide upon one or the other! One results in eternal destruction; the other, eternal life.

Which eternity people will face is totally dependent upon human decision, since God has already given Jesus Christ as a practical expression of His love for all human beings. God already took every necessary action He could to provide for the salvation of man. God the Father planned it, Jesus executed it, and the Holy Spirit applied it to us.

As soon as human beings look in faith to Jesus Christ who has given his life for them on the cross, their destiny changes. They move from eternal destruction to eternal life. However, people who refuse to accept the message of salvation from God face eternal punishment. God gave his only Son to save people from the abyss of destruction. If people still refuse God's love, what else will they face in the end but destruction?

Jesus' death on the cross clearly demonstrates the inevitability of punishment for sin. If not inevitable, God would not have had to give His only Son for man's salvation. Since all sin must be punished, God's Son bore man's sin on the cross. Therefore, the cross calls all sinners to admit their sinfulness and accept God's love for their salvation.

In spite of God's tremendous sacrificial love, there are many people who continue to refuse God's love. Eternal punishment will inevitably follow their decision. Such destruction is not God's will. Another passage of the Bible expresses God's intention: "He is patient with you, not wanting anyone to perish, but everyone to come to repentance" (2 Peter 3:9). If you refuse God's love, the only thing waiting for you is eternal destruction. However, whoever believes in him will have eternal life.

5. A Result

A mother and a daughter lived together. The mother had a very ugly and disfigured face. Daughter, embarrassed by her mother's appearance, would often disregard her mother and treat her very badly. However, the mother loved her daughter very much.

One day the daughter met her mother on the street, while she was walking with her friends. The mother tried to greet her, but the daughter ignored her and passed her by. Her friends asked her who she was. She answered them that she was just her housekeeper. In the distance the mother was able to overhear her daughter's remark.

At dinner time that day the mother talked to her daughter about why she had such an ugly and disfigured face. When the daughter was young, a fire broke out in her house. Without thinking the mother ran out of the house, but then she realized that her daughter was still sleeping inside. The mother ran back to save her daughter. Although she was able to save her daughter, her face was seriously disfigured and burned by the fire.

When the daughter heard this story, she began to sob because she was deeply moved by the love that had made her mother run back into the fire to save her. She asked her mother for forgiveness. Mother and daughter cried together, hugging each other. After that time, the daughter spoke proudly of her mother who had been willing to sacrifice her own life for her daughter.

Chapter 39

God's Love (6)

"For God so loved the world that he gave his one and only Son, that whoever believes in him *shall not perish but have eternal life*" (John 3:16).

1. Unconditional Love

Human beings live on the road to eternal destruction. Why? What is the reason for this destruction? The reason is sin. Paul expressed it clearly: "the wages of sin is death" (Romans 6:23). Sin and destruction (death) are inseparable. Where sin abounds, destruction also abounds! Where there is destruction, sin almost always is seen to be present.

It is here where sin and destruction meet that we find the great power of God's love. If God loved only men such as Nicodemus: excellent in terms of religion, academic ability, and social position, other people would have no chance to experience God's love. However, God's love is unconditionally poured out upon all people; those whom the world judges as being worthy and unworthy. God's love is incomprehensibly great!

God's love is also great from the perspective of justice. In terms of justice, who can stand before a holy God? No one can because "all have sinned" (Romans 3:23). They are to be judged and eternally punished. "Not so," says God! God loves those who face such a destiny, and has offered to set them free. The problem is so many have refused this offer!

2. The Reality of Sin

For one to have a deeper realization of God's love one must know the deep reality of sin. People can appreciate God's love in forgiving man of sin only in proportion to knowing the depth of their own sinfulness. As Paul puts it, "where sin increased, grace increased all the more" (Romans 5:20). It is true! The more people know about, mourn over, and suffer from sin, the more they can realize the depth of God's grace (2 Corinthians 7:10-11).

According to Paul, human beings experience much suffering because of their transgressions and sins. They were dead (Ephesians 2:1)! Transgressions and sins indicate a life of unrighteousness. They refer to intentional violations of God's commandments, doing something that God has forbidden (sin of commission). Ryken claims that man "crosses into forbidden territory by overstepping a moral boundary."

God gave us many prohibitions. God set boundary lines for all human beings. For example, "you shall not have other gods before me" (the first commandment); "you shall not make for yourself an idol" (the second commandment); "you shall not misuse the name of the Lord your God" (the third commandment). These and other commandments are God's boundaries for the relationship between God and human beings. When people cross the boundary lines intentionally, that is transgression.

God also gave us the following commandments of prohibition as regard to relationships with others: "You shall not murder" (the sixth commandment); "you shall not commit adultery" (the seventh commandment); "you shall not steal" (the eighth commandment); "you shall not give false testimony against your neighbor" (the ninth commandment); and "you shall not covet" (the tenth commandment). These commandments are God's moral boundaries for relationships between human beings. Breaking any of these commandments is a transgression which involves the breaking of a human relationship. One does not have to look hard to find innumerable transgressions in human society!

Moreover, God also gave us active commands. The following commandments can be examples: "remember the Sabbath day by keeping it holy" (the fourth commandment) and "honor your father and your mother" (the fifth commandment). Violating these commandments is committing sin against God and against human beings. Therefore, Ryken defines sin as "a failure to do something God has commanded us to do."

In summary, transgressions and sins refer to all kinds of sins which humans commit. Humans cross God's moral boundaries. No one is free from transgressions and sins. No one can claim that he or she has never invaded areas belonging to God and other people.

3. The Meaning of Sin

Leviticus 16 gives us some additional ideas of what sin is. This particular chapter gives us four helpful words. The first word is "uncleanness" (Lev. 16:16, 19). This word signifies not being free of undesirable thoughts, words, or deeds; those things that do not meeting the standards of a holy God. Who can be holy like God is holy? Of course, no one can be.

The second word is "rebellion" (Leviticus 16:21). Rebellion is the intention to do sin, in other word. breaking God-given laws. Human beings that commit this kind of sin know that they should not do it, but they purposely break God's laws. This is similar to treacherously revolting against a king. God is the Creator and Father of all things as well as the Holy One. In addition, God is the Conferrer of laws, and is also the final Judge. Though they know who He is, they defy Him and purposely fight against Him.

The third word in Leviticus that indicates sin is "wickedness" (Leviticus 16:21-22). This word implies a viciousness in sinning. A wicked person is one who is disposed to causing harm, distress, or trouble!

The fourth word of Leviticus 16 is "wrong doing" (Leviticus 16:16, 30, 34). Wrongdoing includes all kinds of sins whether "serious or trivial, deliberate or unintentional, conscious or unconscious, visible or invisible, an act or a disposition, consisting of commission or of omission." Is there anyone who has never done wrong in his or her own life? Of course not! "All have sinned and fallen short of the glory of God" (Romans 3:23).

One more interesting fact can be found in these four words. They are used in plural forms. We see in these words the enormity of sin! We see that the root of sin is too deep and the branches of sin are too high for man to resolve his problem of sin.

4. The Phenomena of Sins

Humans are totally depraved by sin. Every part of man is contaminated by it. They commit sin with their hands, and they go to places where they should not go. They spout out all kinds of evil things from their mouths. They do not have any fear of God in their minds nor their hearts (Romans 3:18). They make up tricks in their heads and hold every kind of sinful desires in their minds. Human beings are totally depraved.

People commit many kinds of sins, and suffer from their sins, often feeling guilty because of them. To make matters worse, they are ashamed of coming to God because of their sins. While not knowing God, they are separated from God. "Your iniquities have separated you from your God" (Isaiah 59:2).

People who are separated from God live their days not knowing the meaning and purpose of life. They, like Solomon in Ecclesiastes, seek after money, pleasure, or power, searching for the purpose of life in all the wrong places. However, these things cannot provide meaning in life. Thus, many serious people turn to religion, but religion, in itself, cannot provide the meaning of life.

Relationships in life? How do people who do not know God and have guilty feelings get along with other people? If they maintain good relationships with other people, why do so many people experience divorce? Why do so many people destroy their societies and countries through violent protests? Why are so many people involved in illegal activities and corruption? Why do so many people cheat other people or sexually abuse children? Nothing is left for people in broken relationship with God, other than emptiness of life.

The problem of pain? Why do so many people experience pain in their lives? Why do so many people die of cancer? Why are so many people mistreated and suffering from economic problems? Why do so many people die or become disabled during war? Doesn't this reflect the reality and enormity of human sinful nature?

What about nature? Why do so many people lose their lives and houses by storms and heavy rain? Why are so many people's lives and property threatened by avalanches or thunderstorms? Why do so many people suffer from yellow dust or vehicle exhaust? Why do many people suffer damage or loss from the green or red tide of the sea? Many of these things happen because of the impact of human sin upon the environment. Sin pervades every area of one's life.

5. Immeasurable Love

Human beings seem to be helpless in terms of spirituality, morality, or their relationship to the natural environment. They are totally corrupt. They cannot escape the abyss of sin, however hard they may try. They are totally incompetent in trying to save themselves. Must they abandon themselves to despair? Of course not! One way still exists to solve the problem of sin, and that way is through seeking God's unconditional love. God still loves human beings, though they flounder in sin and are destined to die in the end. God does not want human beings to die in their sins, to be judged, and to enter eternal hell. God loves them. "For God so loved the world "(John 3:16).

This is true! God unconditionally loves a world worn out by sin. Moreover, He calls people one by one to enter into his loving bosom. John 3:16 claims that "Whoever believes in him shall not perish but have eternal life." Whoever believes in him will be taken out of the abyss of their sins because Jesus Christ resolved all the problems of human sins and judgment on the cross. Why not accept Jesus to be your Savior and Lord? Why not ask Him to come into your heart?

Chapter 40

God's Love (7)

"For God so loved the world that he gave his one and only Son, that whoever believes in him shall not perish but have eternal life" (John 3:16).

1. Perfect Love

God's love is perfect love. Perfect love implies a love not flawed; lacking absolutely nothing. Paul describes God's perfect love in this way: "that you, being rooted and established in love, may have power, together with all the saints, to grasp how wide and long and high and deep is the love of Christ, and to know this love that surpasses knowledge—that you may be filled to the measure of all the fullness of God" (Ephesians 3:17-19). According to this passage, the perfection of God's love is expressed as perfect in every dimension—width, length, height, and depth. In whatever direction you look, His love is there—at work.

John 3:16 can be seen as a similar description of God's love: "God so loved the world"—indicating the width of God's love. "He gave his one and only Son" this signifies the length of God's love. "Whoever believes in him" this refers to the depth of God's love. "Have eternal life" meaning the height of God's love. Through this love, God elevates people who believe in Jesus Christ.

2. Tabernacle

The width, length, depth, and height dimensions which Paul used were used to describe abstract concepts, not concrete objects. Twice in the Old Testament we find God giving specifications, including dimensions, regarding the building of sanctuaries for Him. In Exodus 25, Moses was given a pattern for building Him a tabernacle in the Wilderness. Later in the history of Israel,
God instructed Solomon on how to build the temple in Jerusalem (I Kings 5-6).

After God called the Israelites out of Egypt, He guided them to Mount Sinai. There He gave them commandments, including the Ten Commandments (Exodus 20-23). Then, God gave Moses a blueprint for the tabernacle He wanted them to build (Exodus 25-27).

God gave the pattern because He wanted the Israelites to build the tabernacle exactly las He had told them. Perhaps a lesson to them of perfect obedience! After frequently straying from following God, they finally completed its construction (Exodus 40:33); the glory of God filled the tabernacle as previously promised (Exodus 40:34). God was present in the Most Holy Place (Exodus 25:22)!

The structure of the Most Holy Place was amazing. Its shape? A perfect cube, ten cubits high, ten cubits long, and ten cubits wide. For the Israelites, the shape of a cube symbolized the perfection of God's character. This is very true! Both God and His love are perfect. God was present in His perfect, Most Holy Place!

The purpose for which God brought the Israelites out of Egypt was to bring them into the land God promised to Abraham, Isaac, and Jacob (Deuteronomy 6:23); a land flowing with milk and honey. Often straying off course, they finally arrived and conquered the land. The power of that nation reached its peak in the days of King David. When his son Solomon became king, he built a temple for the Name of the Lord his God (I Kings 5:5).

The Most Holy Place within Solomon's temple was constructed in the same shape as that of the tabernacle in the desert. The only difference was in its size. The Most Holy Place of Solomon's temple was twenty cubits long, twenty wide and twenty high (1 Kings 6:20). Why did Solomon build the Most Holy Place, the place where God was present, in the shape of a cube? It was to symbolize God's perfection and perfect love.

3. Heaven

As mentioned previously, God gave the Ten Commandments and other laws soon after He delivered the Israelites from bondage in Egypt. Why did God not first give the people the directions to the land of Canaanites, or first instruct them on the way to conquer the land? Why did God give commandments and laws first?

The Israelites were to resemble and reflect God's character, to be God's witnesses to the people in the world. One of the strongest characteristics of God was His holiness. If the Israelites wanted to be holy people, they would have learn to obey God's laws and commandments (Deuteronomy 4:1). When they were faithfully following Him, they would be His witnesses. God's presence in the tabernacle and, later, in Solomon's temple encouraged them that, indeed, they were becoming His holy people. The ultimate purpose of God's salvation would be restored and endless fellowship between God and His people would be theirs. God repeatedly commanded them to be holy for this purpose: "I am the Lord who brought you up out of Egypt to be your God; therefore be holy, because I am holy" (Leviticus 11:44, 19:2).

Finally, the time will come when God and His people enjoy endless fellowship between them; that will happen in heaven. Notice that, according to the biblical passages that describe heaven, heaven is also cube-shaped, signifying God's perfectness and God's love in eternity. The book of Revelation illustrates heaven in the following way: The city was laid out like a square, as long as it was wide. He measured the city with the rod and found it to be 12,000 stadia in length, and as wide and high as it is long. He measured its wall and it was 144 cubits thick, by man's measurement, which the angel was using (Revelation 21:16-17).

The above passages gloriously portray God's perfect love and will for man. In heaven, God and His people will enjoy endless fellowship in perfect love. The Apostle John expresses this fellowship: "Now the dwelling of God is with men, and he will live with them. They will be his people, and God himself will be with them and be their God." (Revelation 21:3). Only because of His love!

The Cross

God's love was perfectly demonstrated on the cross. Without the cross, the greatest embodiment of God's love, who would enjoy eternal fellowship with God in heaven? We can find another concrete example that demonstrated the depth, width, length, and height of God's love\ Jesus Christ on the cross. God's perfect love surely is the central theme of the whole Bible.

When Jesus died on the cross a sign written in Hebrew, Greek, and Latin was placed above him. These three languages were representative of the people that reflected the human civilization. Latin, stood for the rule of law, Hebrew symbolizes religion, Greek signified culture.

How did Jesus demonstrate the length of God's love on the cross? Jesus cried out to God that "My God, my God, why have you forsaken me?" (Mark 15:34). How desperate the wail was! The fellowship between Jesus and God had never before been broken, but this time he was separated from God because he was bearing the wrath of God upon himself, in place of sinners.

Jesus' cry indicated the *length* of God's love as well. Although Jesus knew no sin, he died on the cross bearing the full weight of the sin of the world. According to Paul, "God made him who had no sin to be sin for us, so that in him we might become the righteousness of God" (2 Corinthians 5:21). Jesus cried out on the cross, "Why?" In His heart he knew the answer—in order to bring about the transformation of sinners into righteous people. He went to that length so that man might live!

How did Jesus express *the depth and height* of God's love on the cross? We can see the depth of God's love through Jesus' words toward a criminal: "I tell you the truth, today you will be with me in paradise" (Luke 23:43). Why do these words represent the depth of God's love? Jesus hung on the cross between two criminals. While he was in immeasurable pain at that time, he did not turn away his face but reached down to the criminal who cried to him out of the anguish of his own soul. The criminal cried out: "Jesus, remember me when you come into your kingdom" (Luke 23:42). Jesus came down to save sinful people. At the same time, he promised heaven, forgiving the dying criminal and lifting him up high to His Father. How deep and how high is God's perfect love !

5. The Greatest Love

John 3:16 describes God's perfect love and summarizes the whole Bible. This verse is a microcosm of the whole Bible, perfectly depicting God's love. A biblical scholar was so overwhelmed by this verse that he explained it in the following diagram:

God	The greatest lover
so loved	The greatest degree
the world	The greatest company
that he gave	The greatest act
his one and only Son	The greatest gift
that whoever	The greatest opportunity
believes	The greatest simplicity
in him	The greatest attraction
shall not perish	The greatest promise
but	The greatest difference
have	The greatest certainty
eternal life	The greatest possession

Are you experiencing God's great love today? If you are not, talk to Him, repent of your sinful life, and ask for His forgiveness. Then receive Jesus Christ who died for you on the cross as your Savior. You will experience the great love of God.

www.ingramcontent.com/pod-product-compliance
Lightning Source LLC
Chambersburg PA
CBHW021820300426
44114CB00009BA/260